Austin's
Old Three Hundred

HISTORIES OF THE FIRST ANGLO COLONISTS
as written by their descendants

**A Revised and Expanded Edition
with maps of the land grants**

EDITED BY WOLFRAM M. VON-MASZEWSKI

For information about the Descendants of Austin's Old Three Hundred contact:

Genealogy Department
George Memorial Library
1001 Golfview Drive
Richmond, TX 77469
281-342-2608

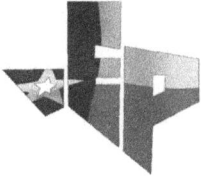

Copyright © 1999
By The Descendents of
Austin' Old Three Hundred
Published By Eakin Press
An Imprint of Wild Horse Media Group
P.O. Box 331779
Fort Worth, Texas 76163
1-817-344-7036
www.EakinPress.com
1 2 3 4 5 6 7 8 9
ISBN-10: 1-681793-42-3
ISBN-13: 978-1-68179-342-9

Stephen F. Austin

Contents

Foreword   ix
Preface   xiii
Acknowledgments   xv
Biographies
    Allen, Martin   3
    Alsbury, Charles G.   4
    Alsbury, Horace A.   5
    Alsbury, Thomas   6
    Andrews, William   7
    Angier, Samuel Tubbs   8
    Bailey, James Britton   9
    Barrett, William   11
    Beason, Benjamin   12
    Best, Isaac   13
    Boatwright, Thomas   14
    Bradley, Edward R.   15
    Breen, Charles C.   16
    Bridges, William   17
    Bright, David   18
    Burnam, Jesse   19
    Byrd, Micajah   20
    Castleman, Sylvanus   21
    Coles, John Prince   22
    Crier, John   24
    Crownover, John Chesney   25
    Cumings, James   26
    Cumings, John   26
    Cumings, Rebekah   27
    Cumings, William   26

Cummins, James 28
Curtis, Jr., James. 29
Curtis, Sr., James 30
DeMoss, Charles. 31
Dyer, Clement C. 33
Edwards, Gustavus Eixon 34
Fitzgerald, David 35
Flowers, Elisha 36
Foster, Isaac. 37
Foster, John 39
Foster, Randolph 41
Fulshear, Sr., Churchill 43
Gates, William 44
George, Freeman 45
Gilleland, Sr., Daniel 46
Gorbet, Chester S. 47
Groce II, Jared Ellison 48
Haddon, John 50
Haddy (Hady), Samuel. 51
Hodge, Alexander 52
Holland, Francis. 53
Holland, William 54
Huff, George. 55
Hunter, John Calhoun. 56
Isaacks, Samuel. 57
Jackson, Alexander 58
Jackson, Sr., Isaac. 59
Jones, Henry 61
Jones, James Wales. 62
Jones, Randall. 65
Kelly, John. 66
Kincheloe, William. 67
Kuykendall, Abner 68
Kuykendall, Barzillai. 69
Kuykendall, Joseph 70
Kuykendall, Robert H. 72
Leakey, Joel. 73
Little, William. 74
Lynch, Nathaniel 75

Marsh, Shubael. 76
McCormick, Arthur. 77
McCrosky, John 78
McNeel, John 79
Mims, Joseph 80
Moore, John H.. 81
Morton, William. 82
Newman, Joseph 83
Pentecost, George S. 84
Phelps, James Aeneas 85
Polley, Joseph H. 87
Pryor, William 88
Rabb, John. 89
Rabb, Thomas. 90
Rabb, William. 91
Roark, Elijah 92
Roberts, Noel Francis 93
Roberts, William. 94
Robinson, George. 95
Scobey, Robert 96
Scott, James. 97
Selkirk, William 99
Shipman, Daniel. 101
Shipman, Moses. 103
Sims, Bartlett S.. 105
Singleton, George Washington 106
Singleton, Phillip 108
Smith, Christian 109
Smith, Cornelius. 110
Smithers, Smeathers, Smothers, William. 111
Stafford, Adam. 113
Stafford, William 115
Teel, George Washington. 117
Thomas, Ezekiel. 118
Thompson, Jesse. 119
Tumlinson, Elizabeth. 120
Tumlinson, Jr., James. 121
Walker, Sr., James 122
Wallace, Caleb 123

White, Amy Comstock 124
Whiteside, Boland 125
Whiteside, Henry 125
Whiteside, James 126
Whiteside, William 127
Whitlock, William 128
Williams, Thomas 129
Woods, Zadock. 130
References 133
Glossary 157
Time Line. 159
Bugbee's Old Three Hundred List. 163
Maps of Land Grants. 178
Descendants of Austin's Old Three Hundred 211
Index. 239

Foreword

On New Year's Day, 1830, Stephen F. Austin sat at his desk in San Felipe composing a petition to Commissioner General Juan Antonio Padilla on behalf of the early settlers of his first colony. As he set forth the arguments in favor of an augmentation of land for these first colonists, the reflections and reminiscences that often color the transition from the old to the new year may have pressed on Austin recollections of the time he was first informed of his father's bold project to settle three hundred families in the Texas wilderness and of the travails that subsequently attended the concretion of this enterprise. Foremost in his thoughts were the settlers who came with him in 1821 and 1822 and the steadfast fortitude they displayed in resisting the privations and dangers they confronted. The enterprising individuals, Austin wrote, laid the foundation of the colony in the heart of the wilderness, and the ensuing advances experienced in Texas were the result of their perseverance. Austin put it succinctly as he argued for his early colonists in the petition to Padilla: ". . . had it not been for the toils of the first [settlers] the others would have never come. In the beginning they risked everything, now there is no risk, no danger, no difficulty whatsoever."

In its inception the Austins conceived the Texas venture as a way to recoup the family fortune, and while Stephen may have eventually subsumed his initial desire for profit to what he came to perceive as his civilizing mission in Texas, most of the first colonists also came to Texas propelled by the hope of economic gain. The Anglo colonization of Texas was driven not by the search for greater political or religious freedom, the conscious advance of some preconceived manifest destiny, or by a utopian dream, but by the pursuit of individual economic self-interest. The glamorous episodes of history are often couched in terms of a struggle for some lofty cause, but the course of history has been changed as much by economic determinations as by the pursuit of these presumably loftier ends, and there can be no doubt that the successful rooting of the first Anglo colonies in Texas changed the history of this region. In retrospect, it was a decisive moment in the events that finally cost Mexico half of its national territory and completed the continental span of the American nation from the Atlantic to the Pacific Ocean.

The lure for these settlers was cheap land, and lots of it, and the distinction of being one of what came to be known as the "Old Three Hundred" emanated directly from being the recipient, through merit, design, or simple good fortune, of a land grant under the terms of Austin's first contract. Capricious fate deprived many other would-be settlers active in the inception of Austin's first colony of a land grant under the first contract and of the distinction this eventually conferred.

Austin's first contract was the only contract approved under the provisions of the 1823 Imperial Colonization Law of Mexico. Austin and a commissioner appointed by the governor were authorized to distribute the land to the settlers and issue titles to them in the name of the Mexican government. The quantity of land allotted to a head of a household was set at a minimum of one *labor* (177 acres) for farmers and one league (4,428 acres) for stock raisers, while those who professed both occupations could obtain a league and a *labor*. This amount could be increased without specified limits to settlers who had large families or to those who established new industries or were useful to the province or nation in other ways. The law stipulated that the land was to be cultivated within two years from the date of the title or run the risk of being forfeited, and several of the first contract grants were, in fact, voided for noncompliance with the provision. In the end, Commissioners Baron de Bastrop and Gaspar Flores issued 297 recognized titles between 1824 and 1828 under the first contract.

The process of distributing the land was not without its difficulties. Austin's desire to have a compact settlement was wracked by the "rambling disposition" of his settlers and the grants were scattered from the Lavaca to the San Jacinto Rivers and from the coast to the San Antonio Road, with concentrations of grants in the most fertile areas. Although this complicated the task of protecting and governing the early colonists, Austin eventually recognized that the dispersion facilitated the settlement of later colonists over an extensive tract of land.

Land selection proved to be another source of difficulties. Every settler wanted a tract of land that was well-watered, fertile, and supplied with good timber and prairie, and disputes over land selections were inevitable and provoked dissension. Some of the settlers also complained about being slighted in the amount of land that Austin allocated them, and others challenged his right to collect from them a fee of twelve and a half cents per acre for surveying the land and obtaining a title. As one might expect, civil disputes also arose among these independent and individualistic settlers, but in hindsight Austin suggested that the colonists had been freer of internal dissension than could be expected under the circumstances. To this assessment he added: ". . . they have borne with the most inflexible fortitude, all the privations, to which their situation exposed them, and have contributed largely, in laying a foundation for the future prosperity of Texas, by commencing the settlement of its wilderness." In many ways the first colony was the testing grounds of the Mexican colonization plan, and its success opened the way for further immigration and set the standard for later colonies.

Although scattered Anglo immigrants had been encroaching on the Texas frontier for years before the arrival of Austin's first settlers, these colonists were the first organized, approved influx of Anglo-American immigrants. Despite the undeniable hardships of the first years, several underlying conditions propitiated their survival and growth. The land was fertile and game was plentiful. The colony was set down in virgin country where there had been no Spanish or Mexican settlement, which precluded conflicts like those that later beset Had Edwards. The colonists were allowed to govern themselves internally under the criminal and civil regulations set down by Austin and, above all, they had the invaluable guidance of a leader who oversaw the quality of settlers entering the colony, served as an intermediary with the Mexican authorities when friction arose over matters such as slave ownership and tariffs, and sought to further their general interests.

Austin's story is well documented, but the story of his hardy

colonists deserves to be expanded. Austin's first settlers consti-
tuted a diverse group of enterprising, persevering individuals,
both men and women, and in the pages that follow the reader will
be able to revive the adventures and contributions of these coura-
geous colonists, through the accounts of the justifiably proud descendants of the pioneering constituents of the "seed colony of
Texas," Austin's Old Three Hundred.

—GALEN GREASER
Archives and Records Division
Texas General Land Office

Preface

Most of the information in this volume was previously published by the Descendants of Austin's Old Three Hundred in two earlier editions, under the title *The First Colony of Texas: Austin's Old 300*. The material in those volumes, now out of print, has been revised and other articles added. An added feature to the present edition is maps showing, county-by-county, the location of land grants awarded the Old Three Hundred settlers.

The basic premise of the earlier books has been retained: to provide glimpses of those who made up Stephen F. Austin's first colony as conveyed in the words of their direct descendants. The sketches reproduced here were either written or the information collected by one or more descendants of each subject.

Over one-third of Austin's "Old Three Hundred" colonists are represented here. Some of the grantees were bachelors and received their land with one or more partners; others were either childless or their direct lineage has run its course. Still others are awaiting the time when their descendants will take up the challenge and provide us with information about their illustrious ancestor.

Please note that names reproduced in this volume are the original spellings as found in state and office records. For updated spellings, where they occur, see the Ancestor Descendant list starting on page 211.

— The Editors

Acknowledgments

You are holding the third edition of what our organization tends to call The Ancestor Book, the second edition published by Eakin Press. We are grateful to Kris Gholson of that publishing house for his cooperation and flexibility in meeting our needs and humoring our wants.

Let me next say that as your immediate past President General, I was proud and pleased at the response from the Descendants when the call went out for biographies of Old Three Hundred colonists not represented in previous editions. We felt that twenty new entries was the minimum number needed to justify a new edition, and you produced thirty-seven! Thank you, thank you! for your unique and invaluable contribution to this book.

This level of response added to the workload facing the Ancestor Book Committee, but it was certainly a nice problem to have. Committee members Wincie Campbell, Tim Cumings, Virginia Scarborough, and Shirley Stedman were aided greatly in their task by the expertise and energy of retired library professional Wolfram M. Von-Maszewski of Richmond. Extra thanks go to Matthew E. Von-Maszewski and A. T. Campbell III for their technical expertise and assistance.

Once again, accuracy was the top goal. Time was invested in verifying the spelling of ancestors' names and place names (and sometimes the result was an arbitrary choice between two equally likely spellings). On those rare occasions when elements in an account were clearly at odds with known fact, known fact won out. But the flavor injected by each contributor has remained.

Among others lending a helping hand were Russell Autrey with original drawings, researcher Clint Drake of the George Memorial Library in Richmond, and James Harkins of the Texas

General Land Office. We also appreciate the permission given by General Land Office archivist Galen Greaser to re-use his fine Foreword from the previous Eakin edition. Inevitably, one or more of the folks who assisted this project in some way will be inadvertently overlooked. Please accept our apologies in advance.

— DOROTHY W. WILBECK
President General, 2006-2010

Biographies

Martin Allen

Martin Allen was born November 28, 1780, in Kentucky. He married Elizabeth Vice on September 27, 1804. She was born in Virginia. They had ten children.

In 1812 Martin joined the Gutierrez-Magee Expedition. His father, Benjamin Allen was killed at the Battle of Medina in 1813. Martin moved to Arkansas Territory in 1817, then to Allen's Settlement, Louisiana, named in his honor. He then joined Stephen F. Austin's First Colony, The Old Three Hundred. In Texas in 1821, he was one of the first settlers on the Colorado River. In 1822, while he was back in the U.S. taking care of his ailing wife, he sent his sons Miles N. and James Bud to plant a crop and claim his land. Martin was granted one *sitio* of land in present-day Wharton County and one *labor* of land in present-day Austin County in July 1824. He and his family were in Texas in 1826 and appear on the first Texas census.

Martin signed the Loyalty Resolution to Mexico in 1827, was made a road supervisor in 1830 and was granted the right to operate a ferry across the Buffalo Bayou near Harrisburg. He also signed the call to the Convention in 1832, was made *regidor* of *ayuntamiento* at San Felipe, Captain in the Civil Militia, and elected justice of the peace and land commissioner. The Allen family operated a "public house" for many years. Martin served in the Texas War for Independence. He gave much in goods and service to help Texas win its freedom from Mexico.

Martin died at his home at Eight Mile Point in Austin County in 1837, leaving an estate of 8,600 acres, animals, wagons, and slaves. Elizabeth died in 1843. Both are buried in the Allen-Johnston Cemetery on Allen's Creek. A Texas State Historical Marker was dedicated in 1993 to his memory and to his accomplishments in early Texas history.

— MRS. H. G. (KATHERINE ALLEN)
HARRISON #2

Charles Grandison Alsbury

One of the elder sons of Captain Thomas Alsbury, Charles Grandison (or Grundison), born in Kanawha County, Virginia, was an early settler of Austin's first colony. He was on the Brazos River when the schooner *Lively* landed in August 1822. He received one half of a league as a part of grant No. 177 located on the west bank of the San Bernard River near the Gulf. He shared the grant with his brothers Horace and Harvey. Today it is a part of a National Wildlife Refuge.

He was politically active in the April 1824 colony election as well as in the December 1824 San Felipe election. In an incident in 1825, he came to the aid of a party of cold, wet and tired Texans who were pursuing a mule thief. Two Kuykendalls, two Gateses, Moses Shipman and others took a rest stop at Aunt Betty Whiteside's house, when all she could offer was cold buttermilk. Charles Alsbury pulled coffee out of his saddlebag and Aunt Betty made hot coffee for all.

Charles unsuccessfully tried to establish a town he called Monticello on his parents' land grant at the mouth of Cow Creek. His land grant was in the eastern end of the Karankawa Indian hunting grounds. In fact, he was killed in 1828 while fighting in the Indian campaigns. His brother Harvey disappeared and was also presumed killed by Indians.

— DELBERT W. WHITAKER #374

The *alcalde* was the chief officer of the local government. As a sign of his office the *alcalde* carried a silver-headed cane, and when he could not appear in person, he could be represented by sending his cane.

Dr. Horace Arlington Alsbury

Land grant No. 177, made on August 3, 1824, gave Horace and his brothers, Charles and Harvey, half a league apiece on the west bank of the San Bernard River. Their father, Thomas Alsbury, also received a grant from Stephen F. Austin.

As a colonist who could understand Spanish, Horace was used on occasion to interpret the language of his adopted country. In August 1835, he authored an open letter warning the people of Texas about Santa Anna's intent to wage war.

Horace married Juana Navarro. She was the niece of Vice-Governor Juan Veramendi, James Bowie's father-in-law. Juana was in the Alamo when it fell, Horace having left her there for safekeeping. Earlier, Horace had taken part in the Siege of Bexar in Captain York's Company.

Horace and his younger brother, Young Perry, served in Texas Army's spy cavalry company during the Battle of San Jacinto. Along with six other men, they reportedly chased Santa Anna and his staff and cornered them at the recently burned bridge on Vince's Bayou (Young helped the scout Deaf Smith with that deed as well). Santa Anna was captured the next day.

In 1842 invading Mexicans captured Horace at Bexar Plaza in San Antonio and imprisoned him at Perote. He was released two years later, and in 1846 he and some of his brothers volunteered for duty in the U.S.-Mexican War. Horace was killed near Saltillo, Mexico, in the bloody last battle of Buena Vista.

— DELBERT W. WHITAKER #374

"G.T.T." was the message left behind in the United States when settlers had GONE TO TEXAS.

Captain Thomas Alsbury

Stephen F. Austin may have seen the potential value in having the Thomas Alsbury family, with its seven sons and three daughters, become part of his colony. He wrote to his mother and sister urging them to have his brother contact and assist the Alsbury family in making the move from Hopkinsville, Kentucky, to Texas.

Long before, Thomas Alsbury had been a company commander in a regiment of the Kentucky Mounted Volunteers during the War of 1812. He married Leah Jane Catlett of a prominent Maryland family. Thomas, born in Virginia in 1773, fathered his own family in Kanawha County, Virginia, and Christian County, Kentucky. He helped found Hopkinsville, Kentucky, where he was a major property owner and ran a sawmill and tavern. He held various public posts.

Thomas settled on grant No. 42 on the west bank of the Brazos River. One of his leagues was in present-day Brazoria County and one in Fort Bend County. He died August 15, 1826. The gravesite is unknown.

— DELBERT W. WHITAKER #374

The Texas Navy

Texas had a three-warship Navy during the Revolution in the spring of 1836. They were the *Invincible* under Capt. Brown, the *Brutus* under Capt. Hurd, and the *Independence* under Capt. Hawkins. Later in the year the Navy added the *Liberty*, captain not stated.

William Andrews

William Andrews received his grant, signed by Stephen F. Austin and Baron de Bastrop, on July 14, 1824. His land lay on the east side of the Brazos River. He was warned of his obligations to live on and cultivate the land for two years.

Andrews married Susan Clark on August 20, 1805, in St. Landry Parish, Louisiana. Six of their children were born there: Richard, Mary Ann, Micah, Joseph Zabulon, William Alexander, and Elizabeth. At least three were born after they came to Texas: Susan, Pamelia, and Walter.

The 1826 Census of Austin's Colony listed him as a farmer/stockraiser, between the age of forty and fifty, wife between thirty and forty, five children under sixteen, and two slaves.

Originally, William was against the idea of independence from Mexico, but he changed his views after the events leading to the battles of Anahuac and Velasco, and the imprisonment of Stephen F. Austin by the Mexican government.

Austin's call to arms came on September 19, 1835, as General Cos was moving his army into Texas. Two of William's sons, Richard and Micah, answered the call from Bastrop County. Both were wounded and Richard died the next day. Richard is said to have been the first casualty of the Revolution. Micah lived to fight in the Battle of San Jacinto.

William Andrews died before January 10, 1840, leaving a substantial estate. Half was to go to his wife and the other half to be divided equally among his children.

— JONETTE HENSON BALLMER #188

Samuel Tubbs Angier

Samuel Tubbs Angier was born in Pembroke, Plymouth County, Massachusetts, on August 26, 1792, the son of Samuel and Mary Tubbs. In 1812, he changed his name to Samuel Tubbs Angier, taking as his surname the maiden name of his paternal grandmother, Katurah (Angier) Tubbs. He received his A.B. degree in 1818 and his M.D. degree from Brown University in 1823. Samuel was married and had two daughters in Massachusetts.

When he came to Texas, Angier, in partnership with Thomas W. Bradley and George B. Hall, received title to a *sitio* of land on August 16, 1824, and in his name only, received a *labor* on August 24, 1824. In a quiet ceremony at the home of James Britton (Brit) Bailey, Samuel married Mrs. Pamelia Picket, a widow who was also one of The Old Hundred, on April 30, 1829.

Angier was one of the four established physicians of Brazoria Municipality who early in the 1830s were appointed by the *ayuntamiento* as a standing committee to examine the qualifications of persons wishing to practice surgery and medicine in the municipality. He was one of several signatories of a memorial to the Congress of the Republic of Texas requesting the establishment of a system of public education. Samuel was active in civic affairs and served as an election judge. He was a Methodist and a Freemason.

Pamelia Angier died September 5, 1837. In 1842 Samuel married Mary Ann Kendall in Monroe County, Alabama, and when they returned to Texas, she became the headmistress of the Columbia Female Seminary. Samuel and Mary Ann Angier had a son, Eugene Luther. Mary Ann died in 1854 and Angier married Mrs. Mary O'Brien Millard on May 25, 1857. Dr. Angier died April 17, 1867, in West Columbia. He is buried in the Columbia Cemetery in West Columbia.

— JAMES PATTON #221

James Britton Bailey

North Carolina was the birthplace of James Britton Bailey in 1779. He was a descendant of Kenneth Bailey, whose ancestor was Robert Bruce, once King of Scotland. Bailey sailed from New Orleans to Anahuac, Texas, with his second wife Nancy and six children. They settled on the Brazos River in 1821, then called the Brazos District. Three years later Stephen F. Austin legalized Bailey's claim by making him one of the Old Three Hundred.

Brit Bailey was a hardy rancher and farmer. He became a friend to the Indians and on many occasions was peacemaker for the settlers.

James Bailey, Brit's youngest son, drowned in a river as a child. Phelps Bailey, the second son, was killed by unfriendly Indians. Smith Bailey, number three son, was killed in the Battle of the Alamo. Elizabeth (Betsy), the oldest daughter, was captured by Indians but escaped unharmed in the darkness of the night. The youngest daughter, Mary "Pollie," married Joseph Henry Polley, another Old Three Hundred grantee.

Stephen F. Austin arranged a meeting of the settlers on the Brazos River, in Bailey's home. Here they took an oath of fidelity

---

Brit Bailey was one of the more colorful characters of the Old Three Hundred. Since his death and burial in 1832 at Bailey's Prairie, there have been numerous reports of his ghost appearing. It is said that the first sighting was in human form to Ann Thomas, who with her husband bought Bailey's place a few years after his death. Beginning in the 1850s the ghost has taken the form of a ball of light that appears on foggy nights and floats over the land and moves away when pursued. There are many stories of people watching the light roam the prairie.

In 1950 a gas well blew out and the fumes caused nearby Highway 35 to be closed for a week. Folks from around there said Brit did not want a well that close to his grave.

If some foggy night you are driving down Highway 35 just west of Angleton, across Bailey's Prairie, slow down and look very carefully. You may see Bailey's Light.

to the Constitution of 1824. At this meeting a group of militia was organized. At Austin's request, Bailey was appointed lieutenant. In 1829 the Governor Jose Maria Viesca bestowed on Bailey a commission as captain. In 1832 Bailey took part in the Battle of Velasco. Bailey had also served in the War of 1812.

Britton Bailey was a straight-shooting pioneer who endured many hardships. In stature he was a large man, feared and respected by the Indians and neighbors. In December 1832, according to his request, he was buried standing up, facing west, with his rifle at his side, in the family graveyard on Bailey's Prairie.

—GEORGE BERT EVERTS #196

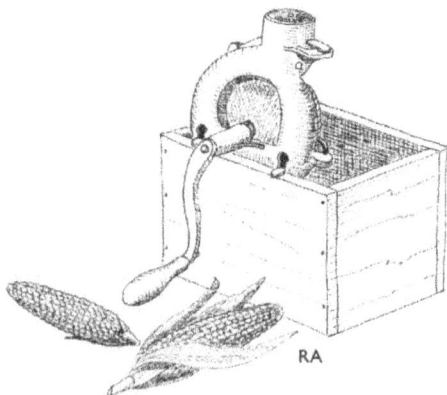

RA

Noah Smithwick wrote, "As one old lady remarked, Texas was a heaven for men and dogs, but a hell for women and oxen."

William Barret (Barrett)

William Barret came to Texas as a single man, aged twenty-six, from Pennsylvania. He and Abner Harris were granted land in Austin's first colony in Fort Bend County on June 4, 1827. Family tradition says that Barret was kin to James Beard, another Old Three Hundred colonist.

One of the few documented acts of Barret's life was his marriage to Elizabeth Wiant on the east bank of the Brazos River. The marriage contract reads:

> Be it known that we William Barret and Elizabeth Wiant of lawful age of Austin Colony and state of [Coahuila] and Texas wishing to unite ourselves in the bonds of matrimony and there being no Priest in the Colony to Celebrate the same,
>
> Therefore I William Barret do agree to take and do hereby take Elizabeth Wiant to be my legal and lawful wife and as such to cherish support and protect forsaking all others and keeping myself true and faithful unto her alone. And I Elizabeth Wiant do agree to take and do hereby take William Barret to be my legal and lawful husband and as such to love honor and obey him forsaking all others keeping myself true and faithful unto him alone, and we also mutually bind ourselves to each other in the sum of five thousand dollars to have our marriage Celebrated by the Priest of the Colony or some other Priest Authorized so to do as soon as an opportunity offer, all of which we do promise in the name of God and in the presence of Alex[ander] Hodge Commissario and the other witnesses Present in Testimony whereof we have hereunto set our hands on the River Brazos this Eighth Day of July in the year of our Lord 1829

To this union were born a son, Thomas William, on April 8, 1831, and a daughter, Elizabeth, who married Reuben Weir in 1846. Barret served in the Texas military offensive against Mexico in late 1835 under Captain W. H. Patton and Commander Edward Burleson. In 1841 he purchased 4,028 acres in Brazoria County. In 1853 Weir was made administrator of Barret's estate.

— DEURENE OATES MORGAN #62

Benjamin Beason

On August 7, 1824, Benjamin Beason received title to one league of land situated in the present county of Colorado, two leagues from the Atascosito Crossing of the Colorado River. He and his family had emigrated to Texas in 1822 from Hardin County, Tennessee. Beason and his wife, Elizabeth, had the following children: Lydia, Nepsey, Collins, Abel, Edward, Leander, Benjamin, and Mary Ann.

Benjamin Beason owned and operated a ferry on the Colorado River at Beason's Crossing, the present site of Columbus. His wife kept a boardinghouse. Sam Houston's army camped at Beason's Crossing on the east side of the river from March 19 to March 26, 1836. When his army moved on toward the Brazos, the Beason family was forced to leave its home as the Mexican army approached. Many people crossed the river on Beason's ferry, after which the ferry and all existing buildings were burned.

The Beason family was in Harrisburg in April 1836. Mrs. Beason was an enterprising woman. On April 10 she wrote David G. Burnet, President of Texas, for permission to open a boardinghouse at Harrisburg for the support of the family until they could return to their home.

Beason died before March 9, 1837. His estate was probated in Colorado County in 1837 with Leander Beason and W. B. Dewees as administrators. Benjamin Beason's will is the oldest one on record in Colorado County.

— Nancy Jane Perry Wooten #242

The first book printed in Texas was Stephen F. Austin's *Establishing Austin's Colony*. It was Austin's account of the establishment of the first Anglo-American settlement of Texas and an English translation of the laws and documents relating to the founding of the colony. It was printed in San Felipe by Godwin B. Cotten in 1829.

Isaac Best

Isaac Best, the son of Stephen Best and probably, Sarah Humphrey, was born about 1774 near Philadelphia, Pennsylvania. His wife was Mary Margaret Wilkins, the daughter of John Wilkins, born about 1776 in Kent County, Maryland.

They were married April 9, 1794, in Madison County, Kentucky. It was in Kentucky that Isaac and Margaret's first seven children were born: John about 1794; Isaac about 1796; Humphrey about 1797; Sarah "Sally," 1800; Phoebe, 1802; Mary "Polly," 1804; and Margaret "Peggy," 1807.

In 1808 Isaac moved his family to the Louisiana Territory. The couple had two more sons while living there: Ebenezer W. "Eben" born in 1808, and Stephen born in 1810.

When Stephen F. Austin sought families to settle his new colony in Texas, Isaac, Margaret, sons Humphrey, Ebenezer, and Stephen, and daughter Margaret, answered the call. They made the 800-mile journey by caravan, carrying not only their regular belongings, but their millstone as well. They arrived at the Brazos River on December 31, 1821. It was not until August 19, 1824, that they received a grant for one *sitio* of land on the east bank of the Brazos River between the Cushatti (Coshate) and La Bahia Roads. This was located near the present town of Hempstead.

Isaac sold his original grant on October 8, 1828, to Jared E. Groce and bought a number of tracts on the east side of the Brazos River near San Felipe. There he built his plantation.

Isaac died intestate on February 8, 1837. Margaret died intestate in February 1852.

The Texas Historical Commission placed a marker to the memory of Isaac Best and Mary Wilkins Best near Pattison in Waller County on September 1, 1974.

—EDDIE WAYNE BADER #277

Thomas Boatwright

Thomas Boatwright was born in Virginia in 1763. He married Amy Rushing in North Carolina about 1792. Five sons and six daughters blessed their marriage.

In autumn 1821, the family of Thomas and Amy Boatwright loaded their wagons and left Miller County, Arkansas, for Stephen F. Austin's Colony. Traveling in a wagon train with the Gilleland and other families, they arrived at the bend of the Red River, left U.S. Territory, and crossed over into Mexico. At that point, Trammel's Trace emerged, a road leading from Arkansas and terminating at the El Camino Real in Nacogdoches. After spending Thanksgiving in Nacogdoches, they followed El Camino Real arriving at La Bahia Crossing on the Brazos River on December 31, 1821. The next morning they crossed over into Austin's land grant, traveling ten miles beyond the crossing, and on the first day of 1822 camped beside a stream known today as New Year Creek in Washington County. On July 27, 1824, Thomas Boatwright received a league of land fronting the Brazos River in what is today Austin County. Thomas' daughter Pricilla married Daniel Gilleland and they received their grant in the southeast corner by Boatwright's grant. Thus, two Old Three Hundred families were united.

About 1829, Thomas and Amy Boatwright returned to Miller County, Arkansas, to protest the United States' agreement with the Choctaw Indians that gave the Indians all of their property in Arkansas. While in Arkansas, Thomas died.

His widow, Amy, and three of her sons, Thomas J., Friend, and Richard were all back in Texas in 1833, making applications for land grants. Amy Boatwright was seventy-two years old. On October 24, 1835, she and each of her sons received a grant of a league of land. Amy Boatwright died about 1839.

— FRANKIE LELAND CARTER #555

Edward R. Bradley

Edward R. Bradley was born in Fayette County, Kentucky, in 1760. His father, also Edward Bradley, came from Pennsylvania and was among those who crossed the mountain with Daniel Boone. Young Edward first married Molly Duncan; after her death, he married Elizabeth Winn around 1795. The twenty-year-old Elizabeth was kin to the prominent Lee family of Virginia. Her father George was wealthy and left land and slaves to all eleven of his children.

The Bradleys and their eight children came to Austin's Colony in 1822 to claim a grant. Oldest son Thomas and three sons-in-law — George Braxton Hall, David Talley, and Chester S. Gorbet — also received grants in the original colony. A daughter, Sarah Bradley Dodson, made the first lone-star flag of Texas in 1836 for her husband, Archeleus B. Dodson.

Edward's league of land was on the east side of the Brazos River, close to that of Talley and Gorbet. He was reportedly buried there in 1826. Elizabeth also buried five of her children before she died in 1843 and was buried alongside her husband.

Bradley has many descendants, but all spring from his five daughters and so none carries the Bradley name.

— JACKIE THOMPSON WAITES #455

Dr. Pleasant Rose said if he were the owner of a wagon he would be one of the aristocracy. He said his neighbors were divided into three classes: those who owned wagons were the aristocracy, the second class owned carts; as he had a sleigh, he belonged to the lower class.

Charles C. Breen

Charles Breen's Mexican grant states that he came to Texas in 1825, to settle in Austin's Colony. The absence of Commissioner Bastrop prevented him from receiving a legal title to his land until May 24, 1827. Gaspar Flores, the new commissioner, and Stephen F. Austin signed his title.

Breen's property is recorded as league #40, on the west side of San Bernardo Creek, on Bay Prairie. Today this land is in Brazoria County, not far from the city of Sweeny. In fact, part is in the city limits.

The Breen family moved to Texas after their fourth child, Calton N. Breen, was born. It is believed that the Christopher Breen who lost his life in the Siege of Bexar was their son. Their two daughters were Mary and Hannah Elizabeth.

On the 1850 census they were listed in Williamson County, giving Charles' age as sixty-three and born in Georgia, and Martha as being born in South Carolina, and her age was fifty-five. Charles Breen died early in the year 1851.

According to the 1860 Williamson County census, Martha was living with her only surviving child, Hannah and husband, John Knox Payne. Martha died February 12, 1890, and is buried in Lawrence Chapel Cemetery in Williamson County. To reach the cemetery, begin just south of Highway 95 overpass in Taylor, Texas, turning right on FM 112. Continue through Noack to Lawrence Chapel sign, 10.6 miles. From this sign to the cemetery is 2.9 miles.

—SHERRILL LOUISE JOHNSON #336

William Bridges

On July 17, 1824, William B. Bridges received a Stephen F. Austin grant of one league of land. This land was located on the Lavaca River, northeast of the present town of Edna, Jackson County, Texas.

Bridges' first wife died in Mississippi. Cynthia Ross and William Bridges were married in Mississippi in 1824. His first child by his second wife was born in Victoria County on December 18, 1825. They had three girls: Mary, Martha, and Elizabeth. Cynthia died in 1831, in Jackson County, Texas. The 1850 Census listed William Bridges' birthplace as North Carolina, and his age as fifty-five.

The War for Texas Independence found Bridges serving in John Alley's Company. His service lasted two terms: October 3, 1835, to an honorable discharge November 25, 1835; then from July 3, 1836, to October 1836.

He was a resident of Gonzales County in May 1838, where he proved that he was entitled to a *labor* of land (177 acres) because he had drawn a colonial grant of one league (4,428 acres) under Mexican law, and now under the Republic of Texas was entitled to another *labor*. He received a patent (deed) for it in Gonzales County in 1841.

Bridges married Eliza Lyons Tribble. They had six children: Amanda, Harriet, William B. Jr., John, Sophronoa, and Carrie.

William Bridges was elected justice of the peace in 1840 and 1845. The family had moved to Black Jack Springs, Fayette County, Texas, where Bridges died in March 1853.

— Violet Ranne McElhinney #342

David Bright

David Bright, the son of George Adam and Mary Bright, was born in Augusta County, Virginia, in 1770. David married Judith Dinsmore, who was born in England and came to Amherst County, Virginia, with her father James Dinsmore. Their marriage on June 6, 1799, was one of the first recorded in Augusta County.

David and Judith Bright's known children were: Sarah Ann, who married Eli Hunter, John McCrosky, and William D. Lacey; Elizabeth, who married Noel Roberts; George was unmarried; Mary, who married Gabriel Straw Snider and Patrick Reels; and Haney, who married Thomas Jamison.

Bright and his family came to Texas from Illinois by way of Arkansas in 1822, landing near the mouth of the Colorado River. On December 20, 1823, he voted in the *alcalde* election at San Felipe de Austin. He was one of the electors in the Colorado District in April 1824 when Baron de Bastrop was chosen the Texas delegate to the state convention of Coahuila and Texas.

In 1823 and 1824, David Bright was a blazer, who cut the brush for the chainmen of surveyor Horatio Chriesman in the Oyster Creek area of Fort Bend County. On July 15, 1824, Bright received one league of land in present Fort Bend County and one *labor* of land in present Austin County. These Old Three Hundred grants are recorded in the General Land Office in Austin, Texas.

The census of 1826 classified Bright as a farmer and stock raiser, age over fifty. His household included his wife, a son, and a daughter.

In April 1836, the Bright family and the Patrick Reels family were camped near Liberty during the Runaway Scrape.

David Bright died September 2, 1837, and the petition of William D. Lacey to administer the estate was filed in Matagorda County on September 14, 1837. Judith Dinsmore Bright died August 15, 1838, in Matagorda County. The final settlement of their estate was filed on March 2, 1842.

— DONNA MCCROSKY JOHNSON # 23

Captain Jesse Burnam

Jesse Burnam was born in Madison County, Kentucky, on September 15, 1792. He moved to Bedford County, Tennessee, with his mother, six brothers and sisters. When Jesse was eighteen years old, his mother died, leaving him no money. On her deathbed, she urged him to be "honest and industrious."

In his twentieth year, Jesse wrote, I married an orphan girl, named Temperance Baker, I made rails for a jack-leg blacksmith and had him make me three knives and three forks and I put handles on them. My wife sold the stockings she was married in, made by her own hands, for a set of plates. I traded a small piece of land and then we were ready for housekeeping. We used gourds for cups.

His family and nine other families headed for Texas, settling at Pecan Point on February 15, 1821. Later they moved across the Colorado River, near La Grange in Fayette County.

Jesse's wife Temperance died May 4, 1837, leaving him with a large family of small children. Their children were William, Mary, John, Hickerson, Minerva, Nancy (said to be the first child born in Austin's Colony), Amanda, James H., and Jesse Bennett.

Jesse married Nancy Cummins Ross, daughter of James Cummins, another colonist, and widow of James J. Ross. Their children were: Emily Maria, Henry, Sadie Ellen, Waddy Linsecum, Adelia Lee, and Alice.

Nancy died on February 3, 1863, and Jesse died on April 30, 1883. They are both buried on the Burnam Ranch in Burnet County.

Captain Jesse Burnam fought in the war with Mexico. He had served as a delegate from Colorado County to the Convention of 1832, the Consultation of 1835, as representative in the second session of the First Congress of the Republic of Texas, and was a member of the Council of the Provisional Government of the Republic of Texas.

—JULIA NAIL MOSS #26

Micajah Byrd

Micajah Byrd was born in Frederick County, Virginia, about 1789. He married Hannah Bradbury, born about 1795. They were among the first arrivals of Austin's colonists at La Bahia Brazos River Crossing in 1821.

In the 1930s my grandmother, who was the granddaughter of Micajah Byrd, said that the Byrds came from Virginia, where they had slaves but none were brought into Texas. Her mother told her also that she would sit on S. F. Austin's lap during his visits to their home. The patent to the 4,428 acres grant was issued on July 10, 1824.

Alden Hatch states in his biography on the Byrds of Virginia (1969) that Micajah Byrd went to Texas with Austin in 1821. In the Texas census of 1823 and 1826, Micajah and Hannah Byrd were enumerated as being farmers and stock raisers with one female child at about six years of age. Stephen F. Austin picked his settlers well as was exemplified by the stalwart Byrd family who took an active part in community affairs. Micajah served as an election judge in 1826-27 to elect an *alcalde*. He was on a committee that registered a protest condemning the Fredonian Rebellion. He was referred to as Major Byrd in the local defense force.

Hannah Byrd was a good, compassionate soul in caring for neighbors. My great-grandmother related the plight of a Mrs. Whiteside to Captain Chriesman, which resulted in the alleviation of much suffering.

Micajah Byrd fathered four daughters, my great-grandmother Nancy Byrd, being the youngest. He died in 1830 during a yellow fever epidemic. Living close to the river with mosquitoes, a carrier of the disease, probably caused his early death. Hannah Byrd later married James Gray of Washington County. She died in 1862.

— JOHN STEVEN HOWARD #75

Sylvanus Castleman

Sylvanus Castleman married Betsy Lucas, in Davidson County, Tennessee. They emigrated to Sainte Genevieve, Missouri, by March 1822. There he signed on with Stephen F. Austin as one of the Old Three Hundred colonists.

Sylvanus first settled in the vicinity of Columbus, on Cummins Creek. He later received title to two *sitios* of land in present-day Wharton County. He also received two *labores* in present Austin County on July 7, 1824.

On March 4, 1823, Stephen F. Austin made a list of American settlers in the Colorado District. Sylvanus Castleman was listed as being forty-six years of age, a farmer with cattle and hogs. His family at that time consisted of Elizabeth (thirty-seven), Nancy (eighteen), Sarah (seventeen), Elizabeth (thirteen), Lavena (eleven), Benjamin (seven), and Jacob (two).

On December 3, 1823, Stephen F. Austin appointed Sylvanus judge for the election held in the Colony for *alcalde*. Castleman was elected by 12 of the 17 votes, and took office on January 26, 1824.

The exact date of death and the place of burial are unknown, but at the July term of court in 1841, in Fayette County, Sylvanus' estate was partitioned between his wife, children, and grandchildren.

It is known that in his latter days, he had moved to the west side of the Brazos, about ten to twelve miles above San Felipe. It was here that he became deranged and committed suicide.

—KATHY FAUL #132

John Prince Coles

"Judge Coles was a man of great learning, courtly and digni-
fied in manners and very popular, both as officer and man."
— *Brenham Banner Press*, July 4, 1890

In 1989, the Texas Historical Commission honored him with
a Historical Marker. The Independence Historical Society restored his 1824 log-hewn house, the oldest home in Washington
County.

Coles was born in Rowan County, North Carolina, in 1793. He
married Mary Eleanor Owen in Georgia in 1816. In 1822, he entered Texas with his wife and two children and in 1824 received a
land grant of eight and one half leagues (37,638 acres) near Yegua
Creek. He died in 1847, at the age of fifty-three, and was buried at
Independence, Texas.

In 1824, he established Coles Settlement, which Stephen F.
Austin came to call the "Athens of Texas" due to its cultural, religious, and educational advantages. After 1835, Coles Settlement
gradually merged into the newly created town of Independence.

Coles was Stephen F. Austin's intimate friend and his agent
for the Upper Settlement. He supervised the building of roads,
bridges, and ferries, organized militias, performed marriages, and
administered elections. He conducted the 1826 Census. Coles was
an original trustee in the establishment of Independence
Academy.

Under Mexican rule, Coles first served as *alcalde* (mayor/
judge) of the Brazos District, then *rigadore* (councilman) for the
municipality of San Felipe. During the Texas Revolution, his family fled in the Runaway Scrape and he later joined William Warner
Hill's Company.

After Texas Independence in 1836, Coles was appointed the
first chief justice (county judge) of Washington County by
President Sam Houston, and in 1840, he was elected to the 5th
Congress of the Republic of Texas. In his twenty-five years in

Texas, John Prince Coles helped shape the political, social, and economic character of Texas, and saw it transform from wilderness to prosperity.

— MARTIN COLES FOR
LUANNE APPEL COLES #755

Judge John P. Coles

John Crier

John Crier was born in 1790, the son of Morgan Cryer and Barbara Morris.

The Crier family moved to Camden County, Georgia, in 1786 and also lived in East Florida where John was baptized in St. Augustine Parish on May 12, 1790. They later moved to West Florida and then to the Arkansas Territory. John's first wife, Cynthia, died some time before he departed Arkansas for Texas. Cynthia was the mother of Andrew and Tolitha.

John Crier received title to one league of land on June 6, 1827, through Stephen F. Austin's first empresario contract with the Mexican government. The land is located in what is now Matagorda County.

John later took up land in Fayette County. He was one of the founders of Fayetteville, along with Judge James Cummins and Captain James Ross. He and Jesse Burnam were the first to plant cotton in Fayette County in 1834.

About 1832 John married again. His second wife was Polly Duty, and they had at least five children.

In 1836 John moved to a home along the Colorado River in Colorado County.

It is reported that John Crier was killed by Indians in March 1856 and buried on the edge of Ross's Prairie, between Ellinger and Fayetteville in Fayette County, Texas.

— MARY ELIZABETH
THOMPSON HAECKER #229

To become a member of Austin's original colony, someone had to swear to the settler's good character. Austin's rules of the colony provided that "no frontiersman who has no other occupation than that of hunter will be received—no drunkard, no gambler, no profane swearer, no idler."

John Chesney Crownover

John Chesney Crownover, born 1799 in Union County, South Carolina, was the third child of John (1774-1842) and Elizabeth Chesney Crownover (1778-1844). He married Nancy Castleman who was born in Franklin, Williamson County, Tennessee, in 1808. She was the daughter of Sylvanus and Elizabeth (Betsy Lucas) Castleman. John Chesney Crownover and Nancy Castleman were the first couple in the new province of Texas to be married by "Bond Marriage." The bond was twenty thousand dollars. It contained a promise to marry on arrival of a priest and fixed a forfeiture sum for a breach by either party. The ceremony took place at San Felipe de Austin on April 29, 1824, and was performed by Stephen F. Austin.

John Chesney Crownover is listed as one of Stephen F. Austin's Old Three Hundred colonists. He received title to a *sitio* of land in present Wharton and Matagorda counties and a *labor* of land in present Austin County on August 3, 1824. John cast his vote for Baron de Bastrop as the Texas Deputy to the Convention of Coahuila and Texas on April 29, 1824. Later, he and Nancy moved to Arkansas where two of their children were born. They returned to Texas where the other four were born. Nancy died during the birth of son John Bunyon on April 1, 1844. Her sisters Sarah Brown and Lavinia Crownover and her son Chesney signed Nancy's nuncupative will in Fayette County, Republic of Texas, on June 5, 1844. She willed to her husband John Chesney the land willed to her by her father Sylvanus Castleman, land that was granted to him by the Mexican government. John Chesney died in 1845. His will, probated in Fayette County on June 16, 1845, lists their six children: Chesney Crownover, Arthur (Arter) Crownover, Jr. (the Jr. was added as he was named for his uncle Arter Crownover), Leona Crownover, Marian R. Crownover, Ruffana Crownover, and John Bunyon Crownover.

John Chesney Crownover was brother to Mary Crownover Rabb, the author of *Reminiscences of Mary Crownover Rabb*.

— MARY ELIZABETH REED #711

James, John, and William Cumings

James, John, and William Cumings, three of Stephen F. Austin's Old Three Hundred colonists, accompanied their mother Rebekah Russel Cumings and sisters Rebecca and Sarah to Texas circa 1822. They all received grants of land in 1824, John and William one league each on July 21 and James six leagues on August 16. These children were born to Anthony and Rebekah Cumings before 1800, in what is now Lewis County, Kentucky; besides the two sisters and three brothers there was another male child. William served in the Kentucky militia in the War of 1812.

After settling in Texas, the three brothers contracted with Stephen F. Austin to construct and operate a gristmill and sawmill on Palmetto (now Mill) Creek in present-day Austin County. In exchange, James Cumings was awarded a five-league grant, or hacienda, and the mills were built on that property.

James died on August 26, 1825, shortly after willing his holdings to John and William. That same year, William journeyed back to Kentucky where, on December 20, 1825, he married Lucinda Ruggles.

The 1826 Texas Census lists John as aged between twenty-five and forty-five, unmarried, and with three slaves. The same census lists William as aged between twenty-five and forty-five, with a wife aged between eighteen and twenty-five, two slaves, and two servants. William had one son, Samuel Anthony, born in 1827. Cumings died at his residence on September 2, 1828, and his widow and child returned to Kentucky.

On at least two occasions, Austin dispatched John Cumings as an emissary to the Cherokee Indians in East Texas. One of these was an attempt by Austin to dissuade the Indians from taking part in the Fredonian Rebellion. John and his sister Rebecca managed the mills as well as an inn, after the death of their brothers, mother, and sister Sarah. The latter was located on the San Felipe-to-Washington road on Mill Creek. John died on April 22, 1839.

— TIMOTHY AUSTIN CUMINGS #18

Rebekah Cumings

Rebekah Cumings (circa 1757-1832), one of Stephen F. Austin's Old Three Hundred colonists and mother of James, William, and John Cumings, also Old Three Hundred colonists, received title to a league and two *labores* of land in present-day Brazoria and Waller counties on July 21, 1824. However, she made her home north of San Felipe in the vicinity of the sawmill and gristmill built by her sons on Palmetto (now Mill) Creek in present-day Austin County.

Rebekah Russel was born in Loudoun County, Virginia, to Samuel and Sarah (Moore) Russel about 1757. Prior to 1777, she married Anthony Cumings, a Loudoun County property owner.

Perhaps also prior to 1777, Anthony and Rebekah Cumings re-located on the Ohio River in what is today Lewis County, Kentucky. The family operated a water-powered sawmill and horse-drawn gristmill prior to 1800.

They had seven sons and two daughters, in this probable order of birth: Samuel, Thomas, Anthony, John, William, James, Rebecca, Sarah, and Robert. Rebekah was widowed prior to 1807.

In 1822, Rebekah, her three unmarried sons James, William and John, and daughters Rebecca and Sarah, traveled to Texas and became part of Austin's original colony. Rebekah, who died in the early part of 1832, outlived all but John and Rebecca. William, who had married in Lewis County, Kentucky, in 1824 and died on Mill Creek in 1828, left the only surviving child of the Texas family members, Samuel Anthony Cumings.

The spelling of Rebekah Cumings' name is taken from the signature on her will, made out in 1825.

— Timothy Austin Cumings #18

James Cummins

James (Jack) Cummins was born in 1774, in North Carolina. He married Elinor Mariah Waller, January 13, 1799, in Davidson County, Tennessee. By June 1822, he was in Texas as one of Austin's Old Three Hundred and was located on the Colorado River. On August 16, 1823, at San Felipe de Austin, he was elected *alcalde* of the Colorado District, and served in this capacity for four years.

Cummins and a group of settlers helped to put down the Fredonian Rebellion at Nacogdoches.

On July 27, 1824, he was granted six leagues of land and one *labor* of land in Colorado and Austin counties after he agreed to build a sawmill and gristmill on Cummins Creek in Colorado County.

Evidently, his first wife, Elinor, died before he came to Texas, leaving him with three small daughters, Maria, Eliza, and Nancy. The March 4, 1823, census of the Colorado District lists him married to Rebecca with a five-year-old son. Rebecca Crier was the daughter of James Crier, another colonist. Beside the five-year-old Willie (or Wylie), James and Rebecca also had two daughters, Harriet and Sarah.

When James Cummins' second daughter, Eliza, married John H. Moore, a famous Indian fighter, on June 14, 1827, her bridal dress was described as the only one worn by a daughter of the Old Three Hundred: it was of fine white muslin brought from the States and trimmed with ruffles and frills of the same. This was according to Julia Sinks.

Because he was forty-nine years of age, James did not take part in the Texas Revolution. He died in 1849. His burial place is unknown.

—JULIA NAIL MOSS #26

James Curtis, Jr.

James Curtis, Jr., was born to Sarah Hercules Curtis and James Curtis, Sr., in Davidson County, Tennessee, near Whites Creek in about 1806. His family later moved to Warren County, Tennessee. The Curtises were stock raisers and farmers. The family later left Tennessee for Alabama.

James married Polly Ann Hide in Jefferson County, Alabama, on June 11, 1823. The couple accompanied James' parents to Texas. James was given land on the east side of the Brazos River in present-day Brazos County. He later moved to Bastrop County near Curtis family members.

Polly Ann and James were recorded on the 1829 Stephen F. Austin Census and were childless at the time. James was married a second time to Tamer C. Gray, daughter of Daniel Gray, sometime before 1843. The couple had one child, Sarah Ann, born in 1843. Tamer and James divorced in 1848. James married a third time, a woman named Rebecca. The third marriage was a short one as he died of consumption the following year.

James shows Republic of Texas service under Burleson from July 27, 1837, to November 9, 1837. He served as a private in Jesse Billingsley's Company in the Texian Army during the Woll Expedition in 1842. James is also mentioned by J. H. Jenkins as one of four men attacked by Comanche Indians during a mustang hunt near Plum Creek in July of 1842.

— CHARLES REID #318

James Curtis, Sr.

James Curtis, Sr., was given land on August 3, 1824, in Burleson County, Texas, on the west side of the Brazos River. He was a stock raiser. In 1831 he moved his family to Bastrop County. He lived with or near to his orphaned grandsons, James and John Stewart. The Stewart land was on the west side of the Colorado River south of the town of Bastrop.

Curtis served in the Texian Army during the Texas Revolution. He participated in the Siege of Bexar. James, Sr. substituted for a son on February 22, 1836. He was under J. J. Tumlinson's command. When the Mexicans came to Bastrop, he went to San Jacinto with Major Williamson and into Jesse Billingsley's company during the battle. Battle officers' reports estimating Curtis' age are incorrect.

James Curtis, Sr., was born circa 1779 in Spotsylvania County, Virginia, to Frances Carter and Rice Curtis III. He married Sarah Hercules in Davidson County, Tennessee, on May 13, 1802. He was twenty-three years old at the time.

Curtis moved his family to Warren County, Tennessee, in about 1811. Sometime after 1820, he moved his family to Alabama. The Curtis family was in Texas by late 1823. Sarah Hercules and James Curtis, Sr., had nine children.

James Curtis, Sr., died in 1836 in Bastrop County, Texas, according to a signed statement by M. Elizabeth Curtis Reid. No gravesite has been found for him or his wife Sarah. It is presumed that he was buried in a family burial ground possibly on Stewart lands in Bastrop County.

— CHARLES REID #318

Charles DeMoss

Charles DeMoss was a man of vision and a true pioneer. At least twice he moved his family into frontiers where they were among the first to domesticate the wilderness.

In 1795, Spain thought it advisable to populate Upper Louisiana Territory as a barrier to the English in Canada, and offered inducements to settlers. A settler could get about 640 acres of land for as little as $41, according to his position, size of his family, and ability to cultivate land.

Taking advantage of this, Charles and his wife Martha and their son Peter, who was born in Ohio, went to Cape Girardeau, Missouri, in 1802. He cultivated this land, raising corn, flax, and hemp. Over the years seven children were born: Sally, Lewis, John, William, Loraharney, Martha, and Elizabeth. They remained in Missouri until 1824, when Stephen F. Austin's colonizing in Mexico beckoned them to move on. Charles and his older son Peter were in the first three hundred families. Son Lewis is listed in an Austin register as arriving as early as 1823, but was not granted land until later.

They landed in Matagorda County, and eventually, all lived on Caney Creek, farming and raising stock.

Unfortunately, Charles' time was short in Texas because he and Martha died in 1826. His sons remained, raised families, and helped in the struggle to make Texas a republic.

— HARDY SANDERS #138

Clement Clinton Dyer

Clement Clinton Dyer

Clement Clinton Dyer was born in Dyersburg, Tennessee, on January 29, 1800. He wrote in his journal that he left Natchez, Mississippi, on May 2, 1822, traveling to Natchitoches, Louisiana. He worked there as a trader for two years. He married Sarah Stafford, daughter of William Stafford, on her fifteenth birthday, June 5, 1824, and they started to Texas. On arriving at San Felipe, he received title to a *sitio* of land in Colorado County on August 10, 1824, and one and one half *labores* of land in Waller County on August 24, 1824.

The Dyers settled on Irons Creek, near San Felipe. After they had a frightening encounter with Indians, the Dyers moved to present Fort Bend County. Dyer became manager of the Stafford Plantation in 1833.

Clement Dyer became a lawyer and was active in politics and government. In 1824, he was one of twelve men to decide on a Plan of Provisional Government. In 1835 he was a delegate from Harrisburg to the Consultation. After the Texas Revolution he was justice of the peace in Harrisburg (now Harris) County. He moved to Richmond in 1839 and was justice of the peace of that county, then later county judge for fourteen years. He was actively involved in the Methodist Church organized in 1839. He was a successful planter.

Clement and Sarah Dyer had twelve children: William, James, Harvey, John Eli, Sarah Jane, Mary, Julia, Josephine, Martha, Pembrook, Florence, and DeWitt Clinton.

Dyer had been suffering for some time with heart trouble and fell in the field one morning while taking a walk. He was dead when field hands brought him to the house. He died April 27, 1864, and Sarah died December 22, 1874. The couple is buried in the family cemetery in Richmond, Texas.

— WINCIE C. CAMPBELL #215

Gustavus Eixon Edwards

Gustavus Eixon Edwards, youngest of five children and third son of John and Susanne (Wroe) Edwards, was born in Bourbon County, Kentucky, circa 1786 or 1789.

Gustavus served one year as a private in the War of 1812. Records reflect that he was in Major V. Ball's Squadron in the state dragoons.

He was married to Hannah Kincheloe, daughter of William and Nancy (Taylor) Kincheloe. She died giving birth to a daughter, Mary Jane, possibly in Louisiana, while en route to Austin's Colony in 1822 or 1823.

Gustavus received a league of land on August 16, 1824, in present-day Wharton County. In 1825, he was operating the Robinson Ferry crossing the river at Washington-on-the-Brazos. That same year he joined Stephen F. Austin in a campaign against the Karankawa Indians. He was postmaster of Pitney, Texas, in October 1836.

When Mary Jane finished school in Nashville, Tennessee, she joined her father in Texas. She married Robert McAlpin "Three-Legged Willie" Williamson in Austin County on April 21, 1837. They had seven children including son, Annexus, so named because his father believed passionately in the annexation of the Republic of Texas to the United States. Their children were: Hoxie Collinsworth, Martha Jane, Julia Rebecca, Patrick Jack, Willie Annexus, James Bennett, and Susan Bruce. Mary Jane died suddenly November 17, 1856, in their home at Independence.

In July of 1837, Edwards sold his Austin County farm and moved to his league in Wharton County. He was living there when his son-in-law, "Three Legged Willie," died at his home on December 22, 1859. Wharton County is where Edwards died after 1859. His burial site is unknown.

— Anna Beth S. Herzer #774

David Fitzgerald

David Fitzgerald, a Georgia planter, was of Scotch-Irish descent. He served under General Francis Marion during the Revolutionary War, and he participated in the War of 1812. He was a widower over the age of fifty when he came to Austin's Colony in December 1821. He arrived at the mouth of the Brazos River in a forty-foot boat and was accompanied by his son John, Joseph Frazier, and two slaves. Upon their arrival they found a group of immigrants who had come on the schooner *Lively*, who were repairing an old log canoe and building other boats. Using these, and Fitzgerald's serviceable craft, these two groups proceeded up the river together with their farms tools, sacks of seed, and other supplies. They arrived in present Fort Bend County sometime in January 1822. Fitzgerald raised crops there, and he received his land grant on July 10, 1824. It was said that Fitzgerald had bushy red hair and that the Indians were afraid of him.

Fitzgerald at first wanted to locate his league of land three miles below Richmond, but he found that William Morton had already chosen this land. So, Fitzgerald's grant was located nineteen miles below Richmond. One-fourth of a league of this land was exchanged with Morton for that amount in his grant near Richmond.

Fitzgerald participated in the Battle of Anahuac in 1832 and he died shortly thereafter. A few months later, his daughter Sarah arrived with her husband Eli Fenn. At first, they lived on the quarter league that Fitzgerald had exchanged with Morton but after the Texas Revolution, they moved down to the Fitzgerald League.

Duke Cemetery is on the quarter of the Fitzgerald league that William Morton received and was dedicated by descendants of Louisiana Morton Perry, daughter of William Morton. It is not known whether Fitzgerald was buried there, but Sarah Fitzgerald Fenn was buried there in 1860.

—JOSEPH JOHNSON FENN III #655

Elisha Flowers

Elisha Flowers, one of Stephen F. Austin's Old Three Hundred settlers, was the son of Edward and Rebekkah Flowers of Kentucky. He married Polly Smalley, daughter of Andrew and Martha Smalley, also of Kentucky, and around 1823 they had a son. Elisha and Polly Flowers, along with their infant son Romulus Orlando, left Kentucky in 1824. Flowers received four reales of land (over 2,000 acres) from Mexico in Matagorda County and a *labor* of land now part of Colorado County on July 19, 1824.

On December 26, 1826, he wrote Stephen F. Austin from Bay Prairie that he had had a *labor* of land in front of his half league surveyed and was plowing it to feed his family. In the winter of 1826-27, when Elisha Flowers, his three-year-old son Romulus and neighbor Charles Cavanah went hunting together, Karankawa Indians massacred their families. When the men returned, they went after the Indians and killed many of them. Polly Flowers, her infant daughter, and Cavanah's wife and daughter were killed in the last recorded Indian raid in Matagorda County. Elisha and his son Romulus stayed in Texas for awhile but eventually Elisha moved back to Kentucky. There he remarried and he and his wife Susannah Baker had a son Martin Van Buren Flowers.

Romulus Flowers returned to his mother's relatives in Matagorda County in his early teens. He lived with Peter and Susannah Bays DeMoss and eventually married their daughter Elizabeth. He also served in the Republic of Texas Army.

—JAMES G. MILLER #714

Isaac Guilford Foster

Isaac Guilford Foster, son of John Foster, Sr., was born in Mississippi. He was one of the three hundred colonists brought by Stephen F. Austin to Texas under contract with the Republic of Mexico. On August 10, 1824, he received title to a league of land in present Matagorda County, but lived at his father's place at Corn Cove, east of the Brazos River. On February 1, 1830, he was ordered to appear before the *ayuntamiento* at San Felipe de Austin to testify concerning improvements on his land. On March 1, 1830, the *ayuntamiento* reported that Foster had made the necessary improvements, but had recently died. He was killed on his father's property. John Sr. was the only heir. Isaac's most valuable asset was his league of land worth $2,914 that his brothers and sisters eventually inherited.

—JUDY MENASCO #648

The Texas cowboy tradition developed because of the number of wild longhorns and mustangs in Texas. The Tejanos perfected horsemanship along with the branding and roundups and cattle drives and the settlers adopted the Hispanic concept of ranching. The cowboy attire was mostly adapted from the Vaqueros: the cowboy hat with the high crowned top and the protective brim, the bandana, the boots with a high top for leg protection, the pointed toe to guide the boot into the stirrup and the high heel to keep the foot from slipping out of the stirrup while working. The cowboys retained some of the livestock handling techniques of the Eastern United States. Another part of the Texas cowboy tradition was the long cattle drive which met the need to get the animals to market.

"... *In short, my mottoes have been*—The redemption of Texas from the wilderness, Fidelity and gratitude to my adopted country, and to be inflexibly true to the interests and just rights of my settlers. *It is my boast to say that I have never deviated from these general principles, and it is a matter of proud gratification to me that my colony has always possessed the confidence of this Govt. ...*"

—From Austin's letter to Thomas F. Leaming

RA

John Foster

John Foster, who was born May 25, 1757, moved to the Natchez District with his family from South Carolina before 1784. They settled along St. Catharine's Creek in Adams County and later he settled in Wilkinson County, Mississippi.

On October 26, 1797, he married Mary Smith, born October 10, 1772, the daughter of Zachariah and Frances (Prestwood) Smith of Anson County, North Carolina.

John Foster's children were as follows: Gideon, John, Sarah, Randolph, Isaac Guilford, Moses A., Elizabeth, Nancy (Ann) D., Barsheba Hetty, John Claiborne, Mary Elizabeth, Augustus Rodney, and George Poindexter.

In 1822, John and two of his sons, Isaac and Randolph, came to Texas as part of Stephen F. Austin's Old Three Hundred settlers. On July 14, 1824, he was granted two and a half leagues and three *labores* of land because of his good qualities, his well-known application to agriculture, stockraising, and industry, and his very large family. This was approximately 12,000 acres, the largest original land grant in present Fort Bend County.

In November 1826, John Foster was commissioned to buy a steel mill in New Orleans. William B. Travis acted as Foster's attorney in January 1834.

Three of John's sons, John Jr., Randolph, and John Claiborne Foster, helped Texas in its struggle for independence. Several of his grandchildren fought in the War Between the States.

Nearing the age of eighty years, John Foster returned for a visit to Wilkinson County, Mississippi, where he died at the home of Major Francis B. Mayes, his son-in-law, on January 26, 1837.

—NADINE FOSTER ZVOLANEK #343

Randolph Foster

Randolph Foster

Randolph Foster, son of John Foster, was born March 12, 1790 in Mississippi. He became friends with Randall Jones when they served together in the War of 1812. After the war he returned to Mississippi.

During the period of 1817-1819 he visited the Fort Bend area prospecting for a place to settle. New Year's Day of 1822 found Foster serving as hunter for Stephen F. Austin's camp. That same year he and family members returned to Texas and applied for land in Austin's Colony. Randolph's grant was on the Brazos River and included his earlier camp.

In 1828 Randolph returned to Mississippi and in Woodville on February 22, 1829, he married Lucy Ruffin Hunter. She was the daughter of William and Lucy Ruffin Hunter. Randolph and his bride returned to Fort Bend and settled on the John Foster Grant.

They were parents of the following children: Isaac Prestwood, Nancy Adaliza, Mary Louise (who married Sid Winston, Jane Long's descendant), Lucretia Collitanius, Caroline Amelia, Lucy Matilda, and Randolph Guilford.

Randolph Foster, known to his family and friends as "Uncle Ran," was no ordinary man. For years he would take his horse and gun, leaving his home to spend months camping in what is now Arkansas.

Foster died August 18, 1876, in the home of his daughter, Mrs. Mary L. Blakely, of Fort Bend County. His wife, Lucy, preceded him in death on March 25, 1872. It is reported that they are buried on the homestead in Fort Bend County. There is a marker in the cemetery at Fulshear, but it bears no evidence that he is buried there.

A painting of Foster with Stephen F. Austin and Deaf Smith hangs near the speaker's stand in the House Chamber at the Capitol building in Austin.

— WINNIE RHEA COWGILL #47

Churchill Fulshear was a generous man with a true warm heart. He had accumulated some money and this fact becoming known, there were frequent calls for loans. If the applicant was a man he wished to oblige, Fulshear would remark that he had "little or none," but would see what he could do and, drawing a purse from his pocket, managed to scrape up the required amount. In other cases, he would solemnly declare that he "hadn't a dollar in the world," and draw out an empty purse to prove it.

According to Noah Smithwick, "You doubtless think me lying when I say I haven't a dollar in the world," said he, in explanation, "but I'll show you that I am not. This," said he, drawing the empty purse from his pocket, "I call 'the world' and you can see for yourself that there isn't a dollar in it. And this," exhibiting one containing money, "I call little or none."

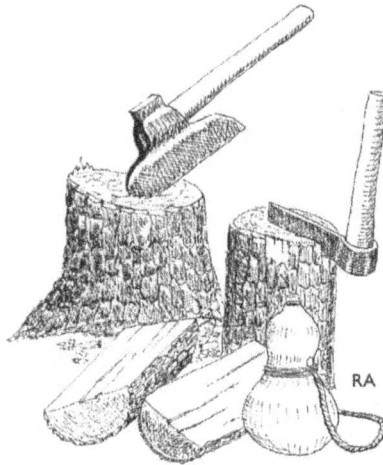

Churchill Fulshear, Sr.

The 1800 Census of Craven County, North Carolina, lists Churchill Fulshear as a single man, but he entered into a marriage bond with Betsy Summers of Craven County in New Bern, North Carolina, December 9, 1800.

In the fall of 1823, the Fulshear family and a weather-beaten band of home-seekers from Tennessee, made their way into Texas to join Stephen F. Austin's seed colony in Coahuila y Tejas, Mexico. When they reached the lower Brazos River, they made their way upstream to the cabin of William Morton where Richmond stands today.

Preserved in Fort Bend County is a faded Mexican Land Grant made out to Churchill Fulshear, the elder, and dated July 16, 1824.

The Census of March 1826 listed Fulshear as a farmer and stock raiser, aged over fifty, and his wife aged forty to fifty. Noah Smithwick was a visitor in the Fulshear home in 1827 and described the old seaman as homely and lame, but noted for his generosity. He was elected *regidor* in 1830 and as such served on a committee to check the merits of land grantees in the Austin Colony. His succession papers state that he died January 18, 1831. No mention is made of his wife, so it is presumed she died between the 1826 Census and his death in 1831. His children were Churchill Fulshear, Jr., Mary L. Fulshear Scobey (married to Robert Scobey, another Old Three Hundred settler), Benjamin Fulshear, and Graves Fulshear.

Several sources state that he was a mariner and a man of considerable property. His succession papers include a detailed inventory of his land holdings, farm equipment, livestock, furnishings, twenty-nine books (including The Holy Bible, *Memoirs of General Jackson, Dilworth's Arithmetic, Acts of Congress 1812, Sequel to the English Reader*, S. F. Austin's pamphlet, Christian Morals, *Treatise for Raising Sheep, Dilworth Spelling Book*), notes due him, and his brand of CF.

— JOHN EMMETTE KIPP #113
— MRS. GERALD FLOYD INMAN #371

William Gates

William Gates was born about 1760. In 1783 he was paid for service as a soldier in the Revolutionary War from the State of North Carolina. Records show he was already married to Catherine Hardin.

Soon after the Revolutionary War, Gates emigrated to Tennessee, where a daughter Sarah and a son Samuel were born, 1783 and 1789 respectively.

Gates left a trail of records as he traveled through Kentucky, where in 1790, as an inhabitant of Lincoln County, on the waters of the Cumberland River, he signed a petition to the General Assembly of Virginia, asking for a county to be laid off south of Green River, to the Ohio River.

While in Kentucky, William and Catherine had more children: Hanna, Charles, Amos, Ransom, Jane, and William.

About the year of 1810, William Gates took his large family to the Cadron Settlement in Arkansas. From there he headed for Texas for free land, wild horses, and game. He reached Nacogdoches December 27, 1821, and continued the journey westward. He found all the rivers fordable and reached the Brazos early January 1822. There in the rich river bottom, near Washington-on-the-Brazos, Gates and his large family made their home.

William Gates received his land grant in 1824 from the Mexican government. While visiting his son Charles in San Augustine County, Gates died on August 6, 1828.

— ELIZABETH L. WHITE #118

Between 1821 and 1836 the population of Texas grew from about 7,000 to more than 35,000.

Freeman George

Freeman George married Elenora, born in Louisiana, and they had eight sons: Jefferson, Holman, James, Freeman, Jr., Nicholas, David, Joseph, and William. This large family left Louisiana in late 1821 to join Stephen F. Austin in his settlement of Texas. Freeman George and his sons appear in the First Census of Texas where Freeman, between forty and fifty years of age, is listed as a farmer and stock raiser. Freeman received title to one *sitio* of land in present Matagorda County and one *labor* in present Waller County on July 7, 1824.

Records indicate that Freeman George died in Matagorda County before April 4, 1837, when an account was filed against his estate. His wife Elenora and her son Nicholas are found in the 1850 Wharton County census living in the home of David George, his wife and children. Only two of the eight sons lived to adulthood, married and had children.

Since there is no record of the location of the burial sites of Freeman and Elenora George, permission was requested and granted for the descendants to place a cenotaph in the Old City Cemetery of San Marcos, Texas. It is located on the plot where their son David George and grandson Jefferson are buried. On this monument is a bronze medallion that says "Stephen F. Austin's Old Three Hundred."

—JACK McCULLOUGH #625

In spite of the Mexican invasion of 1836 and so many farmers in the army, there were good crops that year. The year 1837 was also good and it was estimated that 50,000 bales of cotton were made. The population and the number of towns were increasing rapidly. There was regular steamship service to New Orleans and a fine class of sailing vessels between New York and the Texas coast.

Daniel Gilleland, Sr.

Daniel Gilleland, Sr. was born on June 9, 1795, in Virginia, the son of William Gilleland (1771-1800) and the grandson of James Gilleland (1745-1810). Daniel's father died when he was only five years old, and his mother Nancy Johnson Gilleland soon remarried to Thomas Williams in Davidson County, Tennessee, on September 15, 1802. By 1807, the family had moved to the Arkansas Territory. Daniel married Precilla Boatwright, born to Thomas and Amy Rushing Boatwright, Sr., June 20, 1803, in Old Miller County, Arkansas Territory, on February 3, 1819. The Gillelands left Arkansas for Texas with the Williams, Boatwright, and Kuykendall families in 1821. In November 1821, they arrived at the Brazos River. They first settled near present-day Columbus on Christmas 1821 and claimed land on the Colorado River in 1822. Within a few years, the Gillelands traveled to Arkansas in a failed attempt to reclaim their lands that had been ceded to the Choctaw Indians by the federal government. The family returned to Texas by 1830 and moved around through Wharton, Washington, Harrison, and Montgomery counties before permanently settling in Milam County. Daniel's daughter Nancy and her husband John Demostinie Anders followed them to Milam County.

Daniel and Precilla had 13 children, ten of whom survived to adulthood. Daniel died in Milam County on January 12, 1873, and is buried in the family cemetery. Precilla died on May 9, 1873. The cemetery was rediscovered in 1986 and partially restored in 1987. On October 29, 1988, a Texas historical marker was dedicated a few miles from the cemetery.

(Precilla's parents and Daniel's mother were also members of Austin's Old Three Hundred families.)

— KEVIN THOMPSON #767

Chester Spalding Gorbet

Chester Spalding Gorbet was born in 1790. He was granted a league of land July 19, 1824, according to Brazoria County records. It was situated on the east side of the Brazos River near the Gulf of Mexico. A petition was issued in 1824 by thirty-three men of the lower Brazos, stating that they are in favor of slavery and the privilege of selecting their own officers, both civil and military, and all cases to be tried by jury. The first signature on this document is Chester S. Gorbet.

The marital history of Gorbet is confusing. Among the Gorbet Papers is a certificate of marriage to Ann R. Bradley, dated September 2, 1831, and signed by Father Muldoon. The 1836 census of Austin's Colony listed Chester S. Gorbet with wife Nancy and son Edward. They actually had five children: Dulcenia, Elizabeth, Edward B., Juliana, and Susan B.

It has been recorded that Gorbet was in the Grass Fight, the Battle of Bexar. He was one of the three hundred who answered the call of Old Ben Milam. He had joined the Texas Revolutionary Army on October 3, 1835. He was discharged on February 20 or 28, 1836, missing the Battle of San Jacinto by only a few months. He served in the regiment of the Rangers from June 1, 1836, to January 11, 1838.

On June 24, 1844, he married Nancy White Wilson, a widow with six children. This is recorded in Montgomery County.

Gorbet was one of seven Baptists in the first Old Three Hundred families, and a charter member of the Reliance Baptist Church, in Anderson, Texas, 1847.

Chester and the second Nancy had two sons: John T. and Lorenzo W. Gorbet. Chester died on October 23, 1878. His burial place is unknown.

—LAWRENCE A. MADDOX, JR.,
for his son
FREDERICK ANDREW MADDOX #276

Col. Jared Ellison Groce

Jared Ellison Groce II was born in Halifax County, Virginia, to Jared E. and Sarah (Shepherd) Groce on October 17, 1792. Before coming to Texas, Groce was active in business and politics in Georgia and Alabama. In Alabama he became a substantial planter and slaveholder.

Groce set out for Texas in the fall of 1821, with a hundred slaves as well as cattle, sheep, hogs, horses, and a caravan of fifty wagons. He was granted ten leagues of land by the Mexican government in 1824 "on account of the property he has brought with him." Three leagues of land were in present Brazoria County, five in Waller County, and two in Grimes County.

Groce located Bernardo Plantation on the east bank of the Brazos River, below the present-day town of Hempstead.

His rambling home was crafted so that it did not resemble what it was, a log house. Rooms were twenty feet square, floored with ash and equipped with fireplaces. For many years it was the showplace of the colony.

The first cotton in Texas was raised there and the first bale ginned in 1826. Groce has been called "Father of Agriculture" in Texas. In 1831 he divided his holdings among his sons and built another home, which he called Retreat. Early in 1836 the fleeing provisional government of Texas found refuge for a while at Retreat, and from Groce's fields Sam Houston's army was fed, even though Groce in 1833 had opposed separation from Mexico.

Groce died of malaria on November 20, 1836. His grave is in the Hempstead Cemetery, marked by a section of the Bernardo Plantation entry gates.

— MRS. JOHN EMMETTE KIPP #3

Jared Groce was the wealthiest of the Old Three Hundred and lived in a splendid home. In 1827 his daughter Sarah Ann graduated from a finishing school in New York and was coming to Texas. As the servants prepared the house for her arrival, they bemoaned the fact that the china was cracked and broken from the trip to Texas. A houseguest, Mr. White, who was a silversmith, provided a solution to the problem. Mr. Groce had a large collection of Mexican silver dollars, which Mr. White converted to bowls, cups, and plates.

When Sarah married William H. Wharton, she asked her father if she could convert the rest of the silver dollars to knives, forks, and spoons. The silver, with instructions, was sent to a New York silversmith. These silver pieces have been handed down through the generations.

Dilue Rose Harris records that just after the fall of the Alamo, a large herd of buffaloes came by—three or four thousand of them. They crossed the Brazos River above Fort Bend and came out of the bottom at Stafford's Point, making their first appearance before day. They passed in sight of the Rose house, but folks could see only a dark cloud of dust, which looked like a sandstorm. As the night was very dark no one could tell when the last buffalo passed. The buffaloes went on to the coast, and the prairie looked afterwards as if it had been plowed.

In Texas in 1823 dress material or any kind of cloth sold for seven to ten dollars a yard, a cake of soap was a dollar and a quarter, buttons were a dollar a dozen, men's socks were a dollar and a quarter a pair, and silk handkerchiefs were two dollars each. Few Texians could afford these things.

John B. Haddon

John B. Haddon, the firstborn son of Colonel John Haddon and Isabella Elliott, was probably born in Randolph County, Virginia, about 1786. In about 1806, Colonel Haddon took his wife and six sons and moved to the Busseron Settlement in Indiana Territory.

John B. Haddon married Anna (last name unknown) before 1810, and several children were born to the Haddons while still in Indiana. John served in the War of 1812 with the Indiana Volunteers (31st Rangers) from 1813-1815. In 1816, John, his wife and children became the first settlers in Washington Township, Greene County, Indiana. John built a small log cabin, which afterwards became the schoolhouse of the township.

Described as standing five feet ten inches, with blond hair and blue eyes, he was known throughout the area as an experienced hunter and trapper. Legend has it that he killed two deer with one shot, reloaded and killed another without stepping out of his tracks. The Indians often visited his cabin for warmth, or to beg food, tobacco, or ammunition. He hunted with the Indians and could beat them shooting at a mark.

In June 1822, John left Indiana for Texas, and the first known record of him in Texas was in February 1823. John was chosen lieutenant of the San Felipe Company of the Austin Colony in 1824. He received title to a *sitio* of land on the east bank of the Colorado River a few miles below Columbus in what is now Colorado County on July 29, 1824. John lived on his land in Colorado County until his death in November 1834, leaving his wife Anna, sons William, Jackson, and Henry, and daughters Catherine, Helen, and Elizabeth.

Although John did not live to participate in the Texas Revolution, two of his sons fought for Texas' Independence.

— PAIGE FONTAINE #775

Samuel Haddy (Hady)

The origins of the Haddy family or how they arrived in Texas are not known. Samuel's wife was Elizabeth Chatham. They had four children: Eunice Haddy, Arnold William, Sarah Haddy Kelly, and Susan Haddy Callihan.

Haddy is listed as a stock raiser and farmer in various censuses. He died in February of 1831. He received a Mexican land grant of one *sitio* on August 19, 1824. This grant was located six miles east of San Felipe in what is now Waller County near the town of Pattison.

In 1842 the Austin County Probate Court appointed William Kelly administrator of Haddy's estate.

— CAROLYN MARBLE #364

When Sam Houston heard of the fall of the Alamo, he sent a dispatch for the people to flee from Santa Anna and his army. This was the beginning of the Runaway Scrape. People left things just as they were, took keepsakes and a few supplies and traveled in any transportation available. They were panicked and faced crowds, hunger, floods, getting stuck in the mud, and bottlenecks at ferries. There were diseases and injuries and deaths. Dilue Rose Harris's little sister was one of many who died and were buried where they died. Alexander Hodge, who had never before had time, always walked with a frightened grandchild's hand in his, a granddaughter remembered. Settlers helped each other with many acts of kindness.

A messenger came with the news that the war was over. The colonists returned home to begin rebuilding. The recovery was remarkably fast.

Alexander Hodge

The Hodge family was camped in a grove of trees near Lynch's Ferry when the Battle of San Jacinto erupted. Alexander Hodge stood silent near a pine tree. At last, a rider passed their camp and called to them the war was over, the Mexicans defeated. They all fell to their knees, crying, and prayed their thanks to God, even the grandfather. These are the memories recorded by his granddaughter, Clarenda Pevehouse Kegans.

Judge Hodge returned to Hodge's Bend on Oyster Creek, but the exposure and strain of the Runaway Scrape took its toll. He died August 17, 1836, and is buried in the family cemetery beside his wife, Ruth, who died in 1831.

Hodge's Bend Cemetery, one of the oldest in Fort Bend County, has been marked by the Daughters of the American Revolution as well as the Texas Historical Commission.

Hodge was born 1760 in Cumberland County, Pennsylvania, the son of William Hodge, grandson of John Hodge, residents of West Pennsborough Township. There is evidence that his mother was Mary Elliott, daughter of James Elliott also of Cumberland County.

Alexander migrated as a youth to Edgefield District, South Carolina, and served under General Francis Marion during the American Revolution. He married Ruth, then moved to Oglethorpe County, Georgia, where his children were born: Archibald born 1790 married Charlotte Reeves; William born 1792 married Margaret Welch; Ruth born 1793 married William Harris; Nancy born 1794; John born 1796 married Elsie Smith; Alexander Elliott born 1800 married Elizabeth Barnhill; Mary born 1801 married James Pevehouse; James born 1803 married Zulema Kuykendall; Cynthia born 1805; and Lucinda born 1809 married Stephen Richardson.

Hodge and his family arrived in Austin's Colony in 1826. Austin granted Hodge one of the leagues he had reserved for himself. Hodge's Bend was situated on the road running from Fort Bend to Harrisburg and was a gathering place for family and friends alike.

— MARGUERITE CRAIN #30

Francis Holland

The Hollands came from Canada, settling on what is now Holland Creek in Ohio. Francis Holland married Margaret Buck on October 29, 1804, and raised six children. Susanna was born about 1806, James in 1808; Tapley in 1810, Francis, Jr., "Frank" in 1812, William in 1817, and Nancy in 1819. Francis, Sr., served in the War of 1812 as a private under Captain John H. Lindsey. The Holland clan left for Texas passing through Louisiana and arrived in Texas early in 1822. They camped by a cabin set atop a hill overlooking Ten-Mile Creek. Andrew Millican had built the "dog-trot" cabin in 1821 but wanted to relocate so he sold his improvements to Francis Holland. Holland aligned his land grant on each side of the creek and it was approved as a grant on August 10, 1824. This simple shelter, the local polling place by March 21, 1829, proved to be the center for the community for years and home to several generations of Holland descendants. The original structure still stands as a testament to the pioneer's enduring spirit.

Francis served in the First Company militia, later was elected *comisario* on December 13, 1830, then a delegate from present Washington County to the Convention of 1833 at San Felipe. The cholera epidemic that took James Bowie's family, took the life of Francis and Margaret Holland. Their son William, a lifelong invalid, died shortly after them. The other three sons joined the Texas militia, fighting under Bowie. Several sources that gave accounts of William B. Travis drawing the line in the sand, accredit Tapley Holland as the first to cross over and pledge to defend the Alamo. He is listed as a private in the artillery company of Captain W. R. Carey when he died at the Alamo. Frank Holland was killed by Indians and his brother James died of natural causes. The two Holland girls married and raised families.

— DOROTHY SHEPPERD TATE #617

William Holland

William Holland came from Canada with his brother Francis and sister Mary. They settled in the Northwest Territory that later became Scioto County, Ohio. The Holland brothers courted the Buck sisters. William married Susannah Buck on June 16, 1808. They had three daughters born in Ohio but only two are recorded as coming to Texas: Catherine "Katy" born about 1815 and Sarah born about 1818. The Holland sister, Mary, married William Peterson on September 26, 1805, and after his death, she and her two sons, William, Jr., and John born 1806 were in the Holland caravan when they left Ohio to join Stephen F. Austin in Texas. Arriving in what is now Grimes County in 1822, William received his land grant on August 10, 1824, for one league of land adjoining Francis Holland's land grant on the creek, now known as Holland Creek. The young men, John Peterson, William Burney, and James Holland, who came along at that time, later received grants adjoining those of Francis and William creating 29 square miles of Holland family land that became known as Hollandale and had a U.S. Post Office from 1859-1865. In later years the town's name was changed to Navasota.

William and Susannah became ill and died; the date is not known but a deal was made to sell his land to Freeman Pettus as early as 1824. Katy and Sarah lived in the Francis Holland cabin until Katy married Mill McDowell in 1835 and Sarah married W. H. Grissett about 1837.

Of the ten Holland children, who came to Texas as part of the Old Three Hundred, only one boy, Mary Holland Peterson's son, John Peterson lived to raise a family. He married Susan Fisher Reid on April 1, 1830.

— DOROTHY SHEPPERD TATE #617

George Huff

George Huff, a blacksmith and mechanic in Austin's Colony, was born in Wilkinson County, Mississippi, in 1781. He shows up in 1811 as a resident of neighboring Amite County.

Huff received one and one-half leagues occupying either side of Bernard and Peach Creeks in present Fort Bend and Wharton counties. The extra land may have been awarded because of Huff's agreement to build a sawmill and a gristmill. In the first census of Texas, Huff is listed as between forty and fifty years of age. His wife (not named, but believed to be Mary) is of the same age. Also listed in the household are two males, aged seven to sixteen, one male, sixteen to twenty-five, and two females, also sixteen to twenty-five. One of his sons, Jacob, preceded the rest of the family to Austin's Colony in order to clear and prepare the land. Jacob died in 1833.

By 1825, George Huff had constructed a sawmill on the property. He opened a store in San Felipe de Austin with his son William. In 1835 he was in charge of provisions sent to the headquarters of the Texian volunteer force at Gonzales.

George Huff is listed on the 1840 tax roll in Austin County as owning eight town lots, four slaves, a horse, and a gold watch. He died before 1850.

— JOYCE GRAY CLEGG ROBINSON #440

Dr. Johnson Calhoun Hunter

Johnson Calhoun Hunter was born May 22, 1787, in Charleston, South Carolina. There, he married Martha Harbert of Wythe County, Virginia. After receiving his diploma in medicine, Hunter moved first to southeastern Ohio and then to New Madrid, Missouri. In 1820 or 1821, Hunter joined an expedition that traveled to San Antonio, where he had dealings with the Veramendi family.

Hunter decided to relocate in Texas, and attempted to take his family there by way of water from New Orleans. They were shipwrecked on an island, where they remained until rescued by a passing vessel. Hunter was granted land by the Mexican government at Morgan's Point on Galveston Bay, and there he built his first Texas home.

In 1829 the Hunters moved to present Fort Bend County. Hunter's Plantation, outside of Richmond, lay on Oyster Creek and at the edge of the prairie. In early 1836, the Hunters abandoned their home in advance of Santa Anna's invading army, driving their cattle herd. Their route brought them close to the Battle of San Jacinto.

They returned to the plantation, which had been temporarily occupied by the Mexican troops. Dr. Hunter died there on May 29, 1855.

Between 1811 and 1836, the Hunters had thirteen children: Jacob, Robert Hancock, Mary, John Calhoun, Harriet Harbert, Thomas Jefferson, Thaddeus Warsaw, Messina, Martha, Latisia, William, Amanda Wilson Calhoun, and Walter Crockett.

— LOUISE SCHOENER #197

Samuel Isaacks

At seventeen years of age, Samuel Isaacks was on the Brazos River with his friend William Andrews when Stephen F. Austin brought the first colonists there in December 1821. He was included in Austin's Old Three Hundred.

Isaacks returned to Louisiana, where he married Nancy Allen. They had two sons. Nancy died in 1828. He remarried and is shown in records with his second wife Martha (Patsy) Richardson and their children. Also shown is the eldest son of the first marriage, William.

Samuel enlisted in the Jasper Volunteers. He received several grants of land and also a veteran pension for himself and wife Martha for his service during the Texas Revolution.

About 1850 he secured land at Lynchburg, adjacent to the San Jacinto Battleground. He established a freight line between Coldsprings and Lynchburg. He stayed there until after the Civil War, when he sold his property and moved to Taylor's Bayou in Seabrook, where he lived until his death in 1878.

Samuel Isaacks' grandson writes:

As I remember him, he was probably six feet tall, raw-boned, or stalwart, and very active for a man of more than 72 years old.... His wife, Martha ... small of stature, probably never balancing the scales at as much as 100 pounds, she was one of the most kindly and motherly souls ... She smoked a clay pipe, and my greatest delight was to help her fill and light it.

—BETTY J. MOCZYGEMBA #264

Alexander Jackson

Alexander Jackson was born in 1786 and raised in Ballybay, Ireland. His parents were Hugh and Letitia Thompson who had nine children, including Alexander and his brother Humphrey, both of whom emigrated to the United States in 1808, settling in New Orleans, before later joining Austin's Colony.

Alexander was an active participant in Austin's Colony. By 1822, he was serving as a lieutenant in the militia in the Colorado District. On December 15, 1823, elections for militia officers were held at his home near Peach Creek. Jackson also took part in efforts to protect the colony from disputes with neighboring Indians.

Stephen F. Austin granted Jackson two leagues of land on July 16, 1824. One was near the Colorado River, the other across West Bernard Creek. Originally, the land was located in Colorado County, but in 1846 became part of Wharton County.

The 1823 Census of Colorado County lists Alexander as a farmer, living with his wife Anna Knox Jackson and their four children, Mary Ann, Martha, Alexander, Jr., and Esther, ages eleven, nine, seven, and one respectively. Three servants — Charlotte, Sim, and Sharper were included. Tragically, Alexander's wife died in 1825, at the age of thirty-four, leaving him a single parent with four young children. Shortly after, his daughter Martha passed away.

On January 4, 1827, Jackson and 48 other men signed a declaration of loyalty to the Mexican government, strongly condemning the Fredonian Rebellion and avoiding what could have been a military conflict with the Mexican government.

Jackson died in 1829 and was survived by his three children — Mary Ann, Alexander, Jr., and Esther. The court awarded Alexander's land to his children on October 24, 1834.

Esther Jackson lived out her life on the original Jackson land, marrying Thomas Thatcher, a congressman in the Fifth Congress of the Republic.

— WILLIAM H. PLAGEMAN, JR. #706
— LAURA PLAGEMAN #707

Isaac Jackson, Sr.

There has been no record found of the birthplace of Isaac Jackson, Sr. (1771-1846). However, he appears in the first census of Greene County, Georgia, in 1790, where a younger brother, Henry, was born in 1797.

Isaac and his wife, Elizabeth, had five children: Isaac C., James, John, Job, and Nancy (Pollard). In 1824, Isaac, Sr., received a league of land on the east side of the Brazos River in present-day Grimes County, opposite the town of Washington. He was first listed as a family man in Texas, but Elizabeth may never have joined him. She is listed in the 1850 Greene County census as age seventy, living with her son Isaac C. Later records in Texas list Isaac, Sr., as a single farmer and stock raiser.

Proof that Isaac, Sr., took part in the Texas Revolution is the award of another league of land, this one in Caldwell County, for being permanently disabled in the conflict. He died in 1846 and was buried in present Grimes County. Although he probably never saw the Caldwell County grant, sons Isaac C. and James came to Texas from Georgia and claimed it in 1861.

— JOY MELLIE GOOCH DOTSON #383

Henry Jones

Henry Jones

Henry Jones was born March 15, 1789, in Madison County, Virginia, near "Blue Ridge." He married Nancy Stiles on January 31, 1821. Early in 1822, they came to Texas with Austin's Old Three Hundred colonists. They first settled in present Washington County, near Independence. Later that year, Henry Jones traveled down to what is now Fort Bend County. There he selected a league of land, just below what is present-day Richmond.

Henry and Nancy built their home on the prairie. Their children were: William, James, Mary Moore (Polly), John Henry, Nettie Ellen, Virginia Claudine, Ruth, Elizabeth, Vivian Ann, Susan (Sudie), Wiley Powell, Nancy Timelia, Emily Laura, Henry, and Thomas Walter.

Henry Jones was responsible for the first road to East and West Columbia. He also served on the first grand jury held in Fort Bend County.

In the 1850 Fort Bend County census, Henry's real estate had a value of almost $32,000. In the 1860 census, he was listed as seventy-three years of age, a farmer whose real estate was valued at $193,999, and his personal property at $96,000.

Nancy died August 5, 1851. When Henry died in June 8, 1861, intestate, his possessions were listed as forty-five slaves, several hundred hogs and horses, 4,344 acres of land, valued at $162,862.50, and 1,110 acres of land, including a homestead, valued at $15,165.

Henry and Nancy Jones are buried in Jones Cemetery, located on the George Ranch, near Richmond, Fort Bend County, Texas.

— Virginia Scarborough #160

James Wales Jones

James Wales Jones was born January 13, 1797, in Columbia County, Georgia. He joined Austin's Colony in January 1822. He settled in what is now Wharton County. He received one *sitio* of land in the rich bottomland of the Brazos River, and a *labor* in what is now Fort Bend County.

Jones married Hetty Stiles on August 24, 1825, in the fort settlement. They later had to be married by the Catholic Church, in accordance with the Mexican law. They had the following children: Ann Elizabeth, William Thomas, Robert Ellis, James Randall, Stephen Austin, Richard Henry, John Stiles, James Walter, and Polly White Jones.

James and Hetty Jones built a home near present-day Richmond and called it "Jones Heights." In 1835, when the colonies began their revolt against the Mexican government, James joined the company of Captain Wiley Martin, who was ordered by General Sam Houston to raise a force of men to defend the ferry at Thompson's Crossing on the Brazos. James was granted a bounty grant certificate for 320 acres of land in Atascosa County for his service in the Army of the Republic of Texas, from July 8, 1835, to June 7, 1836.

James Wales Jones died September 29, 1847, from pneumonia. He was buried in a family cemetery in Prairie Lea, Texas. Hetty Stiles Jones lived to be ninety-one. Her death date was April 9, 1899. She, too, was buried in the family plot. Both bodies were later moved to the State Cemetery in Austin, Texas.

— REBECCA B. LEE #130

May 29th 1829

D. G. Burnet Esq.

N. B. This splendid City "en embrio" has been born since your departure. It is on the Brasos river about 25 miles up from the mouth by water—Sam Williams has a fine daughter—he goes in to New Orleans tomorrow with Cap John Austin—Parker has a fine daughter—J. H. Bell has been very sick with the Rheumatism, tho he has another fine boy—in short this has been quite a prolific season amongst the Ladies and it is truly gratifying to say that I never saw healthier children in my life—Miss Sarah Cummins married Mr. Dennet a short time since in *defiance* of the old woman her mother who is *very* wrathy—you know she has made a rule to *discard* every child who marries right or wrong—Sarah did right as I think—

—S. F. Austin

Captain Randall Jones

Captain Randall Jones

Randall Jones was born August 19, 1786, in Columbia County, Georgia, the son of Thomas and second wife, Sarah Story Smith.

Randall and brother James arrived in San Felipe on January 17, 1822. A year's search provided a suitable location on the Brazos River bend near Richmond. In January 1823 land was cleared and cabins erected. Randall received a Mexican title to a league and a *labor* that was patented July 15, 1824. He went back to Louisiana and returned with Fort Bend's first large shipment of stock.

On October 11, 1824, Randall married Mary (Polly) Andrews (Andrus), daughter of William and Susan Andrews in a "bond ceremony" performed by Stephen F. Austin. Father Michael Muldoon performed a formal ceremony on June 3, 1831. Nine children were born to Randall and Polly Jones: Wiley Martin, James Austin, Martha, Pamelia Ann, Sudie E., Sam Houston, James Miller, Eliza M., and Sallie C. Jones.

His service to Texas was long and varied. He participated in the Anahuac Expedition in 1832, was a member of the General Consultation of 1835-1836 and of the *ayuntamiento* of San Felipe, and served in the Texas Army 1835-1837 and again in 1842 during the second Mexican invasion. He received a bounty warrant for 320 acres for that service.

Polly Andrews Jones died on April 17, 1861, and Randall died in Houston at the home of his son-in-law, Gustave Cook, on June 3, 1873.

They were buried on the Jones *labor*, but their remains and those of their daughter, Martha Jones Beale, were removed to the State Cemetery, Austin. Gravesites are C-AO 5 and C-AO 4.

— MRS. LESLIE B. DUNCAN #83

John Kelly

The Austin Colony Census of 1826 lists John Kelly as between 40-50 years old and wife Sarah (Fisher?) as between 25-40 years old. Based on the 1880 Federal Texas Census for their surviving children, John was born in either Pennsylvania or Missouri and Sarah in either Missouri or Georgia.

John and Sarah resided in Missouri and Louisiana before coming to Texas. John Kelly received title to two *labores* (354.2 acres) of land on the Navasota River in present-day Brazos County on July 19, 1824.

The 1826 Census classified John Kelly as a farmer and stock raiser with a wife, four sons, and three daughters. One daughter, Margaretta, married Daniel Shipman, another original Austin colonist. John later received a head-right grant of one league from the Mexican government.

In 1837 John Kelly's petition was granted in Probate Court at Harrisburg to be appointed guardian of the four minor children of Elijah and Cynthia (Fisher) Roark. Indians killed Elijah Roark in 1829 and Cynthia died in the winter of 1836. In her reminiscences, Dilue Rose Harris stated that the Roark children would go and live with their aunt Sarah Kelly. At the July Term 1838, the Probate Court discharged John Kelly from the guardianship.

John Kelly died in Lavaca County, without having a will. When his widow petitioned the Court to name an administrator of his estate, she stated that he died January 18, 1844. The Succession of John Kelly, deceased, filed at the Lavaca County Courthouse in Hallettsville listed the following heirs: widow Sarah Kelly and children William Kelly, Elijah Kelly, Polly Guthrie, Cynthia Smothers, Mrs. Shipman, deceased, and James Kelly, deceased. Sarah Kelly died in Lavaca County in 1848.

—JOE DARRELL WILSON #647

William Kincheloe

William Kincheloe, oldest son of Colonel Thomas Ludwell Kincheloe, was born in Fauquier County, Virginia, on July 12, 1781. The family relocated to Kentucky where William married Nancy Taylor in 1799. This union produced four daughters and a son. Nancy died while the family was residing in Missouri. William and his second wife, Mary Betts, who accompanied him to Texas, had three sons.

Stephen F. Austin enlisted Kincheloe in the Texas colonial project in 1821. Austin sent him to scout out farming and home sites within the colony. Kincheloe then returned with a hired crew to plant the colony's first crops in advance of the settlers. His vessel *Only Son* transported prospective colonists from New Orleans to the Colorado River in 1822.

Kincheloe chose for himself the site of his two one-league grants in present-day Wharton County, awarded on July 8, 1824. The Wharton County courthouse is located on land donated by Kincheloe from his grant. The road between Matagorda and San Felipe crossed Peach Creek at Kincheloe Crossing. William died on his home site in 1835, at which time his estate was valued at $17,558.

William was a blacksmith, a surveyor, a farmer and a stock raiser and was holding the position of *alcalde* in 1826. In 1827, at the time of the Fredonian Rebellion in Nacogdoches, he signed a resolution of loyalty to Mexico. In 1828 William was elected as a police commissioner for the colony.

Two of William's daughters married future Old Three Hundred colonists, but both died en route to Texas. Hannah, married to Gustavus Edwards, is believed to have died in Louisiana. Mary, wife of Horatio Chriesman, died and is buried in New Madrid, Missouri.

William Kincheloe was closely associated with the Baptist Church and his log cabin on Peach Creek near the Colorado is remembered as the site of early Baptist preaching in Texas.

— Anna Beth S. Herzer #774

Captain Abner Kuykendall

Captain Abner Kuykendall, one of Stephen F. Austin's colonists, was the son of Adam and Margaret (Hardin) Kuykendall. He was born in Rutherford County, North Carolina, about 1777. The family moved to Arkansas Territory about 1808. Abner married Sarah (Sally) Gates, the daughter of William and Catherine Hardin Gates. Abner and his extended family left for Texas in October 1821. At Nacogdoches, they were joined by Robert H. Kuykendall and their younger brother Joseph. The three brothers, Abner, Robert, and Joseph, were among the first of Stephen F. Austin's Old Three Hundred colonists.

Abner and Thomas Boatwright moved ten miles west of the Brazos River and on January 1, 1822, established a settlement on New Year Creek. Sarah Gates died about 1823 and Abner never remarried. In November 1823 Abner Kuykendall moved back to the Brazos River and settled above San Felipe. He received title to one and one half leagues and two *labores* of land located now in Fort Bend, Washington, and Austin counties on July 4, 1824. The census of March 1826 classified him as a stock raiser and farmer, and a widower aged over fifty. His grown sons, Gibson, Barzillai, and William, were all members of the Old Three Hundred.

Abner commanded the militia of Austin's colony. In 1824 and 1826 Kuykendall went on campaigns against the Indians. In 1827 he was sent by Austin as a member of a delegation to try to persuade leaders of the Fredonian Rebellion to give up their plans. In 1830 he served on a committee at San Felipe to superintend the building of a jail. He was a public official at San Felipe in February 1832. Kuykendall was stabbed by Joseph Clayton at San Felipe in June 1834 and died in late July 1834. Clayton was convicted and hanged in what was probably the first legal execution in Texas.

Abner was probably buried just north of San Felipe on land he owned on the west side of the Brazos River. No gravestone has ever been found. Ten known children survived him.

—MARSHALL E. KUYKENDALL #29

Barzillai Kuykendall

Barzillai Kuykendall came to Texas as an adult with his father, Abner. Barzillai received title to a *labor* of land in Austin County about six miles north of San Felipe. A second tract of land, a one-fourth league located about six miles west of Bellville, was granted on April 27, 1824. Barzillai farmed, raised cattle, and fought the Indians.

Barzillai married a cousin, Katherine Kuykendall, in 1828. Their children were: Lucinda, Martha, Sarah, and Joseph. Lucinda, the youngest daughter, was born in 1840, and Katherine died soon after that. Barzillai next married a woman named Elizabeth, about 1847-48. They had three children.

On February 5, 1836, Barzillai received another three-fourth league of land in what is now Lee County, between Giddings and Manheim.

During the Battle of San Jacinto, Barzillai was a member of his brother's company, Captain Gibson Kuykendall's. They were to guard the baggage and to care for the wounded at Harrisburg.

The 1860 and 1870 censuses show that Barzillai was a farmer. These same records show that he, Elizabeth, and their children, Solomon, William H., and Nancy (Nannie), lived in Evergreen, Lee County, on a league of land that was granted to his father, Abner Kuykendall.

Barzillai died March 31, 1873, and Elizabeth died April 10, 1873.

—ORRELL LEE PATRICK, JR. #320

Joseph Kuykendall

Joseph Kuykendall, one of the Stephen F. Austin's Old Three Hundred colonists, was born in Kentucky about 1794, the son of Adam and Margaret (Hardin) Kuykendall. The family moved to Arkansas Territory in 1808. In October 1821 Joseph and his wife, Rosanna, and his brother Abner Kuykendall left with family members for Texas. At Nacogdoches they joined their brother Robert H. Kuykendall, who had been living west of the Sabine for some time. In June 1822 they traveled to the mouth of the Colorado River to pick up supplies for the Austin Colony. In August 1823 he received from the Mexican government a *labor* of land, and on July 8, 1824, he received title to a *sitio* of land in the area that became Fort Bend County. In November 1830 the *ayuntamiento* of San Felipe de Austin appointed him a commissioner to choose the best route for a road from San Felipe to Marion.

Kuykendall apparently was a cripple and attempted to remain neutral during the Texas Revolution. He was successful to some degree, for on April 12, 1836, after the Runaway Scrape, Colonel Juan Bringas, commander of the vanguard unit of the Mexican army, wrote Kuykendall "a pass" assuring him that, since he had never taken up arms against the Centralists, his rights as a Mexican citizen would be respected, and that he had nothing to fear from the Mexican troops under Bringas's command. Kuykendall did not, however, emerge unscathed. Ironically, on the same day Bringas guaranteed that his rights would be respected, David G. Burnet wrote Thomas J. Rusk that the Mexicans had captured about thirty of the finest horses in Texas, a portion of which belonged to "Mr. Kyrkendal." Kuykendall lived about five miles south of Richmond. His first wife, Rosanna, died in 1848 and is buried on the line separating Joseph Kuykendall's and Jane Long's leagues. The stone over the crypt reads:

> Rosanah Kuykendall, Consort of Joseph Kuykendall—Born February 1, 1800—Died May 29, 1848.

He married Eliza Jane Jones in January 1849. Kuykendall died circa 1873 and he was probably buried in the same crypt as Rosanah but no marker has ever been found.

— MARSHALL E. KUYKENDALL #29

Though 1821 and 1822 were years of hardship and hunger for some, there was a spirit of kindness and sharing among the colonists. Horatio Chriesman, later Austin's surveyor, heard that a woman and her two sons were surviving on lettuce and little else and her husband was away in the United States on business. Chriesman was staying with Martin Varner, who was a very good hunter. When he told Varner of the situation, the hunter picked up his rifle and went into the woods. He soon was back with a large buck. Chriesman threw the buck on the back of his horse and immediately took it twenty miles to the family.

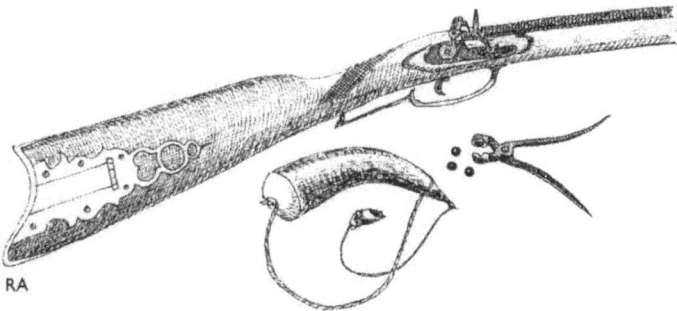

RA

Captain Robert H. Kuykendall

Robert H. Kuykendall (1790-1830) was the son of Adam and Margaret (Hardin) Kuykendall, probably born near Princeton, Kentucky. About 1814, Robert married Sarah Ann Gilleland, daughter of William and Nancy (Johnson) Gilleland of Davidson County, Tennessee.

In the fall of 1821, the Kuykendalls, relatives, and friends moved into the Mexican province of Texas, reaching the Brazos River in November. On January 1, 1822, Robert, brother-in-law Daniel Gilleland, and others proceeded down to the east bank of the Colorado River and settled at what became Beason's Crossing. Under colonial organization, Robert was chosen as Captain of the militia for the district. He led colonists into several Indian battles between 1822 and 1824.

On July 16, 1824, Robert received two leagues of land along the Colorado River. Stephen F. Austin wrote that Kuykendall deserved the larger grant because he has a large family, was one of the first settlers, and has always protected the other settlers from the savage Indians.

In 1826 Captain Kuykendall incurred an injury in an Indian fight that led to blindness and paralysis despite doctor's efforts. He died and presumably lies in the old cemetery at Matagorda.

Robert and Sarah had six known children to survive infancy: R. H. or "Gill," Mary or "Molly," Jane, Joseph Felix (died young), and Albert and Thomas (twins). Sarah Gilleland Kuykendall died in Matagorda County in 1857 and is buried in the Hawley Cemetery near Blessing.

— MARSHALL E. KUYKENDALL #29

Joel Leakey

Ann Hadley, born March 24, 1754, the daughter of Simon and Bridget Hadley of Surry County, North Carolina, married Thomas Leakey, born June 16, 1751. They had three children: Simon, born August 8, 1778; Joel, born March 1, 1780; and Lydia, born September 16, 1793.

At the age of nineteen, Joel helped Samuel Calloway and others build roads in the county. He and Samuel's daughter, Nancy, were married in 1799 and were parents of a son, Thomas, born about 1800. Thomas died in Walker County, Texas, in 1861. Joel and Nancy also had seven daughters: Leny, Mary Asenith, Elizabeth, Lydia, Anna, Nancy, and Ruth.

Some time after 1804 Joel and his family left Surry County and moved to Natchitoches Parish, Louisiana, in February of 1819. He owned 640 acres on the waters of Negrite Bayou. He made a home for his family there until he came to Texas and joined Stephen F. Austin's Colony.

The Leakey family proceeded to build a permanent home near the Brazos on the present Austin–Washington county line. From all reports, Joel was a very hospitable, caring man who helped his neighbors build ferries, welcomed travelers, and made his home available to engaged couples when a traveling priest could perform marriages. He was one of the most influential men in the Colony.

— RUTH T. FOILES #80

William Little

William Little, a native of Pennsylvania, was born about 1790. As a youth, he came south, and served as captain of a Mississippi River steamboat. He married Jane Edwards, a native of Tennessee.

William Little heard about free land in Texas. He met with fourteen other men and made the journey to Natchitoches, Louisiana, to meet with Stephen F. Austin and Commissioner Don Erasmo Smith. They left Natchitoches on July 5, 1821. In San Antonio they met with Governor Martinez, who recognized Stephen F. Austin as successor of his father's rights. This group looked at the land along the Guadalupe, Lavaca, Navidad, Colorado, Brazos, and San Jacinto rivers, as well as the Gulf Coast. Austin decided this would be the site for his first colony.

They returned to Louisiana and bought a schooner, the *Lively*, and loaded the boat with implements, food, guns, ammunition, and other supplies. William Little was in charge of the little thirty-foot sailboat. With about twenty passengers, they left New Orleans on November 25, 1821.

William Little received his grant of one league and one *labor* on the east side of the Brazos River, about twelve miles below the present town of Richmond on July 10, 1824. There, William and Jane Edwards Little reared a large family. Their children were: John, William, Walter W., Martha Jane, Louisa, James K., Robert, and George.

William Little died at his home on July 8, 1841.

— VIRGINIA DAVIS SCARBOROUGH #160
— ANTOINETTE DAVIS READING #161

Nathaniel Lynch

Nathaniel Lynch was born in New York State in 1786. He married Frances Hubert, also of New York State. They had two sons born in New York, Franklin and William. Before 1820, they migrated to the Missouri Territory, where Elizabeth was born about 1820. Another son was born to the Lynches in Texas in 1824.

Nathaniel and his family came to Texas in 1822. He was granted a league and a *labor* of land, which lay on each side of the San Jacinto River. Lynch had operated a ferry back in Missouri and he soon established one across the San Jacinto River. He did not apply for a license to operate publicly until 1830. During the Runaway Scrape in 1836, hundreds crossed on his ferry to escape Santa Anna.

Lynch built a double-hewed log structure, which housed his family, a store and a tavern. He platted the towns of Lynchburg and San Jacinto. He was postmaster of Lynchburg and was appointed second municipal judge of Harrisburg. During the Texas Revolution, he served three months, despite his age. He received a land grant for his service.

In business with David G. Burnet, Lynch is said to have built the first steam-operated saw mill in Texas. In 1973 parts of the old mill were found in the underbrush at the San Jacinto State Park.

Frances Hubert Lynch sewed the flag of independence for Captain William Scott's Lynchburg Volunteers that they carried to the Siege of Bexar. Some historians believe that it was the first Lone Star flag.

In the first census of Austin's Colony, Nathaniel Lynch was listed as a carpenter, farmer, and stockraiser. Lynch died February 14, 1837, and is buried in the old Lynchburg Cemetery.

— FLOSSIE STANLEY KEELS #131

Shubael Marsh

Shubael Marsh (1797?-1868) was raised by his parents, Shubael and Elizabeth (Foxcroft) Marsh, in Portland, Maine. Tradition says that all of his family, except for young Shubael, remained in the East.

After coming to Texas from Hannibal, Missouri, where he had taught school, Marsh took an oath of loyalty to Mexico in April 1824 and received a league of land in present Brazoria County on July 8. He was a merchant in the town of Brazoria for several years. The census of March 1826 lists him as a single man, between twenty-five and forty years of age.

As *sindico procurador*, Marsh presided over an election at Bolivar. He married Lucinda Pitts and they later moved to her family's neighborhood in present Washington County.

In 1835 Marsh applied for another grant. Stephen F. Austin, in supporting the request, wrote: "I shall state that the applicant was one of the first immigrants to this country, and . . . he is a man of good customs, honesty and much industry, and I believe that he has sufficient capital to settle and cultivate the tract he solicits. . . ."

Marsh ultimately owned land in many parts of the state. He died at age seventy-one at the home he built near Independence, with its flower and vegetable gardens and fruit orchards. His granddaughter, Margaret Hall Hicks, wrote extensively about Marsh from personal recollections.

— GENEVIEVE HICKS COONLY #357
— JEAN HICKS RICHEY #356

Arthur McCormick

Arthur McCormick, with his wife Margaret and two sons, Michael and John, emigrated from Ireland to America in 1818 and in that year located in New Orleans. From there they went to Texas in 1822 and located in Harris County on land that afterwards became known as the Arthur McCormick League and *labor*.

He was an early associate of Stephen F. Austin, who persuaded McCormick to consent to return to Ireland and to bring a colony of Irish emigrants. In February 1825 he visited Austin in San Felipe to receive the necessary papers and credentials for carrying out the project. On returning to his home and in crossing Buffalo Bayou near Harrisburg, it was necessary for him to swim. He was caught in a thicket of grapevines and drowned, as did his horse. The widow resided on the home place with her sons until she died some years later.

The McCormick league of land was situated on the west bank of the San Jacinto River, the place where Santa Anna and his army were defeated on April 21, 1836. When Margaret found her land covered with dead Mexican soldiers, she went to General Sam Houston and asked him to remove the stinking corpses. Houston replied, "Why, Lady, your land will be famed in history as the spot where the glorious battle was fought." Margaret was left with the problem to solve of getting the dead Mexicans buried.

— JUNE McCORMICK GAUME #534

John McCrosky

Scotch-Irishman John McCrosky, the son of James and Susan Walker McCrosky, was born November 15, 1792, in Scott County, Kentucky. He came to Texas in 1821 as a tanner and one of Stephen F. Austin's colonists. He received two leagues and a *labor* of land in present Brazoria, Colorado, and Austin counties on August 16, 1824.

His original one-story double log cabin, built in Brazoria County in 1824, now restored, is the oldest log cabin in Texas today. McCrosky sold the Brazoria County property to John Williams in 1825 and moved his tannery to Colorado County. There he married Sarah Ann Bright, widow of Eli Hunter, in 1829. She was the daughter of David and Judith Bright, also colonists. Their son, William Hart McCrosky, was born May 9, 1830, in Colorado County.

McCrosky's tannery, established on the Colorado River near Columbus, was one of the first industries in Texas. A member of the first Texas Rangers in the Colorado District, he was listed in Moses Morrison's Company as a corporal, age thirty, farmer, and courier. He was elected third lieutenant of a company of militia at San Felipe de Austin on July 10, 1824. In January 1827 McCrosky met with other settlers at the home of Bartlett Sims to adopt resolutions and condemn the Fredonian Rebellion.

John McCrosky died about December 1831, and is believed to be buried on his property near the tannery. In 1832, Sarah Ann McCrosky married William D. Lacey, who had worked for John McCrosky at the tannery. Lacey was one of the signers of the Texas Declaration of Independence.

—DONNA MCCROSKY JOHNSON #23

John McNeel

John McNeel was born in or around Cowpens, South Carolina, on November 21, 1770, the son of John McNeel, Sr., and Nancy Devine McNeel. In 1797, the family migrated to Warren County, Kentucky, where they accumulated large tracts of land and raised English longhorn cattle. They later introduced this cattle breed into Austin's Colony.

John McNeel married Elizabeth (Betsy) Mitchell on January 3, 1793, in or around Bowling Green, Kentucky. They had ten children, and those who reached adulthood were: Nancy, Pleasant D., Sterling, John Greenville, George W., and Leander H. Four of the sons would one day be counted among the Old Three Hundred.

In 1822, John McNeel led his family on the overland journey from the Arkansas Territory to the District of Nacogdoches, and joined Austin's first colonists. On August 3, 1824, John McNeel received a league of land on the east margin of the San Bernard River (Gulf Prairie, Brazoria County). In all, six McNeels received land grants in Austin's first colony.

John McNeel established the China Grove Plantation on his grant. He built a cotton gin and shipped his cotton from McNeel's landing on the Brazos River. His cotton crop in 1830 sold for $5,000. McNeel reportedly used an Indian hunter to supply the family with game.

McNeel and the plantation were featured in the early Texas travel book, *Visit to Texas: Being the Journal of a Traveler Through Those Parts Most Interesting to American Settlers* (1830). McNeel is described in the book as having 800 head of cattle, 60 horses, and shipping 30 oxen. His daughter, Elizabeth, is recorded to have just completed college in the Northeast.

McNeel died on August 30, 1833, from cholera. He died intestate and was buried in the McNeel family cemetery in Gulf Prairie, Brazoria County.

—GEORGE WARREN THOMAS #770
—KATHERINE ANN NOONAN #771

Joseph Mims

Joseph Mims was born in Baldwin County, Alabama, in 1790. He served in the War of 1812 as part of Johnson's Company of the Florida Mounted Volunteers. Joseph married Jane O'Neal and she gave birth to a son, Benjamin Franklin Mims. Jane died within a few years of giving birth. Joseph later married Sarah Weakly on January 8, 1821, and they had nine children.

In 1824, after the death of his mother, Joseph and his wife traveled by wagon caravan to Texas. He received a land grant from the Mexican government on authority of Stephen F. Austin later that same year. The grant of 5,222 acres of land was located on the west bank of the San Bernard River, ten miles north of the Gulf of Mexico in present Brazoria County.

James W. Fannin and Joseph Mims were business partners, friends, and neighbors. It is recounted in *Old Plantations and Their Owners of Brazoria County, Texas* that Fannin wrote a letter to Joseph Mims "entrusting his family to Joseph's care while he goes to fight for Texas." Fannin was killed at Goliad and Joseph Mims bought Fannin's estate.

Joseph died in 1844 but his wife Sarah continued to work the plantation and converted the land to a sugar plantation. In 1852, the Mims plantation was the sixth largest producer of sugar in Brazoria County. Sarah died in 1861 and her children lived in the area until they moved later to Galveston and Harris counties. Joseph Mims and his family were not unlike the other families that came to Texas for free land and an opportunity to start anew. It was men like Joseph who were spurred on by their manifest destiny and free enterprise that planted the seed for the great State of Texas.

— MARK JONES #738

John H. Moore

John H. Moore was born in Sumner County, Tennessee, August 13, 1800. At age eighteen, he ran away from Transylvania College in Lexington, Kentucky. His father made him go back, but he again left school and went to Texas in 1821. He fought the Indians in the upper Colorado area and in 1824 secured a land grant from Stephen F. Austin. He and Thomas Gray received title to a league of land in Brazoria County, and a *labor* in Colorado County.

John H. Moore and Eliza Cummins, born April 23, 1803, whom he married on June 14, 1827, made their first home in Columbus. Later they moved to present LaGrange. Their children were: William Bowen, Tabitha B., Eliza, John Henry, Jr., Robert J., and Mary E.

Moore built a twin blockhouse on his plantation, which was known as Moore's Fort. He organized and named Fayette County, and gave the land for the town of LaGrange.

It is known that Moore owned one hundred slaves; when they were freed, most of them stayed with the Moore family.

Moore was a patriot and an advocate of the independence of Texas. There are numerous accounts of the "Come and Take It Flag," which he is attributed to have signed. Austin ordered him to organize a cavalry and Moore was elected colonel of the volunteer army, becoming the commander of the Battle of Gonzales. He then returned to the United States for financial aid and reinforcements. Moore died in LaGrange on December 2, 1880, and is buried on the plantation. Eliza died February 25, 1877.

— KATHLEEN FISK HALE #355
— DONNA L. MCCROSKY JOHNSON #23

William Morton

William Morton arrived in Texas in 1822. He had sailed from Mobile, Alabama, with his wife, Jane, and five children. The family was shipwrecked near present-day Galveston and joined the members of the *Lively* expedition, which followed the Brazos River upstream.

Morton settled in what is now Fort Bend County, on the east side of the Brazos River. As one of the original Old Three Hundred, he received one and one half leagues and one *labor* of land in Fort Bend County. Morton was a brick mason, farmer, and cattle raiser. As a brick mason he was authorized to plan an academy at San Felipe. He was commissioned to build the jail at San Felipe.

Morton was a member of the Masonic Lodge. The Morton Lodge No. 72, chartered January 24, 1851, located in Richmond, was named after him. William Morton drowned in the Brazos River in 1833 while attempting to cross the flooded river. His body was never recovered.

One of the Morton girls married William Little. Daughter Marian (Mary) married William P. Huff. She was baptized by Father Michael Muldoon. Her baptism certificate is on file at the Center for American History, The University of Texas at Austin.

— Mrs. W. T. Robinson, Jr. #440

Texas first participated in the U.S. census in 1850. At that time, the census counted not only more than 200,000 people, but also the agricultural animals. The state had: 12,364 asses and mules, 50,482 working oxen, 75,403 horses, 99,099 sheep, 214,868 milk cows, 652,174 other cattle, and 683,604 swine.

Joseph Newman

Joseph Newman's land grant was No. 57 and it was received on August 10, 1824. It consisted of one league on the east bank of the Colorado River near present-day Egypt, in Wharton County, and one *labor* on the Brazos River, near San Felipe de Austin.

The earliest documentation on Joseph Newman is his marriage at age nineteen to sixteen-year-old Rachel Rabb, daughter of William Rabb, on June 21, 1806, in Warren County, Ohio. From Ohio, the Rabbs and the Newmans moved to Illinois Territory, and by 1820 they had moved to what was known as the Jonesborough settlement, now in Red River County, Texas.

Problems soon arose in this area. Officials in Miller County, Arkansas, tried to collect taxes from the settlers and to govern them while settlers on the south side of Red River believed themselves to be in Spanish territory. In 1821 William Rabb wrote a letter to the Spanish governor of Texas, complaining about this situation. A petition (or memorial) from Pecan Point settlement accompanied this letter. The people there were asking that the Spanish Government send a commandant and an *alcalde* to govern the settlement. In the event this was not possible, they asked permission to elect someone to fill these offices. The petition, known as the "Joseph Newman Memorial," carried the signatures of about eighty settlers.

The Rabbs and Joseph Newman received land grants in Austin's Colony in 1824. Joseph Newman's grant adjoined that of his brother-in-law, Andrew Rabb.

Joseph Newman lived only about six years after settling in the colony. In his last will and testament, signed on February 15, 1831, he requested to be buried in the cemetery on his property. His will left his property to his wife Rachel Rabb Newman and their children: Mary, William, Eliza, Minerva, Sally, Elizabeth, Thomas, Ali Joseph, Jr., and Andrew. The three youngest sons were born in Austin's Colony. Andrew Rabb was named executor and Rachel Newman, executrix, of Joseph's estate.

— COLEMAN C. NEWMAN #116

George Samuel Pentecost

George Samuel Pentecost and his wife Martha Ellen (Denley) left their home in Alabama to join the original colonists of Stephen F. Austin, acquiring a *sitio* of land, in August 1824, in present Matagorda County.

Dissatisfied with the first homesite near the Colorado River and with a second homesite near the San Bernard River, Pentecost established a flourishing plantation in the Big Creek Community in Fort Bend County, on land purchased from Samuel Pharr, husband of daughter Lucy Pentecost.

Pentecost had been a resident of Monroe County, Alabama, prior to the War of 1812 and served in the Mississippi Volunteers during this war, as did two brothers of Martha Denley Pentecost, James and John Denley.

In 1827 Pentecost was opposed to the Fredonian Rebellion and declared loyalty to the Mexican government. He later joined the call for independence and a son, George Washington Pentecost, was among the heroes at the Battle of San Jacinto, along with a son-in-law, Andrew Jackson Beard, husband of Sally Pentecost.

George S. Pentecost is buried in the Brown Cemetery near Big Creek, having passed away in 1841 in the fiftieth year of life. His wife Martha is thought to be buried at the second homesite near the San Bernard River.

Children named in his will were: Lucy Ellen, Gracey Elizabeth, George Washington, Mary Jane, James Denley, Sara (Sally) Jane, Susan Evelyn, and William Walter.

—SALLY BRUMBELOW BELL #422
— MRS. SIDNEY B. BEARD for
SIDNEY BEARD #94

Dr. James Aeneas Phelps

Dr. James Aeneas Phelps was born in Grandy, Connecticut, in 1793. After college, he moved to Wilkinson County, Mississippi, where he was listed in the 1820 census. He married Rosetta Adeline Yerby, on April 18, 1821.

Dr. Phelps came to Texas on the *Lively*, as one of Stephen F. Austin's Old Three Hundred colonists. He received a league of land and two *labores*, on the Brazos River, in what is now Brazoria County.

Dr. Phelps built a large two-story house for his family and named his plantation "Orozimbo." The house stood about ten miles northeast of the present town of West Columbia.

In March 1835, six Master Masons: Phelps, John A. Wharton, Asa Brigham, Alexander Russell, Anson Jones, and James P. Campbell, met in Brazoria to establish a lodge. Although it was forbidden under the Mexican law, they signed a petition to the Grand Lodge of Louisiana. Holland Lodge No. 36, U.D., opened on December 27, 1835, with Dr. Phelps as treasurer.

On March 19, 1836, Dr. Phelps and Dr. Anson Jones left Brazoria to join the army. Dr. Phelps was attached to the medical staff during the Battle of San Jacinto. After Santa Anna was captured, he was prisoner at Orozimbo, from July to November 1836.

In 1842, Santa Anna showed his gratitude to Dr. Phelps, when their oldest son Orlando was captured in the ill-fated Mier Expedition. During the drawing of the black beans, Santa Anna heard the name Phelps mentioned. He saved the young man's life and sent him home.

Dr. Phelps is buried at Orozimbo. His will was probated on November 9, 1847. In 1936 the State of Texas erected two monuments at the site.

— A. FREDERICK RENAUD #235

Joseph Henry Polley

Joseph Henry Polley

The adventurous Joseph Henry Polley left home in Whitehall, New York, at age fifteen. He was a teamster at seventeen in the War of 1812. At the close of the war he emigrated to Missouri.

In 1820 Polley joined Moses Austin for a look at Texas. In 1824 he received a 4,587-acre grant of land from Stephen F. Austin near present Richmond.

Polley competed patiently with Stephen F. Austin for the hand of Pollie Bailey, the daughter of Brit Bailey, another Old Three Hundred colonist. His persistence won out and they were soon married.

Polley served several terms as sheriff of Brazoria District. He also was a farmer, rancher and in the freighting business in Brazoria. At the time of his demise in 1859 his herds were the most extensive in Texas.

In October of 1836 the first Congress of Texas met in Joseph and Pollie's home. The question of creating a seal was posed. Henry Smith, the provisional governor, was wearing a coat with buttons displaying a single star. It was decided that the star would be an appropriate symbol for the flag and the seal.

Polley and his wife, in 1847, moved to the Cibolo Valley in what is now Wilson County, where he constructed a permanent home. They are buried there in a family plot.

— GEORGE B. EVERTS #196

John Henry
Polley's brand,
Bexar County,
1850

William Pryor

William Pryor was one of Stephen F. Austin's Old Three Hundred colonists but received his Mexican land grant somewhat uniquely. He received his *labor* of land on August 24, 1824. It lay on the east bank of the Brazos River directly across from the town of San Felipe de Austin. Later, he received his league of land in Washington County in 1828. Stephen F. Austin and the Baron de Bastrop signed it.

William Pryor was born about 1780 to Joseph Pryor and Mary Fleming in Botetourt County, Virginia. He married Betsy Green Trammell about 1808. They had eleven children, six of whom survived to adulthood: Althea Laura, Trammell, Mary, Harriet, Rosannah, and Elizabeth. In 1826 Harriet married Noel F. Roberts, another of the Old Three Hundred families. In 1834 Elizabeth married Noel's son William by a previous marriage. Both marriages produced children, thus combining two Old Three Hundred families.

William Barret Travis noted in his diary that he "sat with old Pryor" on September 9 and attended his funeral the next day in San Felipe de Austin. Thus we know that William died on September 9, 1833, leaving a remarkable will that contains an abundance of family information. William Pryor disowned his only son in the will because he "stained my honor and seized without my leave and dissipated my property." He left his estate to his five daughters. The will was somehow lost for seventeen years during the revolution and the years of the Republic. It was written under Mexican rule, was continued during the Republic of Texas, and was finally probated in 1850 after Texas became a state.

—James Edgar Roberts #488

John Rabb

John Rabb was born December 31, 1798, in Fayette County, Pennsylvania. He settled in Miller County, Arkansas, at a young age. In 1823 he came to Texas with his wife, Mary Crownover Rabb; his son; his father William; his brothers Andrew and Thomas; his sister Rachel, together with Rachel's husband, Joseph Newman, and family.

As members of the first Three Hundred families all of the men received land grants from the Mexican government through Stephen F. Austin.

John Rabb and family spent most of their lives in and around LaGrange, Texas. He built one of the first grist mills erected in Texas. As a bonus for the enterprise he received a league of land.

John Rabb is known as the first Methodist convert in Austin's Colony. He was one of the founders of Rutersville College in Rutersville, Texas.

On August 10, 1860, he decided to sell his gristmill and placed the following advertisement in the LaGrange paper and in *Harper's New Monthly Magazine*:

> Can't get the kind of miller I want. Won't have any other sort. Too pushing a business for an old man. Can't get time to pray enough. Too far from Church. Intend, by the will of God, to sell out and quit business. A good flouring, corn and shingling mill for sale!! (Steam Power) With large quantity of cedar timber and any amount of land, from one hundred to four thousand acres. For sale on reasonable terms. Ten miles North of LaGrange, Fayette County, Texas. Aug. 10, 1860.

In 1860 he moved with his wife to Travis County and settled at Barton Springs, in present-day Austin where he died on June 5, 1861.

— LILLIAN BELL RABB #129

Captain Thomas J. Rabb

Captain Rabb was known in Texas as a gentleman, scholar, husband, father, and Christian. Thus reads a newspaper obituary for Thomas Rabb of Fayette County, Pennsylvania, born around 1785 to William and Mary (Smalley) Rabb, and one of several members who were Old Three Hundred grantees.

The Rabbs arrived in Austin's colony by December 1821. The following year, William and Thomas accompanied Stephen F. Austin as far as Bexar, on Austin's trip to Mexico City to confirm his colonization contract. In 1824, the Rabb clan settled near present-day Egypt in Wharton County. That same year, Thomas received a one-league grant and was also named first lieutenant in the colony's militia.

In October 1835, the opening days of the Texas Revolution, Thomas joined the Texian army. He took part in the Battle of Mission Conception; soon after, he was assigned by the General Council of Texas to recruit for the army. As a result, Thomas was not able to take part in the Texas Declaration of Independence even though he had been chosen as the delegate from Mina.

Captain Rabb led his volunteers into Gonzales on the day the Alamo fell. The unit became Company F, First Regiment, Texas Volunteer Army.

In 1840 Thomas served as captain of Rangers in a decisive victory over the Comanche, and again in 1842 to meet a Mexican raid on San Antonio. He died in Fayette County, Texas, in 1846.

Thomas and his first wife, Serena (Gilbert), had Ulysses, Sarah, and Mary Louisa. After Serena's death in 1836, Thomas and second wife Barthenia (maiden name unknown) had Adelia Ann and Angeline Thomas.

—COL. VICTOR C. WEGENHOFT,
USAF (RET.), #114

William Rabb

William Rabb was born in Fayette County, Pennsylvania, on December 27, 1770. He married Mary Polly Smalley. They had five children, Rachel, Andrew, John, Thomas, and Ulysses.

This family came to Texas as Austin's Old Three Hundred colonists, about December 15, 1823. They settled on the Colorado River, near the present town of LaGrange. The place was known as Indian Hills at the time.

William Rabb erected a gristmill and a sawmill on the Colorado River. All the materials came from New Orleans, except the millstones, which were shipped from Scotland.

The first census of Austin's colony lists William Rabb as a farmer and stockraiser, over fifty years of age, with a wife, one son, and one slave.

William Rabb died about 1832, at the age of sixty-two. His wife Mary (Polly) died soon after. Rabb's Creek in Lee County and Rabb's Prairie, a farming community, were named for him. They are near LaGrange, Texas.

— IRENE T. PHILIPS #172
— MRS. JOHN WAYNE REEDY #214
— MARK EDWARD ROBINSON #213
— BETTY NEWMAN WAUER #494

William Rabb was given five *sitios* and two *labores* of land in Austin's Colony on the condition that he build and operate a gristmill. They were unable to build for a few years because of Indian raids. When it was time to build, William Rabb ordered the equipment from New Orleans, except the buhrs or grinding stones. They came from Scotland by ship to Matagorda Bay. It would have been impossible to move the heavy stones in a conventional manner since there were no good roads. Rabb constructed an axle from a tree, mounted the stones as wheels, hitched his teams of oxen, and rolled the stones to the site more than 100 miles away.

Elijah Roark

Elijah Roark was born in North Carolina about 1785-88. He moved to Missouri Territory about 1810. He married Cynthia Fisher circa 1812. While living in the Missouri Territory, three of their children were born.

In 1821, Elijah learned that Stephen F. Austin was enlisting families to move to Texas. Records show that the Roark family was in the colony on October 13, 1822. The family lived on Oyster Creek in present Fort Bend County. On July 10, 1824, Elijah received title to a league and a *labor* of land. Twin daughters were born to them there. In all, there were seven children: Leo, Andrew Jackson, Rebecca, twins Lucinda and Louisa, Andy, and Mary, who was born a few months after Elijah was murdered by Indians.

In 1829, Elijah and his son Leo, and a friend loaded a wagon and driving the hogs, began the long trip to San Antonio, about two hundred miles. They had crossed the Guadalupe River and made camp for the night when they were attacked by Indians. Elijah and his friend were murdered, but Leo escaped in the underbrush. He made his way to San Antonio, where he told of the attack. He and others went back to the scene of the campsite, where they found the two men scalped and their wagon burned. The Indians had taken their stock. Wolves were eating on the corpses, a very gruesome picture.

Cynthia Roark died on December 25, 1836.

— DORIS BALLARD DRAKE #272

Noel Francis Roberts

Noel F. Roberts, an Old Three Hundred colonist, received his Mexican land grant of one and one-fourth leagues on July 15, 1824. Stephen F. Austin and the Baron de Bastrop signed the document. His land stretched for about one and a half miles along the north or east bank of the Brazos River and stretched about five miles north. The present-day town of Simonton in Fort Bend County is situated on the old Noel F. Roberts League.

Roberts first married Highley Carter on March 10, 1808, in Clarke County, Georgia. They had three sons: John Hardin, William Taylor, and Josiah. John Hardin and his mother both died in 1817. William and Josiah went to Texas with their father.

Roberts next married Morning Harper in Lawrence County, Mississippi, on November 19, 1820. There were probably a son and a daughter born to this marriage as the 1826 census of Austin's Colony lists Noel F. as widower age forty to fifty, farmer and stockraiser. He had four slaves, one son under seven years of age, two sons between seven and sixteen, and one daughter under seven. If Morning Harper came to Texas, she died before 1826.

He next married Harriet Pryor by marriage bond on July 26, 1826. Harriet was the oldest child of William Pryor, another of the Old Three Hundred families. To this marriage were born Elisha, Hirma, John, Mary, and Thomas.

Noel's son William married Elizabeth "Betsy" Pryor, William Pryor's youngest daughter. William and Josiah fought in the Texas Revolution. William was in the Battle of San Jacinto. He and Betsy walked the battlefield the next day with Betsy carrying her first-born son.

Noel died in the fall of 1843, leaving a large estate.

—JAMES EDGAR ROBERTS #488

William Roberts

William Roberts, born between 1755 and 1765, was one of Stephen Austin's Old Three Hundred colonists, who lived on the lower Brazos River. He received title to a *sitio* and a *labor* of land in present day Brazoria County. The Census of March 1826 lists him, his wife Peggy (born 1770), grown son Andrew, and one servant. He also had a daughter Elizabeth who was married to Cornelius Smith, another Old Three Hundred colonist.

William Roberts died intestate in the spring of 1826. His probate record filed in Brazoria County in 1833, shows as his heirs his son Andrew and his son-in-law Cornelius Smith. William's wife Peggy died in 1832.

—LaNell Lee Moses Wright #570

The first year was a hard one for the colonists. There was a shortage of tools, insufficient seeds for planting, and little rain, so the first corn crop was a failure. Families did without bread. Martin Varner told a story about his little son's first experience with a biscuit. Mr. Varner had managed to buy or trade for a barrel of flour. "Mrs. Varner made a batch of biscuits, which considering the resources of the country, were doubtless heavy as lead and hard as wood. When they were done Mrs. Varner set them on the table," according to Noah Smithwick. The boy picked one up, looked at it, and headed for the door. In a few minutes he came back and got another. Mr. Varner followed him outside to see what he was doing. He punched holes through the center, inserted an axle, and trumphantly displayed a miniature Mexican cart.

George Robinson

George Robinson was born June 2, 1796. He went from Tennessee, in 1816 or 1817, to Louisiana where he married Lucinda Galloway. From Louisiana he went to present Fayette County, Texas, in 1820, where he filled the office of sheriff. He received title to a *sitio* of land from the Mexican government in present Brazoria County on July 8, 1824. The census in 1826 classified George Robinson as a farmer and stock raiser, aged between twenty-five and forty. His household included his wife and three sons.

He served in the War of Independence and received bounty land of 320 acres for three months of service in the army, from October 1835 to January 1836. He was later given, to his heirs, sixty-five acres of land in Fayette County.

He provided ferriage and hospitality to an Indian expedition that passed through and was sent as a token of their gratitude, a tea service along with a letter from the company of Matagorda Volunteers that reads in part:

To Mrs. George Robinson,

RESOLVED: As Mr. Robinson declined receiving any recompense for Ferriage, horse-feed and refreshments for the volunteers, as a token of the high estimations in which he is held by the company for his kindness and Patriotic feeling that ____ to him, and as a solid token of esteem that this Company present to Mrs. George Robinson a Tea Service of China.

George Robinson died intestate on February 20, 1848, at the age of fifty-two. His widow, Lucinda, settled the estate. It is believed that she spent the remainder of her life on the property near LaGrange. She lived to be seventy-five. George, Lucinda, and four of their sons are buried in a gravesite in a pasture in Rutersville surrounded by a wrought-iron fence. They had a total of eight children.

— CAROLYN GRIFFIN #710

Robert Scobey

Robert Scobey was born circa 1802 in Tennessee, the son of Robert Scobey and Lucy Debow. He married Mary L. Fulshear, daughter of Churchill Fulshear and Betsy Summers Fulshear, September 5, 1821, in Tennessee.

Young Scobey and his wife traveled with his father-in-law's family to Texas and had their first child, Andrew Wilkinson Scobey, in Arkansas on August 12, 1823. They made it to Texas in time to join Stephen F. Austin's Old Three Hundred, receiving a *sitio* of land in present-day Wharton County, August 3, 1824.

By the 1826 Census, he and his wife had another son, Matthew, born January 1, 1826. After they had met their obligations on their land grant in Wharton County, they sold it and moved to Brazoria County, between West Columbia and Angleton.

Scobey opened a tavern between San Felipe and Harrisburg in January 1832. He drove a wagon loaded with rifles and ammunitions to Goliad and contributed supplies to the Texas Army during the Texas Revolution.

Mary L. Fulshear Scobey died October 7, 1837, in Brazoria County, Texas. In 1846 Robert Scobey was administrator to the estate of Elisha M. Adcock in Harris County. In 1852 he married Rebecca Adcock. His will was dated August 16, 1855, and probated October 30, 1855, in Brazoria County, leaving his estate to his children: Andrew Wilkinson, who married Rebecca Little on January 23, 1839; Matthew; Elizabeth J., born January 2, 1828, married (a) Stephen Jackson Justice in 1842, and (b) Abraham H. Kipp on November 2, 1857; Sytha Douglas, born 1830, married (a) F. M. Jackson in 1845 and (b) Albert Brown Sweden; Mary Jane, born August 6, 1832, married (a) Harvey N. Little and (b) Harry Newton.

— CHERYL B. (SISSIE) KIPP #3
— JOHN EMMETTE (DICK) KIPP #113

James Scott

Born circa 1789 in Berkeley County, Virginia, to Revolutionary War veteran George Scott and Angeletta (Craighill) Scott, James Scott found new battles to fight in Texas.

In 1822 James and his brother William arrived in Austin's colony, where James received a league of land on the San Bernard River in present-day Fort Bend County and William received two leagues and a *labor* in present-day Harris County. James later left the colony for a period of years, marrying a widow, Jane (Blagrave) McLean in 1827 in Dubois County, Indiana. He was previously married to Mary Lafever in Frederick County, Virginia. James and Jane had three children: William Craighill, George Russell, and James William.

James returned to Texas in 1834. Sometime before February 1836, the family relocated from the San Bernard River to Cedar Bayou, near present-day Baytown in Harris County. He died in 1845 and his widow in 1873. Records indicate James was a Mason.

Records also show that he volunteered for a three-month hitch with the Texas Army after the Battle of Gonzales in October 1835. James probably participated in the "Grass Fight" and other early skirmishes. He was awarded bounty land for taking part in the Siege of Bexar, after which he doubtless decided the war was over and went home to plant crops.

— Esther Smith Halbert #117

In December 1835, the first Masonic order in Texas was initiated into service in Brazoria under the wide spread branches of a huge oak tree, which is still standing today.

Jane Long is known as the "Mother of Texas" because she had the first Anglo child in Texas. Jane was the wife of Dr. James Long, who led several expeditions to free Texas from Spain. On one such trip Jane accompanied her husband into Texas. Dr. Long left her with companions on Bolivar Point, opposite Galveston Island, while he went to Goliad.

After months of waiting for her husband's return, all left except for twenty-three-year-old Jane, six-year-old daughter Ann, and the twelve-year-old servant, Kian. Jane could not be persuaded to leave and spent the winter of 1821-22 at Bolivar existing on birds, fish, and oysters. It was a hard winter and Galveston Bay froze. Indians were near, and when they approached, Jane flew a red skirt (petticoat) as a flag and fired the cannon to frighten them away.

Jane Long became one of the Old Three Hundred, later ran a boardinghouse in Brazoria, and after she moved to Richmond, operated a hotel there. In later years she became a wealthy and influential woman.

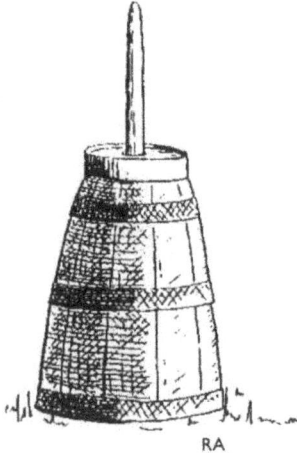

RA

William Selkirk

William Selkirk was born on July 24, 1792, the son of James and Elizabeth (Henry) Selkirk of Selkirk, New York. On November 22, 1813, William married Matilda Hallenbake. They had two children, James Henry and Rachel Elizabeth. Matilda died on August 25, 1820. William left his children under the guardianship of his brother Charles, and came to Texas in 1822 as a surveyor with Stephen F. Austin's Old Three Hundred.

William made surveys throughout the colony, but his principal area was the Gulf Coast where Brazoria, Matagorda, and Jackson counties were eventually organized. The compass that belonged to Elias Wightman and was used by Wightman and William Selkirk to lay out the town of Matagorda is on display in the Matagorda County Museum in Bay City, Texas. Stephen F. Austin paid William $400 for surveying part of the meandering Colorado River.

William was active in the affairs of the colony. In July 1824, he was sent to deliver Austin's "talk" to the Waco Indians. He was elected 2nd sergeant in the Second Company of the colonial militia at an election held at San Felipe on July 10, 1824. On January 4, 1827, William was appointed to a committee of three to wait on the governor of Coahuila and assure him of the loyalty of the citizens of Austin's Colony in regard to recent uprising, the Fredonian Rebellion, in Nacogdoches. William died sometime between June and November 1830.

William Selkirk received a "head right" grant of one league of land on August 10, 1824. The land, called Selkirk Island, was located at the mouth of the Colorado River in Matagorda County. In 1976, during the American Bicentennial, Selkirk Island received a state historical marker from the Texas Historical Commission.

— GEORGEANNA TRIPLETT #843

Daniel Shipman

Daniel Shipman

Daniel Shipman, born in Kentucky on February 20, 1801, was the son of Moses Shipman of North Carolina and Mary Robinson, daughter of John Robinson of South Carolina.

In *Frontier Life*, Shipman wrote: "The 9th of March 1822 we crossed over Red River into Texas; and have lived in Texas ever since. It was a new country, new acquaintances, and new things generally."

He and his family settled on Mill Creek near San Felipe in March 1823.

In 1825 the settlers in the coastal region had trouble with the Karankawa Indians, and Colonel Austin asked for fifty volunteers to drive the Indians out of the area. Daniel was one of the volunteers. The group trailed the Indians to the Guadalupe River before a peace agreement was arranged.

On May 21, 1827, Daniel and his partner, Charles L. Nidever, received title to a league of land in present Brazoria County. They formed one of Austin's Old Three Hundred Families.

On September 23, 1828, Daniel married Margaretta Kelley, the daughter of John and Sarah Kelley, also one of Austin's Old Three Hundred. Daniel and Margaretta had a daughter, Mary Jane, in 1829, and their son, John Kelley, was born October 30, 1831. After the death of his first wife, Margaretta, Daniel married Eliza Hancock, daughter of Thomas Hancock. They had one son, Edward Moses, born January 18, 1840. They lived near Brenham in Washington County and also maintained a ranch in Goliad County. Eliza died on September 11, 1858.

Shipman served Texas well. Under the command of Francis W. Johnson in 1832, he joined the company that attacked Juan Davis Bradburn at Anahuac. When General Cos invaded Texas to establish a stronghold in San Antonio, and Austin issued a call to arms, Daniel, with his brother Moses and his brother-in-law John Owens, enlisted in the Texas Volunteer Army and marched to Bexar. Daniel participated in the fight that caused Cos to surrender and leave Texas.

In the fall of 1870, Daniel wrote a series of articles about his experience in Texas that were published in the *Houston Telegraph*, and in 1879, at the age of seventy-eight, he published *Frontier Life*, his reminiscences of his early life and days in Texas.

Daniel Shipman died March 4, 1881, in Goliad County at the age of seventy-nine. He is buried beside his second wife in a cemetery near Weesatche. On June 15, 1938, Daniel and Eliza were reinterred in the State Cemetery in Austin.

—HELEN SHIPMAN CUNNINGHAM #192

You, in Kentucky, cannot for a moment conceive of the beauty of one of our prairies in the spring. Imagine for yourself a vast plain extending as far as the eye can reach, with nothing but the deep blue sky to bound the prospect, excepting on the east side where runs a broad red stream, with lofty trees rearing themselves upon its banks, and you have our prairie. This is covered with a carpet of the richest verdure, from the midst of which spring up wild flowers of every hue and shade, rendering the scene one of almost fairy-like beauty. Indeed it is impossible to step without crushing these fairest of nature's works. Upon these natural flower gardens feed numerous herds of buffalo, deer, and other wild animals. Here and there may be seen beautiful clumps of trees, and anon, a little thicket comes in view. The flowers of the prairie are certainly the most beautiful which I have ever beheld. Our ladies in Kentucky would feel themselves amply repaid for all the labor which they bestow upon their beautiful flower gardens, could they but afford one half of the beauty of one of our prairies.

Your truly,
W.B.D.

—from *Letters from an Early Settler of Texas*
by William B. Dewees

Moses Shipman

Moses Shipman was born about 1775 in North Carolina. On January 19, 1798, Moses married Mary Robinson of South Carolina, and they became parents of ten children, nine of whom lived to adulthood.

The Shipman family left South Carolina in 1814, moving to Tennessee, Illinois, and Missouri. In October of 1821 the family began their journey to Texas.

The trip was slow and tedious since the roads were bad, with many deep gullies and muddy creeks to cross. In December while traveling through Arkansas, Mary gave birth to their youngest child, Lucinda. Before they reached Texas they sold or gave away everything they could not carry and made the final trip on horseback, crossing the Red River at Jonesboro on March 9, 1822. After receiving a favorable report on Stephen F. Austin's colony, the family moved to the Brazos River and settled near San Felipe in the fork of Mill Creek and the Brazos River.

Moses Shipman received a league of land in present-day Fort Bend County and a *labor* of land in present Austin County on July 19, 1824.

While the family was living on Mill Creek in 1825, Joseph Bays, a Baptist minister and a friend from Missouri, came to visit. Although contrary to Mexican law under which they were living, Reverend Bays was allowed to hold a service in the Shipman home. Probably this was the first Baptist sermon preached west of the Brazos River.

In 1825 the Shipmans moved to their league on Oyster Creek, southeast of the present town of Richmond. They built a house which had two rooms with wooden floors, a lean-to, and a rain barrel. Some of the Shipmans lived on this league for more than fifty years.

The Shipmans were involved in the events leading to the Texas Revolution. Moses Shipman was the president of the election at the home of John Owens to choose delegates to the Convention of 1836 at Washington-on-the-Brazos.

Moses Shipman died in Fort Bend County in late 1836. His wife, Mary, remained on the league until her death.

— HELEN SHIPMAN CUNNINGHAM #192

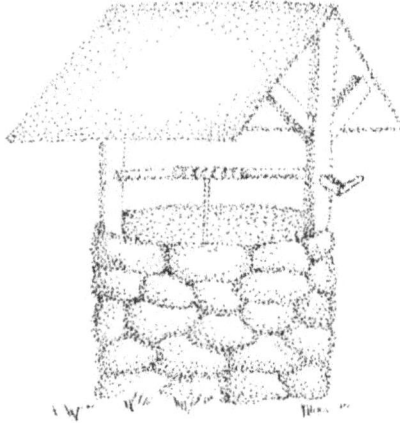

Aylett C. Buckner was a red-haired, 6'6", 250-pound giant of a man. He came to Texas the first time in 1812 and built a house on the Colorado River before Austin arrived. In the beginning, Buckner and Austin had several disagreements but became good friends.

Known for his rough manner and incredible strength, Buckner has been the subject of many stories. It was said that he could kill a yearling with one blow of his fist. He gained a reputation as a great hunter, choosing to use, instead of guns, his bare fist or a tomahawk to get wild game. A Karankawa said he saw Buckner stop a wildcat in midair with one swing.

Buckner was later ranked by *Harper's Magazine* as the equal of Paul Bunyan.

Captain Bartlett Samuel Sims

Captain Bartlett Samuel Sims was born in 1773, in Tennessee. In 1824, two years after coming to Texas, he married Sarah Curtis, the daughter of James Curtis, in Burleson County.

They had three sons: James Curtis, William Anderson, Thomas McKinney; and six daughters: Mary E., Margaret A., Eugenia Missouria, Emily V., Josephine, and Sarah.

In October 1824, Stephen F. Austin contracted with Captain Sims to start the northern part of the colony. At this time, Captain Sims was living in a two-room dirt-floor cabin, south of the Old Spanish Road on the Brazos River. He surveyed roads, *labores*, and leagues of land, most of which are in now Burleson and Washington counties.

Bartlett Sims was treasurer for Mina (Bastrop) County for a number of years, and county surveyor from 1836 to 1840. He also was a Christian gentleman, very generous, with the unusual ability to lead. His devotion to the cause of freedom was outstanding. He is said to be one of the two founders of the famous Texas Rangers.

In 1846, Sims started on a surveying expedition to the Pedernales River, with his nephew, William Sims, and chain-carriers Clark and Grant. They were attacked by a party of Indians and all were killed, except Captain Sims, who managed to escape

Bartlett Sims died circa 1863 at Rice's Crossing. Sarah Curtis Sims died in 1876. Both were buried in a cemetery on a cliff on the old Brushy Creek in Williamson County. The cemetery was washed away during floods in the 1900s.

— CORINE CROSSLAND THOMAS #21

George Washington Singleton

George Washington Singleton and his wife Sarah (Sally) Lusk were living in Mississippi prior to the move to the Mexican territory of Texas-Coahuila. The land grant signed by Stephen F. Austin, empresario, on May 14, 1827, was for 4,428+ acres in what is now Wharton County. Sarah stated in the Decree of Heirship in May 1831, that they resided about twenty-five miles above Gonzales. George Washington and Sarah were related to the Singleton and Whiteside families who received their grants in 1824.

According to the 1826 census of Austin's Colony, Washington Singleton, a farmer and stockraiser, and his wife Sally were between the ages of twenty-five and forty. Seven children, unnamed, are listed: five males between the ages of five and sixteen, one female between the age of seven and sixteen, and one female between the age of sixteen and twenty. Marcella (born circa 1828-1829) must have been born just before her father's death.

As a loyal citizen of Mexico, George condemned the Fredonian Rebellion. In August 1830 he was in San Antonio de Bexar where he made a will dated August 10, 1830. Acting administrator Jose Francisco Flores legalized the will. John Smith was appointed to translate the will "because he (Singleton) was dangerously ill." George declared in the document that Sarah Lusk was his wife and that the two of the six children born to this marriage still living were Amos and Marcella. He made statements about land and livestock owned and other worldly possessions, and money owed to him and debts to be paid. The remaining property was divided between his wife and the two children. Pedro Pablo and James Whiteside were named as executors and administrators. George died on Christmas Day, December 25, 1830, believed killed by Indians, according to Sarah in a statement made in May 1831.

After George's death, Sarah and the two children went to the home of James Walker, east of Brenham, and eventually they moved to Phillip Singleton's home in the Harrisburg District on the San Jacinto River. Here Sarah married Peter Duncan, Amos married Priscilla Faulk, and Marcella married Anderson Smith.

—SHIRLEY JEAN HANAGRIFF STEDMAN
#53

Marriage Bond

Be it known by these present that we John Crownover and Nancy Castleman of lawful age inhabitants of Austin's colony in the Province of Texas wishing to unite ourselves in the bonds of Matrimony, each of our parents have given Their Consent to our Union, and there being no Catholic Priest in the Colony to perform the Ceremony—therefore I said John Crownover do agree to take the said Nancy Castleman for my legal and lawful wife and as such to cherish and support and protect her, forsaking all others and keeping myself true and faithful to her alone, and I the said Nancy Castleman do agree to take the said John Crownover for my legal and lawful husband and as such to love, honor and obey him, forsaking all others and keeping myself true and faithful to him alone. And we do each of us bind and obligate ourselves to the other under the penalty of twenty thousand Dollars to have our Marriage solemnized by the Priest of this or some other Priest authorized to do so as soon as the opportunity offers, all of which we do promise in the name of God, and in the presence of Stephen F. Austin, Judge and Political Chief of this Colony and the other witnesses hereto signed—Witness our hands the 29th of April 1824.

Witnesses present:

—Adapted from Marriage By Bond in Colonial Texas,
by Bennett Smith, Fort Worth, Texas:
The Author, 1972, p. 67

Phillip Singleton

Phillip Singleton was married to Susanna Walker on June 14, 1815, in Wayne County, Kentucky.

On August 16, 1824, Stephen F. Austin granted him his land. Witnessing the transaction were David McCormick and Samuel M. Williams. The land was located on the south and north sides of Yegua Creek, where it empties into the Brazos River. By 1828-29, the family moved to the San Jacinto-Lynchburg area. Phillip had possession of 171+ acres of land across Buffalo Bayou, opposite the San Jacinto battlegrounds. There he built a log house and later covered it with sawmill planks and added glass windows. According to Burke's *Almanac*, it was the first house to have such amenities. It was later sold to Lorenzo de Zavala. This house was used for a hospital for the Texian troops during the Battle of San Jacinto.

The 1826 census shows Phillip as a farmer/stockraiser between forty and fifty years of age; Susana in the same age bracket; two male children between seven and sixteen, two male children between sixteen and twenty-five, one female under seven, and one female between seven and sixteen.

Phillip Singleton spent the last years of his life on the banks of the San Jacinto River. The cause of his death and his burial place are unknown. It is said that he went hunting and never returned. On the legal documents concerning the estate, Spyars, James W., and Phillip Singleton were named as sons.

Many of his descendants have remained in the area of his home.

—SHIRLEY JEAN HANAGRIFF STEDMAN
#53

Christian Smith

Christian Smith was born in 1774 in Stokes County, North Carolina. His father was possibly Christian Schmidt, a German immigrant. He was married to Rachel Poffard or Paffard who was born in North Carolina in 1774.

Smith moved to Kentucky some time between 1803 and 1809 and was in Texas by July 19, 1824, when he received a *sitio* of land in the present area of Harris and Chambers counties. He was residing in the San Jacinto District in November of 1824, when he signed a petition for appointment of a surveyor in the area. He was one of twenty-three men who were recruited to spend three months in Galveston in case Santa Anna sent a fleet of ships there.

In the Atascosito District census of July 31, 1826, Christian Smith was listed as a carpenter, over fifty years of age, with a wife, four sons, and a daughter.

Smith's granddaughter Elizabeth married Edward Este, who went on the Mier Expedition and was one of the unfortunate ones who drew a black bean and was shot.

Christian Smith died in 1839, possibly in Tennessee, where his son Joseph lived. His estate was probated in Harrisburg, Texas. His wife, Rachel, died at Cedar Bayou, Texas, in 1845.

Their children were born in North Carolina: John, circa 1798; Joseph, circa 1800; Elizabeth, 1803; and Eleanor, 1809.

— CHARLES "DOUGLAS" McBEE, JR.
#176

Cornelius Smith

Cornelius Smith was born on December 23, 1783, in Rowan County, North Carolina. He was the son of Thomas B. and Molly Smith. His marriage on January 21, 1808, to Elizabeth Roberts was in Pulaski County, Kentucky. Twelve children were born to them: Margaret Elizabeth, John B., William Robert, Mary (Polly), Lucriata, Cornelius, Rachel, Gaines, C. Henry, Wesley Lee, James, and Elizabeth.

Cornelius was among the Old Three Hundred and appears on the First Census of Texas in 1826 with his family. He received grant No. 191 on August 10, 1824.

Smith died on October 10, 1837, according to the Cornelius Smith Bible. In the 1850 census, his wife Betsy is shown in Brazoria County as head of a household. She died about 1859.

The grave of Cornelius has not been found but is believed to be in Brazoria County. Some of his children emigrated to the West Fork of Plum Creek in Caldwell County to make their home. A chapter of the Daughters of the Republic of Texas in Caldwell County has been named in his honor because so many of his descendants live there today.

— MAXINE MOSES HENDERSON #138

In 1827 there was a drought and the only rain that fell in the area was in present Wharton County on land that had been granted by Stephen F. Austin to John C. Clark. When other colonists heard about it, they would say that they were "going down to Egypt for corn," as matched the story in the Bible. That's how Egypt, Texas, got its name.

William Smithers/ Smeathers/Smothers

William Smothers was born in Virginia circa 1760. He was the first-born child of Smothers and his wife, Anna Marie Chrisman. When he was 12 years old Indians killed his father. His mother died of shock nine days later.

William fought in the American Revolution. He moved to Kentucky in 1781 and then fought in the War of 1812. He was a leader of civil affairs in early Kentucky. It is said that he was well liked and had a great sense of humor. He enjoyed playing jokes on others.

On his second trip to Texas in 1821, he joined Stephen F. Austin and his men in exploring the region to decide on a location for Austin's first colony. Smothers and four other men were left on the Brazos to build Fort Bend while Austin returned to Louisiana for his first group of settlers. On July 16, 1824, William received his land grant on the Brazos River. A large lake nearby was named for him, Smithers Lake. In 1826 he joined DeWitt's Colony and settled in Lavaca County, joined by his two sons. They acquired land adjacent to each other. A small stream in that vicinity still bears the name of Smothers Creek.

William was first married to Nancy Cecelia Fitzpatrick of Virginia and they had four daughters, Jane, Mary, Elizabeth, and Betsy. After Nancy's death he married Mary Winters of Tennessee. They had a daughter, Mary, and two sons, John and Archibald. William Smithers/Smothers died at Columbia, Texas, on August 13, 1837.

Smothers is listed as one of the few veterans of the American Revolution to settle in Texas and was honored by the University of Texas Institute of Texan Cultures. Four historical markers stand in his honor, two in Texas (Lavaca and Fort Bend counties) and two in Kentucky.

— BETTY JOYCE UPCHURCH LYNE #759

Adam Stafford

Adam Stafford

Adam Stafford, the son of William and Martha (Donnell) Stafford, was born February 5, 1806, in North Carolina. In 1824 he journeyed from Tennessee to join his father in Austin's Colony. On August 24, 1824, despite having no wife or partner, he received a *labor* of land located in present Waller County. He farmed in Fort Bend County.

Handicapped at the time of the Texas Revolution, Adam Stafford saw no action. He did, however, furnish supplies to the Texas Army. During the Runaway Scrape, he sent his servants to accompany his family and neighbors while he took the cattle on a different road to ford the San Jacinto River.

Adam married Maria Elizabeth Hankins in 1842 in Richmond. Their children were Sarah, Martha, Margaret (Bettie), Mary Ella, and William Hankins. Only Martha and Bettie would survive their long-lived father. In 1846, reportedly wanting to live in a larger town, the family moved to Victoria, where Adam Stafford became a land owner and horse breeder of note. His wife died there on November 8, 1855. Adam lived until November 21, 1880.

Adam Stafford's obituary reads in part:

The deceased was eccentric in disposition, but warm hearted and kind withal. To his friends he was the truest of friends — his enemies he had none. He attained a ripe old age, respected most by those who knew him best.

— WINCIE CHENAULT CAMPBELL #215

Mary Crownover Rabb wrote that when she was in her first house in Texas, Andrew Rabb made a spinning wheel for her. She was very pleased and got to work making clothes for her family. She would pick cotton with her fingers and spin "600 thread around the reel everyday." When she was lonely and frightened, "I kept my new spinning wheel whisling all day and a good part of the night for while the wheel was rowering it would keep me from hearing the Indians walking around hunting mischieaf."

RA

The first mention of a Texas Ranger force was by Austin in 1823. In 1835 the Provisional Government passed a resolution creating a corps of Rangers. There were three companies of twenty-five men to protect against Indians and bandits. They were paid $1.25 a day and had to furnish their own equipment. The reputation of the Texas Rangers was expressed by famous Ranger Col. John S. Ford, "The Texas Ranger can ride like a Mexican, trail like an Indian, and fight like the very devil."

Asa Mitchell settled at the mouth of the Brazos and had a salt works. He made salt by evaporating gulf water in large, shallow pans. Salt was used to preserve meat.

William Stafford

According to a petition authorized and signed by his friends not long before he died, William Stafford was an "orderly, peaceable, honest, enterprising, patriotic and philanthropic citizen" of the Republic of Texas.

Research indicates that Stafford was born about 1780 in North Carolina. There he married Martha Donnell and they had four children: Adam (also an original grantee), Sarah, Harvey, and Mary. After his wife's death he married Martha Cartwright on May 28, 1818, in Wilson County, Tennessee. Their children were: Martha, William Joseph, Jr., Susan, and John Thomas.

Two years after his arrival in San Felipe, on August 16, 1824, Stafford was granted one and a half leagues on Oyster Creek in present Fort Bend County and a *labor* in present Waller County. He established his plantation on the creek near Stafford Lake, where he built a cane mill and reportedly had the first horse-powered cotton gin in the colony. He has also been credited with introducing sugar cane to the area. A second Stafford home on the nearby prairie (Stafford's Point) sat on the future site of his namesake city.

In 1835 Stafford slayed a man named Moore which caused him to flee the country. In his absence, and after his family abandoned their home in the face of the invading Mexican army in April of 1836, Santa Anna put the plantation buildings to the torch. Stafford returned home in 1838, following the success of his friends' petition to secure an executive clemency for the slaying.

Stafford died in 1840.

— WINCIE CHENAULT CAMPBELL #215

George Washington Teel

George Washington Teel

George Washington Teel was born in Virginia in 1784. He married Nancy Caldwell in Dickson County, Tennessee, where their child, Rachel, was born in 1816. About 1820, the couple immigrated to near Little Rock, Arkansas, where Nancy died on July 12, 1822.

In 1823 George married Rebecca Johnson, born in Missouri on September 26, 1806. They settled near her family in Hempstead County, Arkansas, before they joined Stephen F. Austin's colony in Texas where they received a league of land (4,428.4 acres) in present-day Fort Bend County. In 1826, the Teels relocated six miles west of what is now San Augustine on the El Camino Real. They raised four children here, Wyatt, Lucette, Eliza, and Olive.

The Teels became significant figures in the development of the area. In 1827 George Teel was a member of the board of trustees of San Augustine University. Teel was involved in the Battle of Nacogdoches in August 1832 and was enrolled in Captain William Kimbrough's Company in 1836. The Teels operated a wayside inn where they hosted influential people of the day including Sam Houston. Around 1835 George Teel owned and operated a Whitney cotton gin as well as a blacksmith shop. During 1834-35, the Teel home was the location of services conducted by Methodist missionaries, the Stevensons. This led to the establishment of two churches. Additionally, in 1838 the Jerusalem Memorial Colored Methodist Episcopal Church was built on a town lot belonging to George Teel.

George Teel died on August 20, 1856, and, as he had requested, was buried beneath a pear tree that he had planted. Although the Teel Family Burial Ground lay in ruin for several decades, restoration began in early 2000. On February 27, 2007, it was designated a Texas Historical Cemetery, and on May 2, 2009, a Texas Historical Marker was dedicated.

—SARAH MARSHALL #693

Ezekiel Thomas

Ezekiel Thomas, a native of Edgefield, South Carolina, was in Texas in 1822. The Texas Census of 1826 noted that his occupation was farmer and stock raiser and his age between twenty-five and forty. Also enumerated were his wife Elizabeth and two daughters between one and six years of age.

Ezekiel came to Texas by way of Louisiana, documented by a Louisiana marriage bond and a census record noting the birthplace of his first-born child to be Louisiana. On January 22, 1822, The Reverend Isham Nettles, "a minister of the Baptist order," married Ezekiel Thomas and (Mary) Elizabeth Hennesey, daughter of Mrs. Sarah Robinette. The ceremony most likely took place in or near the city of Opelousas.

Shortly after Ezekiel's marriage, he left his wife, who was pregnant with their first child, in Louisiana and proceeded to establish a residence on Buffalo Bayou, in the San Jacinto area, with Elizabeth's uncle Morris "Moses" Calliham. It is a matter of record that a Mr. Calliham and Mr. Ezekiel Thomas were the first to build homes on Buffalo Bayou. He received his grant of one league of land on August 19, 1824.

Ezekiel brought Elizabeth and their infant daughter Frances "Fanny" Thomas to the colony shortly after the land grant was awarded, known by the fact that the couple's second child, Mary, was born in the colony in 1826. At least four more Thomas children were born in the colony: Rebecca Jane in 1830, William H. and Samuel E. in 1832, and Lindsey in 1833 (she died in 1839). The Thomas children attended school in the colony, according to guardianship records that listed expenses for school supplies, and they became proficient in basic academic skills.

The parents would not live to see their children grown. Elizabeth died in 1833 and Ezekiel died in 1834.

— BLANCHE FRANCES #386

Jesse Thompson

Jesse Thompson was born in Georgia around 1776. Jesse was a big man. He had blue eyes and light colored hair. He married Mary Denley from Alabama where most of their nine children were born: Hiram M., James M., John D., Jesse M., Mary, Grace Elizabeth, Eliza Jane, Henry C., and Lavinia.

In 1823 Jesse and his family moved to Austin's Colony. He located his league in Brazoria County, which was granted to him on August 7, 1824, by the Mexican Government. Austin's 1826 census listed Jesse Thompson as a farmer and stockraiser. His household included his wife Mary, four sons, four daughters, two servants and fifteen slaves.

In about 1828 Jesse came to the Fort Settlement and contracted for one fourth of the Knight & White league on the east side of the Brazos River. This became the Thompson plantation. He also bought from Knight & White's agent the *labor* across the river from the plantation. He put in a ferry there in the early 1830s.

Thompson's Ferry holds a special place in Texas history. According to the diary of Colonel Almonte of the Mexican army, on April 11, 1836, there was firing across the river between General Santa Anna's and Captain Wyly Martin's men at Thompson's Crossing. This confrontation is known as the "Battle at Thompson's Crossing." On April 14, 1836, the ferry was seized by a detachment of Santa Anna's army and used to cross the Brazos River in their pursuit of General Sam Houston. Fort Bend County records show that the Thompson family operated the ferry until 1866.

Jesse Thompson was killed in 1834. Mary died May 2, 1856.

Descendants of Jesse Thompson reportedly lived on the farm as late as 1939. In 1936 the Texas Centennial Commission erected a monument near the site of the ferry on this property.

—Stephen H. Lubojacky #67

Elizabeth Tumlinson

Elizabeth Tumlinson, her husband John Jackson, Sr., three daughters, and three of their sons, originally from North Carolina, arrived at Austin's Colony in 1821.

John Jackson Tumlinson was appointed the first *alcalde* from their district. He was credited with forming a group of men who became the forerunners of the Texas Rangers. He was also the first man from that organization to lose his life in the line of duty. He was killed by Waco Indians on his way to San Antonio for supplies and ammunitions. His body was never found.

Jackson's widow was given a land grant of a league and a *labor* August 16, 1824, on the south bank of the Colorado River, where the town of Columbus is now located. As she was led by the hand and told that by the virtue of the land commissioners and the Mexican government, she now possessed this land for herself, her heirs and successors, she had her dream of a permanent home. But she never imagined her family would have to pay such a high price as John's life. She fought back tears as she followed the ritual requirements and shouted aloud, pulled herbs, threw stones, set stakes, and performed the necessary ceremonies. When it was over, Elizabeth stood tall. She had her children and there was work to do.

Elizabeth died in Colorado County in 1833.

—NADINE FRANCES DEES HAYS #74

James Tumlinson, Jr.

James Tumlinson, Jr., was born in Lincoln County, North Carolina, in July 1781. He married a woman named Elizabeth in North Carolina and they had eleven children. By 1818 the family was living in Jackson County, Illinois, and in 1821 they moved to Texas as one of Stephen F. Austin's Old Three Hundred colonists. On August 19, 1824, he received a land grant of one *sitio* and one *labor* in Colorado County and one-half *sitio* in Wharton County.

After his wife's death, James moved to DeWitt's Colony where he married Diana Mary Wilkerson White. They had one child before Diana's death in Gonzales County in November 1839. James acquired a large amount of property in Gonzales and operated a freighting business. In 1831 he apparently helped transport the cannon sent from Mexican authorities in San Antonio to Green DeWitt in Gonzales.

Several of his sons fought in the Texas Revolution, one of whom, George W. Tumlinson, died at the Alamo on March 6, 1836.

James died in Gonzales County on July 9, 1839, and was buried at Harwood, Texas. Many descendants can still be found in the Harwood area and many of them later became Texas Rangers, sheriffs, and law officers.

— JANE ALICE BELL BOLSTAD #657

James Walker, Sr.

James Walker, Sr. was born in 1762. He married Catherine Miller on September 9, 1783. They had a total of fifteen children: Catherine, Sally, Lucretia, James, John, William, Elizabeth, Sanders, Charles, Andrew, Susanna, Gideon, Lucinda, Thomas, and one child died young.

In 1790 James and his family (which consisted of the wife and three children at that time) left Virginia and settled in Wayne County, Kentucky. The others were apparently born there.

Soon after arriving in Kentucky, rumors were spreading about a greater and better land in Texas, so they began to plan on moving again.

On July 21, 1824, after their trek to Texas, they joined Stephen F. Austin's colonists. Walker's land grant was in Washington County.

After receiving word in 1835 of the impending war with Mexico, James signed up and fought for independence from Mexico.

James Walker died in 1837. His estate was administered by his son Gideon.

— MARILYN R. THACKER #271

Telegraph & Texas Register, August 4, 1841

"Lost Subscribers. Some wiseacres have been lately circulating a report that we have lost upwards of 1,000 subscribers, owing to our opposing the election of Gen. Houston. We have lost only 9 subscribers owing to this cause, viz: Thomas F. McKinney, Dr. Hunter, Thomas Trimmer, A. McFadden, J. Bartlett, T. J. Rucker, James Walker, J. D. Burks, and H. Higgins.

Caleb Wallace

Caleb Wallace (circa 1797-1844), born in Georgia, came to Texas from Virginia in early February 1825. The awarding of his land grant was delayed by Stephen F. Austin's imprisonment in Mexico and by the absence of land commissioner Baron de Bastrop from San Felipe de Austin. In a petition to Gaspar Flores, Bastrop's replacement as commissioner, Wallace stated that he settled his family near Groce's Retreat on a league of land that he selected, settled, and cultivated. His request was approved by Flores and Austin and certified on May 14, 1828. Wallace's league, just below the headwaters of Beason's Creek, lay approximately ten miles southeast of Washington-on-the-Brazos in present-day Grimes County.

Less than a month before being awarded his league, Wallace married Elizabeth Wingfield. She died during the Runaway Scrape a few days after the birth of their fourth child. Wallace later married Elizabeth's sister, Elvira. This marriage produced two children.

He served in the Army of the Republic in mid-1836 and in the militia in 1842. In 1838 Wallace received two tracts of land, 177.1 acres in present-day Grimes County as a headright and the other, 320 acres, in Houston County for his service in the Army of the Republic. Caleb Wallace is believed buried on his league in a family cemetery, now Fairfield Cemetery, near the community of White Hall, Grimes County.

— BETTY McCLELLAND #787

Amy Comstock White

Amy White was born Amelia Comstock on March 10, 1775, in Rhode Island, the daughter of William Comstock and Rachel Aldrich. She was married in St. Martinville, Louisiana, on January 31, 1791, to William White, the son of John White and Sarah Gambill of Virginia. William White was born in North Carolina in 1766 and died on the Vermilion River in 1821 at his land grant in present Vermilion Parish. He and Amy raised a family of 10 children.

The depressed economic conditions of the 1820s made many Louisiana families look west to Texas, where the new Republic of Mexico opened up the land to immigrants. In 1824 Amy, a widow, and seven of her children became a part of Austin's first contract for Three Hundred families to settle in Texas. Daughter Rachel had married Mark Lee and stayed behind, as did son Jesse White, who took care of family business before coming to Texas in 1829. Daughter Mary, who was married to William Whitlock, and married son Reuben White were also among the Old Three Hundred.

Amy White and her children, as well as friends from Louisiana, selected grants along the San Jacinto River, and formed the White Settlement above the present-day town of Highlands. They were listed in the Atascosito Census of 1826.

In about 1827, Amy married a new arrival from Ireland named William Swail. After the death of her second husband in the 1830s, Amy lived for a while with her daughter Mary Whitlock in Liberty County and later with her son William White, Jr., at the White Settlement on the San Jacinto River in Harris County. The 1850 census shows her in his household. She died in 1853.

Her sons William and Jesse White, and sons-in-law, grandson, and other eligible men in the family participated in the Battle of San Jacinto and other actions in the revolution to free Texas.

—GIFFORD WHITE #40

Henry and Boland Whiteside

Henry Whiteside, born October 31, 1801, in Kentucky and Boland Whiteside, born 1806 in Pulaski County, Kentucky, were sons of Jonathan Whiteside and Thankful Anderson, and nephews of William and James Whiteside, both Old Three Hundred colonists. Encouraged by their Uncle James, Henry and Boland Whiteside came to Texas in 1824. They paired up for a land grant that they received title to on August 10, 1824. The league was located in present-day Grimes and Brazos counties.

According to family tradition, Henry left Texas in 1830. He married Zippora Skillen in Tennessee, January 19, 1832. He briefly returned to Texas in 1835 with his wife and two children. He is listed as one of the members forming a new Methodist church in Austin's Colony, under the leadership of John Wesley Kenney. In 1840, Henry is living in Bledsoe, Tennessee. On February 20, 1850, the widower Henry married Letha Hanna, in Camden County, Missouri, and they had four children. He died in Kansas on June 6, 1889, and is buried in the Mount Pleasant Cemetery outside of Waterville, Kansas.

Boland Whiteside, like his brother Robert Henry, did not remain in Texas. He married Nancy Thurman in Tennessee on April 9, 1833. She died in October 1848. Afterwards, Boland married Narcissa Frances Massengale and, according to the census of November 1850, lived in Spadra, Arkansas. His profession is given as physician. His brother, Colonel James Anderson Whiteside was a founder of Chattanooga and by 1860 Boland and his wife were living there where he worked as a hotelkeeper. In the 1870 census he is listed as a retired physician. Boland died in Chattanooga, Tennessee, on March 24, 1875, with no known children.

In family records Boland is referred to as Bolen and in the original 1824 Texas Land Grant records he is referred to as Bowlin but signs as Boland.

— DOUG CHOJECKI for
TRACI CHOJECKI #788

James Whiteside

James Whiteside, eldest son of Robert Whiteside and Elizabeth Coffey, was born in Wilkes County, North Carolina, on July 21, 1771. James' parents moved to Kentucky where he married Elizabeth Dick in Wayne County on January 8, 1811. Elizabeth was born in Virginia on February 10, 1786, and died in Texas on October 23, 1843. The young couple and their children moved to Overton County, Tennessee, where James served as postmaster in 1816. On January 24, 1822, James and his siblings sold the land in Wayne County, Kentucky, that they had inherited from their father.

In either 1821 or 1822, James migrated to Texas as part of Austin's Colony. The 1823 Texas Census shows the family living in what is today Brazos County. On July 16, 1824, James received title to a league and a *labor* of land east of the Brazos River in what are presently Grimes, Brazos, and Waller counties. The 1826 Texas Census shows the family living in Bastrop County.

In 1829 and 1830 James operated a tavern and the Whiteside Hotel in San Felipe. The hotel was a story-and-a-half building that at the time was the tallest structure in the settlement. Daniel Shipman, as early as 1824, and William B. Travis in 1833 reported on visits in the Whiteside home and on "Aunt Betsy's" hospitality. About the mid-1830s James was partner with Joshua Parker, husband of his niece Nancy Whiteside Parker, in a store in Independence. In 1834 and 1835 he signed a petition that called for the creation of Washington County, Texas.

James was a trustee of Independence Female Academy in 1839 and active in land sales. In 1835 he sold a league of land in Austin County to William B. Travis. James Whiteside died in Texas on April 24, 1848. His and Elizabeth's burial site is unknown. "Uncle Jimmie" is recorded to have been an interesting character.

— DOUG CHOJECKI for TRACI CHOJECKI #788

William Whiteside

William Whiteside, son of Robert Whiteside, was born in Wilkes County, North Carolina, in 1773. William married Lavina Singleton in Lincoln County, Kentucky, on March 8, 1802. She was born in Rutherford County, North Carolina, in 1775. Her father was Richard Singleton. The Whitesides and the Singletons are represented by six families of the Old Three Hundred: William and his brother James, nephews Henry and Boland, and Lavina's brothers George Washington and Phillip Singleton.

William operated a mill near Bowling Green, Kentucky, but when the mill burned down he took his family to Texas and joined his brother James in Austin's Colony. He received a league of land on July 15, 1824. It was located just south of present-day Hempstead. William and Lavina brought their nine children to Texas: Davis, Nancy, Elisha, George Washington, Ann Eliza, Mary, John J., Phillip, and William. Shortly after arriving there, William and his wife lost their lives on the Brazos in the month of September. On December 24, 1824, Stephen F. Austin appointed John P. Coles as guardian of the surviving eight orphan children as relatives were unable or unwilling to assist them.

Nancy married Joshua Parker, another Old Three Hundred colonist, in 1829. The family today continues through known descendants of Nancy, George Washington, and Ann Eliza Whiteside.

— DOUG CHOJECKI FOR TRACI CHOJECKI #788

William Whitlock

William Whitlock was born in 1784 in Caswell County, North Carolina. He was the son of Robert and Aggy (Stringer) Whitlock. The family appeared in the Ninety-Six District of South Carolina for the 1790 and 1800 census.

As a young man William came to Louisiana, where on February 16, 1813, he married Mary White, daughter of William and Amy Comstock White. Their marriage is recorded in St. Martin's Church, St. Martinville, Louisiana.

William and Mary Whitlock and their children joined the extended family of the widowed Amy White in the move to Texas in 1824. On August 13, 1824, William Whitlock made his petition for land to Baron de Bastrop and became one of Austin's Old Three Hundred. He was granted a league on the east bank of the San Jacinto River near the grants of the other Amy White family members. William Whitlock and family were in the Atascosito Census of 1826, where he appeared as a farmer and stockraiser.

William and Mary Whitlock had three sons: Robert, Bernard, and Henry; and four daughters: Elizabeth, Amanda, Rachel, and Martha. Three of the children were born in Texas. Son Robert and husbands of the married daughters joined the Texian forces at the Battle of San Jacinto and otherwise aided in the revolution against Mexico.

William died in Liberty County, Texas, in March 1835.

— MARY S. MAXFIELD #46

Thomas Williams

Thomas Williams was born between 1771 and 1773 in Kentucky. He married Nancy Johnson (Gilleland), widow of William Gilleland, in Davidson County, Tennessee, on September 15, 1802. Nancy was born circa 1773-1775 in Kentucky.

By 1807 the Thomas Williams family was living in Arkansas Territory. The children born there were: Benjamin, who died on the way to Texas; Thomas Johnson, born November 7, 1807, and who died October 5, 1889, in Matagorda County; Nancy, born 1809; and Mary Diane, born 1811, who died in Texas.

In 1820 the family left Arkansas for Texas bringing pack horses, cattle, and hogs. Caleb Bostic and John Ingram traveled with them. In January 1821 the travelers crossed the Colorado River and settled about eight miles above present-day Columbus.

In June 1823, Williams, Bostic, Thomas Jamison, and Moses Morrison cut a path down to Bay Prairie and then to Cedar Lake in Matagorda County, where the Williams family relocated. The Karankawa Indians were an ever-present threat to the colonists; members of a neighboring family were killed.

On July 4, 1824 or 1825, Thomas Williams died from exposure at age fifty-three. Nancy was left with three children to rear in a wild new land. On August 16, 1824, Stephen F. Austin granted a league of land to the name of Thomas Williams. In 1833 Nancy divided this land among her children. She died in Travis County about 1854.

— BETTY JO RAY RUSK #532

Zadock Woods

Zadock Woods, son of Jonathan Jr. and Keziah Keith Woods, was born September 18, 1773, in Brookfield, Massachusetts.

In Woodstock, Vermont, in 1796, Woods met Minerva Cottle, daughter of Joseph Cottle. They were married in 1797. The children and spouses are as follows: Minerva, 1798-1897, married William Harrell 1796-1891; Ardelia, 1804, lived seven months; Norman, 1805-1857, married Jane Boyd Wells, 1809-1866; Montraville, 1806-1857, married Isabella Gonzales; Leander, 1809-1832; and Henry Gonsalvo, 1816-1867, married Jane Boyd Wells Woods.

The grant on which the Woods family finally settled was a few miles above LaGrange in the Colorado River Valley, Indian country. A Texas Centennial historical marker has been placed on the site of the Woods Fort, which was used by colonists as protection against Indian attacks. It stands one and a half miles west of West Point on Texas Highway 71.

In September 1842 Captain Dawson called for volunteers to face General Woll in San Antonio. Norman and Gonzalvo immediately hid their father's horse and made an emphatic declaration that the old man was not to undertake the ride to San Antonio. Zadock declared he would ride with them or he would walk without them. Said he, I fought with Andrew Jackson at New Orleans, and with old Sam Houston at San Jacinto, and I'll just give the enemy one more crack at old Zadock. There were five Woods men in this group: Zadock, Norman, Gonzalvo, and Zadock's grandsons, John Wesley Pendleton, and seventeen-year-old Milvern Harrell.

The Battle of San Antonio was fierce. Thirty-five were killed, fifteen wounded and taken prisoner. Two escaped. Norman was wounded and Zadock was killed when he went to his aid. In 1848 their remains were disinterred and entombed in the old Rock Tomb on Monument Hill overlooking the wide sweep of the Colorado River Valley.

Zadock Woods, on his sixty-ninth birthday, died for what he

believed in, liberty and family. Minerva Cottle Woods had died in 1839. She is buried in the Woods Cemetery at Woods Prairie in Fayette County.

— MRS. LEWIS ASBAL PARR #32

Taking of the Land
(Closing statement contained in each grant document)

We put the aforesaid *(name of colonist)* in possession of said tracts, taking him by the hand, leading him over them, telling him in a loud and understandable voice that by virtue of the commission and the authority vested in us, and in the name of the Government of the Mexican Nation, we put him in possession of said tracts, with all their uses, customs, rights, and appurtenances, for him, his heirs, and successor, and the aforementioned *(name of colonist)*, as a token of finding himself in real and personal possession of said tracts without any opposition, shouted, pulled grass, threw stones, set stakes, and performed the other necessary ceremonies, being notified of his obligation to cultivate them within the two-year term prescribed by the law, and in evidence thereof, we have the aforementioned Commissioner Baron de Bastrop and Empresario Estevan F. Austin, hereunto subscribe with attendant witnesses, lacking a notary in the terms of the law, which we certify.

In the Town of San Felipe de Austin, on the 16th day of August of the year 1824.

—William Stafford file, Box 4, Folder 6,
Texas General Land Office, Austin, Texas

References

A word about the source materials for the biographies: There are ten major sources that nearly all Old Three Hundred researchers utilize. Rather than repeat them in each bibliography, we cite them one time, as follows:

Barker, Eugene C., editor. *The Austin Papers*. 2 vols. Washington, D.C.: U.S. Government Printing Office, 1924-28.

Bugbee, Lester G. "The Old 300," *Quarterly of the Texas State Historical Association*, vol. I, no. 2 (October 1897): 108-117.

Mexican Land Grants. Texas General Land Office, Austin, Texas.

Mullins, M. D. *The First Census of Texas, 1829-1836*. Washington, D.C.: National Genealogical Society, 1962.

Ray, Worth S. *Austin Colony Pioneers*. Austin: The Pemberton Press, 1970.

The Handbook of Texas Online, <http://www.tshaonline.org/handbook>.

Tyler, Ron, editor. *The New Handbook of Texas*. 6 vols. Austin: The Texas State Historical Association, 1996.

Webb, Walter P., editor. *The Handbook of Texas*. 3 vols. Austin: The Texas State Historical Association, 1952.

White, Gifford. *1830 Citizens of Texas*. Austin: Eakin Press, 1983.

_____. *1840 Citizens of Texas*. Austin: Pemberton Press, 1984.

Williams, Villamae. *Stephen F. Austin's Register of Families*. Baltimore: Genealogical Publishing Co., Inc., 1989.

Martin Allen

Allen, Miles Newton. Wallis, Texas. Personal interview.

Barker, Eugene C. *The Life of Stephen F. Austin*. Austin, Texas: The University of Texas Press, 1949.

Davis, Robert E., editor. *Diary of William Barret Travis*. Waco, Texas: Texian Press, 1966.

Duval, John C. *Early Times in Texas*. Austin Texas: Steck Co., 1935.

Erickson, Joe E. *Judges of the Republic of Texas*. Dallas, Texas: Taylor Publishing Co., 1980.

Grisham, Noel. *Crossroads at San Felipe*. Burnet, Texas: Eakin Press, 1980.

Harris, Dilue W. and B. M. Hulse. *History of Clairborne Parish*.

Hollon, W. Eugene, and Ruth L. Butler. *William Bollaert's Texas*. Norman, Oklahoma: University of Oklahoma Press, 1956.

Schartz, Fred, and Robert H. Thonhoff. *Forgotten Battlefield*. Austin, Texas: Eakin Press, 1985.

Tracy, Milton Cook, and Richard Havelock-Bailie. *The Colonizer*. El Paso, Texas: Guynes Printing Co., 1941.

Charles G. Alsbury

Lewis, W. S. "Adventures of the Lively Immigrants." *Quarterly of the Texas State Historical Association*, vol. 3 (1899), nos. 1 and 2.

Renner, Helen Ruth. *The Alsbury Gleanings from the Midwest*, p. 231.

Dr. Horace Arlington Alsbury

"The San Jacinto Campaign." *Texas Historical Association Quarterly*, vol. 4 (1900-01), pp. 339-340.

Daughters of the Republic of Texas. *Muster Rolls of the Texas Revolution*. Austin, Texas: DRT, 1986, p. 43.

Dixon, S. H. and L. W. Kemp. *The Heroes of San Jacinto*. Texas: Anson Jones Press, 1932, p. 308.

Gronemann, Bill. *Alamo Defenders*. Austin, Texas: Eakin Press, 1990, p. 5.

_____. *Roll Call at the Alamo*, p. 83.

Letter of Y. P. Alsbury of October 1, 1859. Center for American History, The University of Texas, Austin, Texas.

Roll of Captain Thomas Alsbury's Company, First Regiment Kentucky Mounted Militia. Soldiers of the War of 1812, Kentucky Archives.

Spurlin, Charles D. *Texas Veterans in the Mexican War*. Austin, Texas: Eakin Press, 1998.

Texas Almanac 1861, pp. 55-58.

Texas as Province and Republic. Reel 1, Texas Imprints nos. 1-120.

Texas State Archives. Petition for pension for Mrs. Juana Alsbury.

_____. *San Jacinto List*. Major General Sam Houston's Army Roster, p. 30.

Capt. Thomas Alsbury

Brazoria Board of Land Commissioners. Land Certificate, March 15, 1832.

Daughters of the Republic of Texas. "York's Company," *Muster Rolls of Texas Revolution*. Austin, Texas: DRT, Inc., 1986.

"Hanson Alsbury to S. F. Austin, June 1, 1827." *Austin Papers*. Center for American History, The University of Texas at Austin.

"Juana Navarro Alsbury, September 18, 1870." Pension Applications. Texas State Archives.

Killebrew, J. T. Court Order Book, Christian County, Kentucky.

_____. Deed Book, Christian County, Kentucky.

Perrin, W. H. *County of Christian, Kentucky*.

Point Pleasant Battle Commission, Charleston, West Virginia.

Renner, Helen Ruth. *Alsbury Gleanings from the Midwest*.

Roll of Captain Thomas Alsbury's Company, First Regiment Kentucky Mounted Militia. Soldier of the War of 1812, Kentucky Archives.

Spurlin, Charles D. *Texas Veterans in the Mexican War*. Austin: Eakin Press, 1998.

Stephen F. Austin's letter to Alsbury dated May 4, 1824. Center for American History, The University of Texas, Austin.

Texas State Archives. *San Jacinto List.*

William Andrews

Hebert, Rev. Donald J. *Southwest Louisiana Records.* Vol. 2. Eunice, Louisiana: The author, 1974.

Moore, Bill. *Bastrop County 1691-1900.* Wichita Falls: Nortex Press, 1977.

Resolution of the House of Representatives, May 24, 1838.

U. S. Census. 1810. St. Landry Parish, Louisiana.

Wharton. Clarence R. *History of Fort Bend County.* Houston: Anson Jones Press, 1939.

Samuel Tubbs Angier

Taylor, Virginia H. *The Spanish Archives of the General Land Office of Texas.* Austin, Texas: Lone Star, 1955.

Telegraph and Texas Register, October 4, 1837, August 11, 1838, and March 20, 1844.

James Britton Bailey

Gholson, Josephine Polley. *Bailey's Light.* San Antonio: Naylor, 1950. pp. 33-82.

Wharton, Clarence R. *History of Fort Bend County.* Houston: Anson Jones Press, 1939, p. 50.

William Barret (Barrett)

Bible data furnished by Edgar Barrett, who resides on the Thomas William Barrett farm between Nixon and Stockdale where Thomas William Barrett's body is buried.

Brazoria County, Texas. Barrett *et al.,* Vol. G, File 177.

_____. Deed Book, Vol. A, p. 423.

_____. Vol. A, 1829-1852, p. 30, #4.

_____. Vol. A, p. 200, #134.

Wilson County (Texas) Courthouse. File 182.

Benjamin Beason

Johnson, Frank W., and E. C. Barker. *The History of Texas and Texans.* Chicago: American Historical Society, 1914.

Williams, Amelia, and E. C. Barker, editors. *The Writings of Sam Houston.* Austin: The University of Texas Press, 1938.

Isaac Best

Best, Isaac. File. Waller County Historical Museum.

Bryan, William C., and Robert Rose. *A History of the Pioneer Families of Missouri.* Reprint. Baltimore: 1984.

Mouser, Lafrona Foshee. *A Genealogy of the Mouser Ancestry Including the Best and Other Families.* Oklahoma City: 1978.

Shuman, Mrs. Sam. *A History of Waller County, Texas.*

Taylor, Virginia H. *The Spanish Archives of the General Land Office of Texas.* Austin: 1955.

Thomas Boatwright

1818 Crawford County, Illinois, census.
1819 Miller County, Arkansas, census.
1830 Pope County, Arkansas, census.
Hatley, Allen G. *The Indian Wars in Stephen F. Austin's Texas Colony, 1822-1835.*
Wilbarger, I. *Early Depredations in Texas.* p. 214.

Edward R. Bradley

Bradley/Dodson Family Bible.
French Tipton Papers. Eastern Kentucky University, Richmond, Kentucky.
Kentucky Tax Rolls, 1788.
Letter from Archeleus B. Dodson to Mrs. Looscan, 1892.
Lincoln County, Kentucky. Marriage Records, 1787
Winn, George. Will probated in Clark County, Kentucky, 1803.

Charles C. Breen

U.S. Census 1850. Williamson County, Texas. National Archives Microfilm M 432, Roll 916.
_____. 1860. Williamson County, Texas. National Archives Microfilm M653, Roll 1308.

William B. Bridges

Circuit Court Records of Clark County, Arkansas. Deposition #3615, P. B. Lyons *et al.* Vs. William S. Lyons *et al.*, Book B, p. 81.
Clerk of the Court's Office, LaGrange, Fayette County, Texas, Vol. C, p. 354.
Ericson, Joe E. *Judges of the Republic of Texas 1836-1846.* Dallas: Taylor Publishing Co., 1980.
Texas State Archives. Discharge papers, William B. Bridges, File #743 3.

David Bright

Augusta County, Virginia, Court Records. Marriage Book I.
First Census of Texas/ Residents of the Colorado District, March 4, 1823.
Hawley Cemetery Association. Deming's Bridge Cemetery-Howley Cemetery-Tres Palacios Baptist Church, 1977, p. 6.
Matagorda County Probate Record filed March 2, 1842.
Matagorda County Probate Record, Book A, filed September 14, 1837.
U.S. Census, Matagorda County, Texas. 1850. National Archives Microfilm M432, Roll 912.
_____. 1860. National Archives Microfilm M653, Roll 1300.
_____. 1870. National Archives Microfilm M593, Roll 1597.
Wharton, Clarence R. *History of Fort Bend County.* Houston: Anson Jones Press, 1939.

Capt. Jesse Burnam

"Reminiscences of Captain Jesse Burnam." *Quarterly of the Texas State Historical Association*, Vol. V (1901-1902).

Colorado County Historical Survey Committee. *Early Settlers and Bits of History of Columbus and Colorado County, 1821-1845.*

Shuffler, R. Henderson. "Winedale Inn, at Early Texas' Cultural Crossroad." *Texas Quarterly* (Summer 1965), vol. VIII: no 2, pp. 132-134.

Sinks, Julia Lee. *Chronicles of Fayette.*

Weyand, Leonie Rummel, and Houston Wade. "An Early History of Fayette County." LaGrange, Texas: *LaGrange Journal*, 1936, pp. 85-92.

Williams, Marjorie L., editor. *Fayette County: Past & Present.* LaGrange, Texas: The author, 1976, pp. 328-329.

Micajah Byrd

The Galveston News, November 11, 1884, quoting the *Navasota Tabloid.*

Hatch Aldon. *The Byrds of Virginia.* 1969.

Pollard, Charleen Plumly. "Civil War letters of George W. Allen." *Southwestern Quarterly of the Texas State Historical Association*, vol. LXXXIII, No. 1 (July 1979).

Quarterly of the Texas State Historical Association, vol. VI, pp. 23 6-237.

Star of the Republic, vol. XLII, no. 2.

Thrall, Homer S. *Pictorial History of Texas.*

Sylvanus Castleman

Davidson County [Tennessee], Marriage Book I, January 2, 1789–December 13, 1837.

Davidson County [Tennessee], Minutes Book 1809-1812, p. 826.

Gulick, Charles Adam, Jr., editor. *Papers of Mirabeau B. Lamar.* Vol. IV. Austin: Von Boeckmann-Jones, 1920.

Weyand, Leonie Rummel, and Houston Wade. "History of Fayette County." LaGrange, Texas: *LaGrange Journal*, 1936.

Williams, Annie Lee. *History of Wharton County 1846-1961.* Austin: Von Boeckmann-Jones, 1964.

Winkler, Ernest W. *Manuscript Letters & Documents of Early Texians, 1821-1845.* Austin: The Steck Co., 1937.

John Prince Coles

Brenham Banner Press. May 24, 1989, p. 5.

Burleson, Georgia L. *The Life and Writings of Rufus C. Burleson.* 1901.

Fehrenbach. *Lone Star.* De Capo Press, 2000.

Hatcher, Mattie Austin. *Letters of an Early American Traveler, Mary Austin Holley, Her Life and Her Works, 1784-1848.* Dallas: Southwest Press, 1933.

Historical marker at Coles' home to honor founder of Independence.

Maddox, Joseph T. *Early Georgia Marriages*, Book 4, not dated.

Moore, Mary Ann. *Framing Independence.* Houston: MAM Publications, 1994.

_____. *Politicians on Horseback.* Houston: MAM Publications, 1996.

Murray, Lois Smith. *Baylor at Independence.* Waco: Baylor University Press, 1972.

Toland, Gracey Booker. *Austin Knew His Athens*. Brenham: Independence Historical Society, 1958, 1977, 1985.

John Crier

Church Archives, St. Augustine Parish, Florida. Historical Records Survey, Entry 383.
Colorado County, Texas, Marriage Records, Vol. B, p. 131.
Colorado County, Texas, Probate Court Case #307, 11-14-1856.
Fayette County, Texas. County Clerk Records, vol. J, p. 214, #3 144.
Weyand, Leonie R., and Houston Wade. "Early History of Fayette County." LaGrange, Texas: *LaGrange Journal*, 1936.
Salley, A. S. *History of Orangeburg County, S.C., 1704-1782*. Baltimore: Genealogical Publishing Co., 1978.
Texas State Library, Austin, Texas. Manuscript notes of Louis W. Kemp.
Veteran's Administration, Washington, D.C. Pension Claim S31635.

John Crownover

American Historical Association. Annual Report 1919. Bastrop Election, April 1824 (p. 771- 772).
Fayette County, Texas. Probate Court. Nuncupative Will of Nancy (Castleman) Crownover. Probate Court Records Index Book #Z, case 86, p. 22; Probate Book A. p. 309.
Fayette County, Texas. Probate Records, Book A.
"Reminiscences of Mary Crownover Rabb." Texas State Archives, Austin, Texas.

John, William, and James Cumings

Ragan, O. G. *History of Lewis County, Kentucky*. Press of Jennings and Graham, Cincinnati, Ohio, no date.
W. C. Dugan's History of Lewis County. Reprint. Lewis County Historical Society, Vanceburg, Kentucky, no date.
Marriage Records (William Cumings/Lucinda Ruggels), Lewis County Clerk's Office, Vanceburg, Kentucky.
Probate Records (James, John, William, and Rebecca Cumings), Austin County Clerk's Office, Bellville, Texas.
Veterans' Administration service records (William Cummins, Lewis County, Kentucky, militia, War of 1812), Washington, D. C.

Rebekah Cumings

Austin County Colonial Archives. Bellville, Texas. Book II, pp. 306-311.
Austin County Wills. File Drawer 8, Packet 28.
Haskew, Corrie Pattison. *Historical Records of Austin and Waller Counties*. Houston: 1969.
Henderson County, Kentucky. Deed Book E, p. 282.
Jackson, Evelyn, and William Talley. *Eastern Kentucky References*. Owensboro, Kentucky, 1980, p. 109.

Lewis County, Kentucky. Tax List. 1807.
Private correspondence, May Biggs to Mrs. B. L. Smythe and Mrs. J. R. Sanders, October 31, 1951.

James (Jack) Cummins

Colorado County Historical Commission. *Colorado County Chronicles*. Austin: Nortex Press, 1986, vol. I, p. 43.
Lucas, Silas Emmett, Jr., editor. *Davidson County, Tennessee, Marriage Book I*. Southern Historical Press: 1979.
Matagorda County Historical Society. *Historic Matagorda*. Houston: D. Armstrong, Co., Inc., 1986, vol. I, pp. 32-34.
Sinks, Julia. *Chronicles of Fayette*, p. 10.

James Curtis, Jr.

Curtis, James, 1849-1857. Probate Index and Minute Book C: Holdings of the Bastrop County Courthouse.
_____. File papers. Texas State Archives. Austin, Texas.
_____. Land Record Files. Texas General Land Office, Austin, Texas.
Jenkins, John H. III, editor. *Recollections of Early Texas*. Austin: The University of Texas Press, 1958, p. 157.
Kesselus, K. *Bastrop County Before Statehood*. Austin: Jenkins Publishing Company, 1986, p. 153.
U. S. Census 1850. Bastrop County, Texas National Archives Microfilm M432, Roll 908.
_____. 1860. Bastrop County, Texas National Archives Microfilm M653, Roll 1288.

James Curtis, Sr.

Crozier, W. A., editor. *Spotsylvania County Records, 1721-1800*. Baltimore: Genealogical Publishing Company, 1965.
Curtis, James. File Papers and Land Record Files. Texas State Archives and Texas General Land Office, Austin, Texas.
Daughters of the Republic of Texas. *Muster Rolls of the Texas Revolution*. Austin: DRT, Inc., 1986.
Dixon, S. H., and L. W. Kemp. *Heroes of San Jacinto*. Houston: Anson Jones Press, 1932, pp. 54, 58, 212, 221,375.
Eddlemon, S. K., compiler. *Genealogical Abstracts from Tennessee Newspapers, 1803-1812*. Heritage Books, Inc., 1989, p. 156.
Gandrud, P. J. *Marriage Records of Jefferson County, Alabama, 1818-1864*. Memphis: Milestone Press, 1979, p. 29.
Kesselus, K. *Bastrop County Before Statehood*. Austin: Jenkins Publishing Company, 1986, p. 153.
Lucus, S. E., Jr. *Marriage Book I: January 2, 1789–December 13, 1839, Davidson County, Tennessee*. Easley, South Carolina: Southern Historical Press, 1979.
Moore, J. T. *Record of Commissions of Officers in the Tennessee Militia (1796-1815)*. Baltimore: Genealogical Publishing Company, 1977, p. 71.

Sistler, B., and S. Sistler. *Tennesseans in the War of 1812*. Nashville: Byron Sistler & Associates, Inc. 1992, p. 549.

U.S. Census. 1820 Warren County, Tennessee. National Archives Microfilm M33, Roll 122.

_____. 1850. Bastrop County, Texas National Archives Microfilm M432, Roll 908.

_____. 1860. Bastrop County, Texas National Archives Microfilm M653, Roll 1288.

_____. 1870. Bastrop County, Texas National Archives Microfilm M593, Roll 1574.

Charles DeMoss

Goodspeed's History of Southeast Missouri.

Second Census of Missouri, 1803

Settlers of Matagorda County.

Clement C. Dyer's Journal. Manuscript in private possession.

Harris, Dilue Rose. "The Reminiscences of Mrs. Dilue Harris." *The Quarterly of the Texas State Historical Association*, Vol. IV, No. 1, 1900.

Sowell, A. J. *The History of Fort Bend County*. Houston: W. H. Coyle & Co., 1904.

Wharton, Clarence R. *History of Fort Bend County*. Houston: Anson Jones Press, 1939.

Gustavus Eixon Edwards

Davis, Robert E., editor. *Diary of William Barret Travis*. Waco, Texas: Texian Press, 1966.

Edwards, Georgia Hortense. *The Edwards & Todd Families & Their Descendants 1523-1895*.

History of Wharton County, Texas.

Robinson, Duncan W. *Judge Robert McAlpin Williams*. Austin: Texas State Historical Association, 1948.

Scott, Harrison & Nicholas. *History of Bourbon County, Kentucky*.

David Fitzgerald

Creighton, James A. *A Narrative of Brazoria County*. Waco, Texas: Texian Press, 1975, p. 16.

Fitzgeral Land Grant. Abstract of Title, Fort Bend County. 1918.

Sowell, A. J. *The History of Fort Bend County*. Houston: W. H. Coyle & Co., 1904, pp. 187-188.

Wharton, Clarence R. *History of Fort Bend County*. Houston: Anson Jones Press, 1939, pp. 5-6.

Elisha Flowers

Matagorda County Historical Commission. *Historic Matagorda County*. Three volumes, 1986-1988.

Isaac Guilford Foster

Barker, Eugene C. "Minutes of the Ayuntamiento of San Felipe de Austin, 1828-

1832." *Southwestern Historical Quarterly*, volumes 21-24 (January 1918-October 1920).

Matagorda County Historical Commission. *Historic Matagorda County*. Three volumes, 1986-1988.

John Foster

1821 Smith Family Tree, in possession of T. J. Foster, Natchez, Mississippi.

Casey, *Amite County, Mississippi*. Vol. I, p. 476.

Dunbar, Rowland. *Mississippi, Heart of the South*.

Mayes Family Bible in possession of Felix C. Kelly, Houston, Texas.

McBee, Mae Wilson. *Natchez Court Records 1767-1805*. Baltimore: Genealogical Publishing Co., 1979.

Order of the First Families of Mississippi 1699-1817, p. 72.

Succession of John Foster, Probate Minutes, Vol. A, p. 120, #50.

Sydnor, Charles S. *Gentleman of the Old Natchez Region*, p. 4.

Texas State Archives. Vouchers, Texas War of Independence.

Woodville Republican Newpapers, volume XIV, p. 3, February 18, 1837.

Randolph Foster

Ericson, Carolyn. *First Settlers of the Republic of Texas*. St. Louis: Ingmire Publications, vol. I, 1982.

Sowell, A. J. *The History of Fort Bend County*. Houston: W. H. Coyle & Co., 1904.

Churchill Fulshear, Sr.

Austin County, Texas. Succession Records.

Craven County, North Carolina. Marriage Bonds.

Fort Bend Museum. *History of Fulshear, Texas*. Richmond, Texas.

Herald-Coaster [Richmond-Rosenberg, Texas], newspaper, September 1, 1972.

Houston Chronicle [Houston, Texas], newspaper, July 5, 1936.

William Gates

"Arkansas Territory." *The Pulaski County Historical Review*. Vol. XIX, pp. 384-387.

Moss, Booby Gilmer. *The Patriot's at King's Mountain*. Blacksburg, South Carolina: Scotia Hibernia, 1990.

Robertson. *Petitions of Early Inhabitants of Kentucky to the General Assembly of Virginia 1769-1792*.

Starling, Edmund L. *History of Henderson County*. Kentucky Census, tax and court records.

Freeman George

1820 Federal Census of St. Helena Parish, Louisiana.

Jeter, Loraine Bruce. *Matagorda, Early History*. Baltimore: Gateway Press, Inc., 1974, p. 7.

Nacogdoches Archives, July 2, 1832. R. B. Blake Collection, vol. XIII, pp. 3-4.

Taylor, Virginia H. *The Spanish Archives of the General Land Office of Texas.* 1955, p. 189.

U.S. Federal Census. 1850 Wharton County, Texas.

U.S. Federal Census. 1860 Wharton County, Texas.

Daniel Gilleland

Carter, Clarence Edwin. *The Territorial Papers of the United States, The Territory Of Arkansas, 1825-1829.* Vol. XX. Washington, D.C.: Government Printing Office, 1954, pp. 136-142.

Holman, Norinne Holder. *170 Years of Cemetery Records in Milam County, Texas.* Vol. 1. Austin, Texas: Armstrong Printing, Inc., 2001, p. 326.

Whitley, Edythe Rucker. *Marriages of Davidson County, Tennessee, 1789-1847.* Baltimore: Genealogical Publishing Co., 1981, p. 10.

Young, Patricia Gilleland, and L. Richard Scroggins. *The Tree and Vine, Gilleland Branches from Texas Roots.*

Chester Spalding Gorbet

Carroll, J. M. *History of Texas Baptists.* Dallas: 1923.

Fort Bend County, Texas. Probate records. Gorbet Papers, in possession of the family.

Oinnell, Mrs. Sarah A. Affidavit, May 10, 1894.

Pension application, dated August 1871.

Col. Jared Ellison Groce II

Berlet, Sarah Wharton Groce. *Autobiography of a Spoon, 1828-1956.* Port Arthur, Texas: LaBelle Printing Company, 1977, pp. 96-97.

Davis, Joe Tim. *Legendary Texians.* Austin: Eakin Press, 1982, vol. III, pp. 48-63.

History of Grimes County, Retreat, Texas, not dated.

History of Waller County, Texas. 1973.

Texas Almanac, 1980-81, pp. 562-563.

Texas Parade, vol. XI, 1950.

John B. Haddon

Baker. *A Texas Scrap-Book.*

Brevoort, Eliza Haddon. *Our Haddon, McClure, Curry, and Allied Families.*

Brown. *A History of Texas 1685-1892.*

Hoke, Bessie. *Pioneer Indiana Ancestors of Richard Jerome Hoke.*

Huston, Hubert, *Captain Phillip Dimmit's Commandancy of Goliad.*

Jenkins, John. *The Papers of the Texas Revolution.*

Stein, Bill. *Colorado County Chronicles: From the Beginning to 1923.*

Randolph County Historical Magazine, 1929

Samuel C. Haddy (Hady, Heady)

Austin County, Texas Deed Record, vol. A, pp. 49-50. Deed of Partition, Book B, p. 465.

_____. Samuel C. Hady Probate, Probate Minute Book B, pp. 55 & 170, Probate File 22(1).
Colonial Census 1820-29, Bastrop.

Alexander Hodge

Barker, Eugene C. *The Life of Stephen F. Austin*. Austin, 1926.
Cumberland County, Pennsylvania. Will Book, vol. B, pp. 105-106 (James Elliott's will).
_____. Will Book, vol. K, part I, p. 11 (P.O.A. by William Hodge).
Department of State. *Territorial Papers of the United States*. Vol. XIX, Arkansas Territory 181?-1825.
Elbert County, Georgia. Will Book 1791-1803, pp. 53-54 (William Hodge's will).
Harris County, Texas. Probate Book, vol. A, p. 36 (Alexander Hodge's will)
Kegans, Clarinda Pevehouse. *Memoirs*. Housed in Nita Stewart Haley Memorial Library, Midland, Texas.
Kemp, L. W. *Honor Roll of the Battle*. San Jacinto, Texas: San Jacinto Museum of History, 1974.
Oglethorpe County, Georgia. Tax Roll 1796-1805.
Texas Telegraph and Register, September 13, 1836.
Travis, William Barret. *The Travis Diary 1833-1834*. Austin: Barker Texas History Center, n.d.
Texas and the American Revolution. University of Texas Institute of Texan Cultures. San Antonio, Texas: 1975.

Francis Holland

Blair, E. L. *Early History of Grimes County*. 1930.
Boyd, Bob. *The Texas Revolution, A Day-by-Day Account*. 1986.
Gibson, Roy E. *Hollands of Austin's Colony*. DRT Library, 1973.
Groneman, Bill. *Alamo Defenders*. 1990.
Marriage Records, Scioto County, Ohio.
Peterson, Carl. *Now's the Day and Now's the Hour*. 2004.
Williams, Daniel W. *History of Jackson County, Ohio*. 1900.

William Holland

Blair, E. L. *Early History of Grimes County*. 1930.
Burney, Cecil E. *Homes of Heroes*. East Texas Historical Association (October 1971)
Gibson, Roy E. *Hollands of Austin's Colony*. DRT Library, 1973.
Marriage Records, Scioto County, Ohio.
Veteran's Biographies. San Jacinto Museum, 1952.
Williams, Daniel W. *History of Jackson County, Ohio*. 1900.

George Huff

Founders and Patriots of the Republic of Texas. Vol. II. San Antonio: Daughters of the Republic of Texas, n.d.
Geiser, S. W. *Collectors of Pleistocene Vertebrates in Early Texas* (William P. Huff, 1811-1886). Dallas: Southern Methodist University, n.d.

Sowell, A. J. *History of Fort Bend County*. Houston: W. H. Coyle & Co., 1904.

Wharton, Clarence R. *History of Fort Bend County*. San Antonio: Naylor Company, 1939.

Johnson Calhoun Hunter

Goodspeed Brothers. *Memorial and Biographical Record of Southwest Texas*. Chicago, 1894.

Hunter, Robert Hancock. *Narrative of Robert Hancock Hunter*. Austin: Cook Printing Company, 1936.

Red, George Plunkett. *Medicine Man in Texas*. Houston, 1930.

Sowell, A. J. *History of Fort Bend County*. Houston: W. H. Coyle & Co., 1904.

Speer, William S., and John H. Brown. *Encyclopedia of the New West*. Marshall: 1881.

Samuel Isaacks

Isaacks, S. J. *The Isaacks Clan in America and Texas*. El Paso: 1935.

Martin, Madeleine. *More Early Southeast Texas Families*. Quanah, Texas: Nortex Press, 1978.

Martin, Mrs. Charles. "Jasper Countians in the Army of the Republic of Texas." *Kirbyville Banner*, Kirbyville, Texas, 1971.

_____. "The First to Arrive." *Kirbyville Banner*, Kirbyville, Texas, 1971.

Alexander Jackson

Ardoin, Robert Bruce L., compiler. *Louisiana Census Records. Iberville, Natchtoches, Point Coupe, and Rapides Parishes 1810 & 1820*. Vol. 2. Baltimore: Genealogical Publishing Co., Inc., 1972.

Dewees, W. B. *Letters from an Early Settler of Texas*. Waco, Texas: Texian Press, 1968

Jackson, Ralph Semmes. *Home on the Double Bayou*. Austin: University of Texas Press, 1961.

Kuykendall, J. H. "Reminiscences of Early Texans. A Collection from the Austin Papers." *Quarterly of the Texas State Historical Association* 6-7 (January, April, July 1903).

Partition of Property of Alexander Jackson, 12 January 1835, Wharton County, Texas, Deed Book K/444. County Recorder's Office, Wharton, Texas.

Stein, Bill. "Consider the Lily: The Ungilded History of Colorado County, Texas. Part 1: 1821-1828." *Nesbitt Memorial Library Journal* 6.1 (January 1996).

Texas Gazette, January 23 & July 10, 1830.

Isaac Jackson, Sr.

Blair, E. L. *Early History of Grimes County, Texas*. Trinity: 1930.

First Census of the United States. Greene County, Georgia.

Murray, Joyce Martin. Deed Abstracts of Washington County, Texas. Dallas: The author, 1986.

U.S. Census. 1850 Green County, Georgia. National Archives Microfilm M432, Roll 71.

U.S. Census. 1850. Grimes County, Texas. National Archives Microfilm M432, Roll 910.

U.S. Census. 1880. Caldwell County, Texas. National Archives Microfilm T9, Roll 1293.
Wortham, L. J. "Wilderness to Commonwealth." *Texas Historical and Biographical Record.*

Henry Jones

Diary of Mary (Polly) Moore Jones Ryon.
Fort Bend County, Texas. Probate Record, vol. G. pp. 337-347, 417-453.
Sowell, A. J. *History of Fort Bend County.* Houston: W. H. Coyle & Co., 1904.
Steely, Skipper. *Six Months from Tennessee.* Wolfe City: 1983.

James Wales Jones

Dobie, Frank J. "Jane Long Was Mother of Texas and Servants." *Fort Worth Star Telegram,* March 1, 1964.
Syer, Ed. "Off the Beaten Trail." *San Antonio Express-News,* September 3, 1965.

Capt. Randall Jones

Sayers, William Edward. *Off Beaten Trails.* Waco: 1971.
Texas State Library, Archives Division. Republic of Texas Pension Files.
Wharton, Clarence R. *History of Fort Bend County.* San Antonio: 1939.

John Kelly

Fisseler, Brenda Lincke. *Documented Deaths Lavaca County, Texas 1846-1859.* Hallettsville, Texas: Old Homestead Publishing Co., 2003, Sec. K.
Harris, Dilue Rose. "The Reminiscences of Mrs. Dilue Harris." *The Quarterly of the Texas State Historical Association,* Vol. IV, No. 1, 1900.
Harrisburg (Harris) County, Texas, Probate Court Book a, pp. 83-84.
"Minors of Elijah Roark." Lavaca County, Texas, Deed Book B, pp. 72-74
"Phillip Howard vs. Kelly Heirs—Succession of John Kelly, deceased."
Shipman, Daniel. *Frontier Life – 58 Years in Texas.* Reprint. Pasadena, Texas: The Abbotsford Publishing Co., 1965, p. 58.
Smith, W. Broadus. *Pioneers of Brazos County, Texas 1800-1850.* Bryan, Texas: Scribe Shop, 1962, p. 110.

William Kincheloe

1850 Census of Wharton County, Texas.
Carroll, J. M. *History of Texas Baptists.* Baptist Standard Publishing Co., 1923.
Wharton County Historical Commission. *Wharton County Pictorial History 1846-1946.*
Williams, Annie Lee. *A History of Wharton County 1846-1961.*

Abner Kuykendall

Kuykendall, J. H. "Reminiscences of Early Texans." *Quarterly of the Texas State Historical Association.* Vols. 6-7 (January, April, July 1903).

Thrall, Homer S. *A Pictorial History of Texas*. St. Louis: Thompson, 1879.

Barzillai Kuykendall

U.S. Census. 1850. Washington County, Texas. National Archives Microfilm M432, Roll 916.
U.S. Census. 1860. Washington County, Texas. National Archives Microfilm M653, Roll 1307
_____ Washington County, Texas. Probate Records. Book J, p. 569.

Joseph Kuykendall

Gulick, Charles Adams, et al., editors. *The Papers of Mirabeau Buonaparte Lamar*. Six volumes. Austin, Texas: Pemberton Press, 1968.
Jenkins, John H., editor. *The Papers of the Texas Revolution, 1835-1836*. Ten volumes. Austin: Presidial Press, 1973.
Kuykendall, J. H. "Reminiscences of Early Texans." *Quarterly of the Texas State Historical Association*. Vols. 6-7 (January, April, July 1903).
Smithwick, Noah. *The Evolution of a State, or Recollection of Old Texas Days*. Reprint. Austin: The University of Texas Press, 1983.
Sowell. Andrew Jackson. *History of Fort Bend County*. Reprint. Richmond, Texas: Fort Bend County Historical Museum, 1974.
Texas Gazette, November 6, 1830.
Texas State Gazette, March 5 and July 2, 1853.
Wharton, Clarence. *Wharton's History of Fort Bend County*. San Antonio: Naylor Co., 1939.
Winkler, E. W., compiler. *Manuscript Letters and Documents of Early Texians*. Austin: The Steck Co., 1937.

Robert H. Kuykendall

Texas State Archives, Austin. "The Papers of M. B. Lamar."
Kuykendall, J. H. "The Recollection of Gibson Kuykendall." Center for American History, The University of Texas at Austin.
Steely, Skipper. *Six Months from Tennessee*. Wolfe City: 1983.
Winkler, E. W. *Letters and Documents of Early Texians, 1821-1845*. Austin: 1937.

Joel Leakey

Lakey (Leakey) Bible records.
Leakey, Joel. Will.
Swensom, Helen. "Early Texas News."

William Little

Johnson, Frank W. *A History of Texas and Texans*. Vol. III. Chicago: 1914.
Wharton, Clarence. *Wharton's History of Fort Bend County*. San Antonio: Naylor Co., 1939.

Nathaniel Lynch

Department of Texas. Atascosito District, 1826.
Harris County, Texas. Deed Records. Vol. B, p. 48; Vol. I, pp. 32-87; Vol. L, pp. 280-3 18.

Shubael Marsh

Genealogy of the Family of George Marsh.
Hicks, Margaret Hall. *Memories of Ancestors*. Center for American History, University of Texas, Austin.

Arthur McCormick

Gaume, June B. McCormick. "The Battleground McCormick." Manuscript in the possession of the author.
Johnson Frank W. *A History of Texas and Texans*. Chicago: The American Historical Society, 1916, vol. IV, pp. 1593-1595.
"The Late Capt. Michael McCormick." *Galveston Daily News*, November 11, 1874, p. 2, col. 3.

John McCrosky

Brazoria County, Texas. Court records, February 12, 1833.
Colorado County, Texas. Court records, 1832.
Colorado County Historical Association. *Colorado County Chronicles*. Columbus, Texas.
Justice Court, Town of San Felipe de Austin, April 12, 1825.
Kilgore, Dan E. *A Ranger Legacy*. Austin: Madrona Press, 1973, p. 73.
Matagorda County, Texas. Probate Court, October 31, 1859.
McCrosky Bible record.
"Notes and Fragments." *Southwestern Historical Quarterly*, vol. XXVI (1922-1923).
White, Emma Siggins. *Descendants of John Walker of Wiginton, Scotland*, p. 550.

John McNeel

McNeel file papers, Brazoria County Historical Museum.
Smithwick, Noah. *The Evolution of a State, or Recollection of Old Texas Days*. Reprint. Austin: The University of Texas Press, 1983.
Strobel, Abner J. *The Old Plantations and Their Owners of Brazoria County, Texas*. 1926.
Visit to Texas: Being the Journal of a Traveler Through Those Parts Most Interesting to American Settlers. New York: Goodrich and Wiley, 1834.

Joseph Mims

Creighton, James A. *A Narrative History of Brazoria County*. Waco, Texas: Texian Press, 1975.
Hamilton, Peter J. *Colonial Mobile: A Study of Southwestern History*. Cambridge, Mass.: The Riverside Press, 1910, p. 421.
Mims, Sam. *Leaves of the Mims Family Tree: A Genealogic History*. Page 31.

John H. Moore

"Come and Take It." *Washington-on-the-Brazos Quarterly*, 1981.
Des Cognets, Anne R. *William Russell and His Descendants*. Louisville, Kentucky: 1884.
DeShields, James T. *Tall Men with Long Rifles*. San Antonio: The Naylor Co., 1971.
Jones, William Moses. *Texas History in Stone*. Houston: Monument Publishing Co., 1958.
Wallace, Ernest, and David Vigness. *Documents of Texas History*. Austin: Steck Co., 1963.

William Morton

Carter, James David. *Masonry in Texas: Background, History, and Influence to 1846*. Waco: Grand Lodge of Texas, 1955.
Daughters of the Republic of Texas. *Founders and Patriots of the Republic of Texas*. Vol. II. San Antonio, 1974.
Geiser, Samuel W. *Collectors of Pleistocene Vertebrates in Early Texas* (William P. Huff, 1811-86). Dallas: Southern Methodist University.
Sowell, A. J. *History of Fort Bend County*. Houston: Coyle & Co., 1904.
Transactions Texas Lodge of Research A.F. & A.M., June 17, 1978–March 17, 1979, vol. XIV. Waco: Texas Lodge of Research, 1979.
Wharton, Clarence R. *History of Fort Bend County*. San Antonio: Naylor Company, 1939.

Joseph Newman

Austin County Courthouse, Bellville, Texas. Joseph Newman file.
Davy (Salt Creek) Cemetery, Karnes County, Texas.
History of Madison County, Illinois, and county records.
Rabb, Mary Crownover. *Travels and Adventures in Texas in the 1820s*. Waco: 1962.
Warren County, Ohio. Marriage Records.

George Samuel Pentecost

Fort Bend County, Texas. Deed Records. Book A, p. 140; Book B, p. 121.
_____. Probate Book A, p. 247.

Dr. James Aeneas Phelps

Abstract of Annual Return of Mississippi Free and Accepted Masons, 1819-1849, p. 40.
Brazoria County, Texas. Index to Probate Cases, No. 20.
Carter, James D. "The Men Who Introduced Organized Free Masonry Into Texas." *The Texas Freemason*, Spring 1987.
Plunkett, Mrs. George. *The Medicine Men in Texas, Surgeons at San Jacinto*, p. 69.
Wall, Bernard. *Following General Sam Houston 1793-1863*. Houston: Clayton Library.

Joseph Henry Polley

Clapp, Marjorie. "Old Mansions Hold Ghost of Texas Past." *The Light*, San Antonio, September 13, 1955, p. 25.

Golson, Josephine Polley. *Bailey's Light*. San Antonio: Naylor, 1950, p. 65.
"Whitehall Mansion." *The Floresville Chronicle*, Floresville, Texas.
Wharton, Clarence R. *History of Fort Bend County*. San Antonio: Naylor Company, 1939.

William Pryor

Austin County Courthouse. Austin Colony marriage records.
_____. Probate Records for William Pryor.
Mississippi Territory Census for Clarke County. 1816.

John Rabb

Allen, Beverly W. "Beginning of Methodism in West Texas." *West Texas Conference Journal*, 1928.
Brown, John Henry. *Indian Wars and Pioneers of Texas*. Austin: 1880.
Harper's New Monthly Magazine, vol. XXII, December 1860.
Rabb, Lilliam Bell, editor. *Reminiscences of Mary Crownover Rabb*. Austin: Privately printed, Austin 1931.

Capt. Thomas J. Rabb

Brown, John Henry. *Indian Wars and Pioneers of Texas*. Austin: 1895, p. 650.
Gulick, Charles A., editor. *Lamar Papers*, vol. IV, part 1, p. 215.
Jenkins, John H., ed., *Papers of the Texas Revolution 1835-1836*. Austin: 1973, vol. III, pp. 142- 144.
Kemp, Louis Wiltz. *The Signers of the Texas Declaration of Independence*. Houston: Anson Jones Press, 1944, p. 72.
Kuykendall, J. H. "Reminiscences of Early Texas." *Quarterly of the Texas State Historical Association*, vol. VI, pp. 321-324.
Memorial and Genealogical Records of Southwest Texas. Chicago: Goodspeed Brother, 1894, pp. 337-338.
Rabb, Mary Crownover. *Travels and Adventures in Texas in the 1820's*. Waco: Morrison, 1962, pp. 1-2.
Texas General Land Office. Roll of officers of First Regiment, Texas Volunteer Army.
Texas Methodist Historical Quarterly, vol. I, no. 1 (1909).
Texas Presbyterian, The. Victoria, Texas, January 2, 1847.
Texas State Library, Archives Division. Certificates of Service dated November 23, 1835, and August 29, 1836.
Webb, Walter P. *The Texas Rangers*. Cambridge: 1935.
Weyand, Leonie R., and Houston Wade. "An Early History of Fayette County." LaGrange, Texas: *LaGrange Journal*, 1936, p. 124.

William Rabb

Bexar Archives, Microfilm 68 for 1821.
Brown, John Henry. *Indian Wars and Pioneers of Texas*, pp. 650-65 1.
Chronicles of Oklahoma, p. 35.

Dunlevy, J. H., and James H. Anderson. *Dunlevy History*, p. 104.
Ellis, Thomas, ed., *History of Fayette County, Pennsylvania*. 1882
German Township, Fayette County, Pennsylvania. Property Rolls, 1804.
Gulick, Charles A., ed. *Lamar Papers*. Vol. IV, part 1, p. 215.
History of Madison County, Illinois, 1882, p. 122.
History of Refugio County, 1836-1936, Centennial.
Kilgore, Dan. *Kilgore Express*, August 25, 1971, p. 6.
Madison County, Illinois. Courthouse Records, Book B, pp. 491, 508-509. Isaac
    West to William Rabb.
_____. Deed Records, April 3, 1818. Wm. Rabb to Chr. Wilt.
Pennsylvania Vital Records. Will of William Scott, 1739.
Rabb, Lillian Bell. *Reminiscences of Mary Crownover Rabb*, 1931, pp. 3-4.
Smalley, Benjamin, letter to John Smalley, 10-13-1810. File No. 6 on Smalley,
    Rutgers University.
U.S. Archives. Military Records, War of 1812, p. 252.
Warren County, Ohio. Marriage Records, vol. I, p. 12.
Wilson, Paul C. *Forgotten Mission to the Indians*, pp. 53-57.

Elijah Roark

Austin County papers. Charge receipt in "Elijah Roark, deceased, #38."
Brown, John Henry. *History of Texas*. St. Louis: 1892.
Harrisburg County. Probate Records.
Quarterly of the Texas Historical Association, vol. IV, pp. 93-95.
Texas State Archives. Navarro County Records.
Wharton, Clarence R. *History of Fort Bend County*, pp. 40-41.

Noel Francis Roberts

Austin County Courthouse. Austin Colony marriage records.
Clarke County, Georgia. Marriage Register, Book A.
Daughters of the Republic of Texas. *Muster Rolls of the Texas Revolution*.
Family story of Elizabeth Pryor Roberts walking the battlefield.
Fort Bend County probate records, George Memorial Library. Noel F. Roberts,
    Harriet Roberts, and William Roberts.
Marriages and Deaths, 1763-1820. Abstracted from extant Georgia Newspapers
    by Mary Warren.

William Roberts

Brazoria County Courthouse. Probate filed in 1833.
Brazoria County Courthouse. Sale of land to his son Andrew and son-in-law
    Cornelius Smith.
Copy of letter from Governor Bullock granting 65 acres to George Robinson and
    heirs in 1871.
Letter from Volunteers.
Probate cases in Fayette County: Case #100, Estate of George Robinson and the
    widow Lucinda Robinson; Case #314, Guardianship of Minors; Case #315,
    Succession of O. V. Robinson.

Robert Scobey

Ericson, Carolyn, and Francis T. Ingmire. *Citizens of the Republic of Texas*. St. Louis: 1982.

Memorial and Biographical History of Dallas County, Texas. Chicago: Lewis Publishing Company, 1892, pp. 938-939.

Texas Gazette, January 10, 1892.

James Scott

Berkeley County, West Virginia. Deeds.

Carter, James David. *Masonry in Texas*. Waco: 1958.

Family and Bible records.

Fort Bend County, Texas. Deeds.

Frederick County, Virginia. Deeds.

Wharton, Clarence R. *History of Fort Bend County*. Houston: The Anson Jones Press, 1939.

William Selkirk

Ingram, Mary Belle. "Matagorda's James H. Selkirk: A Man for All Seasons." *Daily Tribune*, Bay City, Texas, October 7, 2001.

Matagorda Historical Commission. *Historic Matagorda County*, vol. I.

New York American Deaths and Marriages 1784-1899.

Records of Albany Rural Cemetery, Menands, Albany County, New York.

Records of First and Second Reformed Churches of Albany, New York.

Daniel Shipman

Goliad County Historical Commission. *History and Heritage of Goliad County*. 1983.

Harris, Dilue Rose, "The Reminiscences of Dilue Harris." *Quarterly of the Texas State Historical Association*, vol. IV, 1900-1901.

McCutchen, Joseph D. *Mier Expedition Diary*. The University of Texas Press.

Shipman, Daniel. *Frontier Life*. 1879.

Bartlett S. Sims

Gamel, H. P. N. *Laws of Texas*. Vol. I. Austin, 1898.

McLean, Malcolm D. *Papers Concerning Robertson's Colony*. Vol. XII. Arlington: 1985.

Southwestern Historical Quarterly, Texas State Historical Association, vol. LXV, p. 291.

Texas State Library. Archives Division. Papers of Bartlett Sims.

Tolbert, Frank X. *Informal History of Texas*. New York: 1961.

Watkins, Sue, ed. *One League to Each Wind*. Austin: n.d.

White, Gifford. *Character Certificate in the General Land Office*. Baltimore: 1988.

George Washington Singleton

Degree of Heirship, Department of Bexar, Wharton County Courthouse, and the Bexar Archives.

Harris County Marriages, Volume A.
Will of Joseph George Singleton, Wharton County Courthouse and the Bexar
    Archives.

Phillip Singleton

Clay County, Kentucky. Deed Book A, p. 39.
Harris County, Texas. Deed Records. Vol. B, p. 103; Vol. E, p. 159.
Kentucky Military Records. *Kentucky Genealogical*, vol. 22, p. 32.
Wayne County, Kentucky. Green Book, p. 85.

Christian Smith

Atascosito District Census of 1826.
Early Pioneers and Settlers in Washington County.

Cornelius Smith

Daughters of the Republic of Texas. Dedication of Citizen of Texas marker.
Pulaski County, Kentucky. Marriage Record.
U.S. Census for Texas. 1850.

William Smithers, Smeathers, Smothers

Historical Marker Files, Texas Historical Commission, Austin, 1996.
Houston Telegraph, 1837. Obituary of William Smeathers.
Texas and American Revolution. San Antonio: The University of Texas Institute of
    Texan Cultures, 1975.

Adam Stafford

Fort Bend County, Texas. Marriage Records.
Harris, Dilue Rose. "Reminiscences of Dilue Harris." *Quarterly of the Texas State
    Historical Association*, vol. IV, 1900-1901.
Stafford, Adam. Family Bible.
_____. Papers, Center for American History, The University of Texas at Austin.
Victoria Advocate, November 27, 1880. Obituary of Adam Stafford.

William Stafford

Gulick, Charles A., and Harriet Smither, eds. *Papers of Mirabeau Buonoparte Lamar.*
    Vol. V. Austin: The Pemberton Press, 1968.
Harris, Dilue Rose. "Reminiscences of Dilue Harris." *Quarterly of the Texas State
    Historical Association*, vol. IV, 1900-1901.
Sowell, A. J. *History of Fort Bend County.* Houston: W. H. Coyle & Co., 1904.
Stafford, Adam. Family Bible.
Wharton, Clarence R. *History of Fort Bend County.* Houston: The Anson Jones
    Press, 1939.
Wilson County, Tennessee. Marriage Records.

George Washington Teel

"Death Notices," *Arkansas Gazette*, July 16 1822, vol. III, Whole No. 134.
Dickinson County, Tennessee. Deed Book B, pp. 197-198; Deed Book C, p. 102 and 251.
"George Teel Obituary." Newspaper unknown.
Hope, Hempstead County, Arkansas. Book H, Administration of Deborah Johnson's Will, November 14, 1848.
_____. Settlement of Estate. Edward Johnson's Will, January 25, 1846, p. 463.
San Augustine County, Texas, Deed and Survey transferring land to George Teal, August 5, 1854.

Ezekiel Thomas

Burke's Texas Almanac and Immigrants Handbook for 1879. Austin: Steck-Warlick, 1969.
Harris County, Texas. Guardianship Records.
McAshan, Marie Phelps, *A Houston Legacy: On the Corner of Main and Texas*. Houston: Gulf Publishing, 1985.
Southwestern Historical Quarterly, "Harris County, 1822-1825." Vol. XVIII.

Jesse Thompson

Fort Bend County, Texas. Court Minutes, Book A.
_____. Deed Records, Book B, pp. 23-25.
Hocker, Irene Feris. Bible records.
Wharton, Clarence R. *Gail Borden, Pioneer*. San Antonio: 1941.
_____. *History of Fort Bend County*, p. 74.

Elizabeth Tumlinson

"Limestone Genealogy." *The Gusher*, vol. IV, no. 1. Midland County Library.
White, Lucille Latham. *The Tumlinsons, A Fearless Family of Gunfighters*.

James Tumlinson

Bell, Verner Lee. *From Whence We Came*.
Groneman, Bill. *Alamo Defenders*.

James Walker, Sr.

Greenbriar County, West Virginia. Marriage Records.
Washington County, Texas. Deed Records.
_____. Probate Records.

Caleb Wallace

1880 Census, Navarro County, Texas.
Montgomery County. Probate Records, Black Box, Packet 174.
Texas State Library. Archives Division. "Texas Adjutant General Service Records, 1835-1836, Call No. 401-12.

Amy Comstock White

White, Gifford. *James Taylor White of Virginia*. Austin: 1982.
_____. *Amy White of the Old 300*. Austin: 1986.

Boland and Henry Whiteside

Austin County, Texas. Deed Records, vol. A.
Barker, Eugene C., editor. "Minutes of the Ayuntamient of San Felipe de Austin 1828-1832." *Southwestern Historical Quarterly*, Vol. XXI, p. 419; Vol. XXII, p. 191
Brazos County, Texas. Abstract #56.
Grimes County, Texas. Abstract #508.
Phelan, Macum. *A History of Early Methodism in Texas, 1817-1866*. Nashville: Cokesbury Press, 1924.
Tennessee State Marriages. Davidson, Tennessee, January 19, 1832
Whiteside, Don. *The First Four Generations of Descendants of William and Elizabeth Whiteside of Ireland, Pennsylvania, Virginia, and North Carolina*. Nepean, Ontario, November 1990.

James Whiteside

Nutter, Mildred Moody. *Wills of Wayne County, Kentucky, 1802-1909*. Rushville, Indiana: circa 1972.
Blair, Eric Lee. *Early History of Grimes County*. Austin, Texas: 1930.

William Whiteside

Baldwin, Carl R. *Echoes of Their Voices*. St. Louis, Mo.: Hawthorne Publishing Company, 1978.
Barker, Eugene C., editor. "Minutes of the Ayuntamient of San Felipe de Austin 1828-1832." *Southwestern Historical Quarterly*, Vol. XXI, p. 419; Vol. XXII, p. 191.
Murray, Joyce Martin. *Austin County Deed Abstracts 1837-1852*.
Washington County, Texas. Marriage Records, Volume I

William Whitlock

Family Record of Mrs. Fannie Whitlock Sneed.
Partlow, Miriam. *Liberty, Liberty County and the Atascocito District*. Austin: Pemberton Press, 1974.
St. Martin of Tours Church, St. Martinville, Louisiana. Marriages.
U.S. Census. 1850. Liberty County, Texas. National Archives Microfilm M 432, Roll 912.
U.S. Census. 1860. Liberty County, Texas. National Archives Microfilm M 653, Roll 1300.
White, Gifford. *Amy White of the Old 300*. Austin: 1986.

Thomas Williams

Colorado County Historical Commission. "First Census of the Colorado District." *Colorado County Chronicles*, 1986, vol. II, pp. 722-742.

Matagorda County Historical Commission. *Historic Matagorda County*. 1986, vol. I, pp. 103, 104.
U.S. Census. 1850. Travis County, Texas. Dwelling/Family No. 245, National Archives Microfilm M 432, Roll 915.

Zadock Woods

Daughters of the Republic of Texas Museum and Library. The Woods-Harrell Family.
Spellman, Paul N. *Zadock and Minerva Cottle Woods, American Pioneers*.
Texas State Archives, Austin. Republic of Texas Pension Application Abstracts.

Glossary

alcalde: served in the capacity of judge and mayor.

Anahuac Disturbances: The disturbance of 1832 broke out as the culmination to a series of grievances of the Texas colonists. The disturbance of 1835 marked the end of a period of harmony between the settlers and the Mexican authority.

ayuntamiento: the equivalent of the modern city council.

Bexar, Siege of: preceded battle which drove the Mexican troops from Texas in December 1835.

Census of 1826: the first census of Austin's colony.

"Come and Take It" flag: This flag was flown at the Battle of Gonzales in response to the Mexican demand for the return of a cannon. See also Gonzales, Battle of.

Consultation: A body of representatives that met in San Felipe in November 1835 to discuss their situation. They decided to remain loyal citizens of Mexico but would set up a provisional government.

Convention of 1836: A group of delegates which met at Washington-on-the-Brazos, wrote the Declaration of Independence for Texas and the Constitution of the Republic, and organized the ad interim government.

empresario: a land agent or contractor used by the Mexican government to colonize Texas.

Fredonian Rebellion (1826): the first time independence from Mexico had been proclaimed in Texas.

Gonzales, Battle of: the first encounter of the Texas Revolution; see also "Come and Take It" flag.

Grass Fight: an early incident in the Siege of Bexar.

Gutierrez-Magee Expedition: an early (1812-1813), ill-fated episode in the Mexican Revolution against Spain.

land grant: the patent or title to the land granted by the government to a settler.

land terms:

hacienda	five or more square leagues.
labor	1,000,000 square varas, or 177.1 acres, considered the amount of tillable land for one farmer.
league	a linear measure of 5,000 varas; also a measure of land equal to a plot one league square, equal to 4428.3 acres; see also sitio.
sitio	one square league as needed for a ranching operation; see also league.

vara   a Spanish linear measure of varying value; Texas finally settled on 33¹/₃ inches.

Lively: a schooner hired by Austin at New Orleans to bring settlers and supplies to Texas.

Mier Expedition (1842): the last of the raiding expeditions from Texas into Mexico during the days of the Republic of Texas; best remembered for the "Black Bean Episode."

Muldoon, Father Michael: a Catholic priest assigned to Austin's colony and known for his liberal views.

regidor: a town councilman.

Runaway Scrape: the name used for the spring 1836 flight of Texians from their homes to escape Santa Anna's advancing army.

sindico procurador: an official with the combined duties of notary and city attorney.

Texian: the term used for an Anglo-American colonist.

Velasco, Battle of (1832): preliminary to the Texas Revolution, this battle was the scene of the first bloodshed in relations between Texas and Mexico.

Veramendi family: a wealthy and prominent San Antonio family in colonial Texas.

Woll's Invasion (1842): Gen. Adrian Woll, a French mercenary, led the Mexican army in the capture of San Antonio.

Timeline

1821	Spain grants Moses Austin permission to bring settlers to the Province of Texas.
	Moses Austin dies.
	Mexico wins independence from Spain.
	Earliest colonists arrive in Texas.
1823	The Republic of Mexico grants Stephen F. Austin a colonization contract.
1832	Disturbance at Anahuac.
	Battle of Velasco.
1833	S. F. Austin is imprisoned in Mexico City.
1835	Austin returns to Texas.
	Trouble at Anahuac. Battle of Gonzales.
	Consultation, November 3.
	Grass Fight.
	Siege of Bexar.
1836	Convention, March 1.
	Declaration of Independence, March 2.
	Fall of the Alamo, March 6.
	Goliad Massacre.
	Runaway Scrape.
	Battle of San Jacinto.
	Stephen F. Austin dies.

The
Old Three
Hundred List

Bugbee's Old Three Hundred List

The colonists who settled under the terms of Austin's first contract came to be known as "The Old Three Hundred," because the contract was for the introduction of 300 families. The actual number of families introduced under it, however, was 297. Nine families received two titles each. The table given below is an adaptation of one compiled from the records of the General Land Office at Austin, Texas, by Lester G. Bugbee, and published in *The Quarterly of the Texas State Historical Association* for October 1897 (Volume I). It gives the names of the colonists, the amount of land received by each, the present county in which the land is located, and the date that the title was issued. A *labor* of land was about 177 acres, and a *sitio*, or league, about 4,428 acres.

Name	Amount of Land		Present Location	Date of Title
	sitios	*labores*		
Allcorn, Elijah	1		Fort Bend	July 10, 1824
	½		Washington	July 10, 1824
		1	Waller	July 10, 1824
Allen, Martin	1		Wharton	July 19, 1824
		1	Austin	July 19, 1824
Alley, John	1		Jackson & Lavaca	May 14, 1827
Alley, John	1		Fayette	May 16, 1827
Alley, Rawson	1½		Colorado	Aug. 3, 1824
Alley, Thomas Alley, William	1		Brazoria	July 29, 1824
Alsbury, Charles G. Alsbury, Harvey Alsbury, Horace	1½		Brazoria	Aug. 3, 1824

Name	Amount of Land		Present Location	Date of Title
	sitios	*labores*		
Alsbury, Thomas	2		Fort Bend & Brazoria	July 8, 1824
		1½	Waller	July 8, 1824
Anderson, S. A.	1		Fayette	Aug. 10, 1824
Andrews, John	1		Fayette & Colorado	July 7, 1824
		1	Waller	July 7, 1824
Andrews, William	1		Fort Bend	July 15, 1824
		1	Fort Bend	July 15, 1824
Angier, Samuel T.	1		Brazoria	Aug. 16, 1824
		1	Brazoria	Aug. 24, 1824
Austin, John	2		Harris	July 21, 1824
		1	Brazoria	Aug. 24, 1824
Austin, Santiago E. B.	3		Brazoria	Aug. 19, 1824
		1	Brazoria	Aug. 19, 1824
Austin, Santiago B.		1	Waller	Aug. 24, 1824
Austin, Estevan F.	5		Brazoria	Sept. 1, 1824
	7½		Brazoria	Sept. 1, 1824
	⅓		Brazoria	Sept. 1, 1824
	½		Brazoria	Sept. 1, 1824
	¼		Brazoria	Sept. 1, 1824
	1¾		Brazoria	Sept. 1, 1824
	2⅙		Brazoria	Sept. 1, 1824
	3⅙		Wharton	Sept. 1, 1824
	2		Wharton	Sept. 1, 1824
		3	Brazoria	Sept. 1, 1824
Baily, James B.	1		Brazoria	July 7, 1824
Balis, Daniel E.	1		Matagorda	April 14, 1828
Baratt, William	1		Fort Bend	June 4, 1827
Barnet, Thomas	1		Fort Bend	July 10, 1824
Battle, M. M.	1		Matagorda	Aug. 10, 1824
Battle, Mills M.	1		Fort Bend	May 31, 1827
Beard, James	1		Fort Bend	Aug. 10, 1824
Beason, Benejani	1		Colorado	Aug. 7, 1824
Belknap, Charles	1		Fort Bend	May 22, 1827
Bell, Josiah H.	1½		Brazoria	Aug. 7, 1824
Bell, Thomas B.	1		Brazoria	Aug. 16, 1824
Berry, M.			(Partner of M. M. Battle)	

Name	Amount of Land		Present Location	Date of Title
	sitios	labores		
Best, Isaac	1		Waller	Aug. 19, 1824
Betts, Jacob	1		Matagorda	Aug. 19, 1824
Biggam, Fras	1		Wharton	July 10, 1824
	1		Brazoria	July 10, 1824
		1	Waller	July 10, 1824
Bloodgood, Wm.	1		Chambers & Harris	Aug. 10, 1824
Boatwright, Thomas	1		Austin	July 27, 1824
Borden, Thos.	1		Brazoria	July 29, 1824
Bostick, Caleb R.	1		Matagorda	July 24, 1824
Bowman, John T.	1		Matagorda	Aug. 21, 1824
Bradley, Edward R.	1		Brazoria	Aug. 10, 1824
Bradley, John	1		Brazoria	July 8, 1824
Bradley, Thomas			(Partner of S. T. Angier)	
Breen, Charles	1		Brazoria	May 24, 1824
Brias, Patrick	1		Harris	May 1, 1827
Bridges, Wm. B.	1		Jackson	July 21, 1824
Bright, David	1		Fort Bend	July 15, 1824
		1	Austin	July 15, 1824
Brinson, Enoch	1		Harris	Aug. 7, 1824
Brooks, Bluford	1		(Forfeited)	Aug. 10, 1824
Brotherington, Robt.			(Partner of Caleb R. Bostick)	
Brown, George			(Partner of Charles Belknap)	
Brown, John	1		Harris	Aug. 19, 1824
		1	Waller	Aug. 19, 1824
Brown, William S.	1		Washington	July 29, 1824
Buckner, Aylett C.	1		Matagorda	July 24, 1824
		2	Matagorda	Aug. 24, 1824
Burnet, Pumphrey	1		Matagorda	July 24, 1824
Burnam, Jesse	1		Fayette	Aug. 16, 1824
		1	Colorado	Aug. 16, 1824
Byrd, Micajah	1		Washington	July 16, 1824
Calliham, Mosis A.	1		Harris	Aug. 3, 1824
Calvit, Alexr.	1		Brazoria	Aug. 3, 1824
		1	Waller	Aug. 3, 1824
		1	Brazoria	Aug. 3, 1824

Name	Amount of Land		Present Location	Date of Title
	sitios	*labores*		
Carpenter, David	1		Harris	Aug. 16, 1824
Carson, Wm. C.	1		Brazoria	May 15, 1827
Carter, Saml.	1		Brazoria	July 8, 1824
Cartwright, Jesse H.	1		Fort Bend	Mar. 31, 1828
		1	Lavaca	Mar. 31, 1828
Cartwright, Thomas	1		Colorado	Aug. 10, 1824
		1	Austin	Aug. 10, 1824
Castleman, Sylvenus	2		Wharton	July 7, 1824
	½		Fayette	July 7, 1824
		2	Austin	July 7, 1824
Chance, Samuel	1		Brazoria	July 27, 1824
Charles, Isaac N.	1		Brazoria	May 21, 1827
Chriesman, Horatio	1		Fort Bend	July 8, 1824
		2	Austin	July 8, 1824
Clark, John C.	1		Wharton	July 16, 1824
Clarke, Antony R.		1	Brazoria	Aug. 24, 1824
Coats, Merit M.	1		Waller	July 19, 1824
Coles, Jno. P.	7½		Burleson & Washington	Aug. 19, 1824
	½		Washington	Aug. 19, 1824
	½		Brazoria	Aug. 19, 1824
Cook, James	1		Colorado	Aug. 3, 1824
Cooke, Jno.	1		(Partner of Isaac Hughes)	Aug. 10, 1824
		1	Harris	Aug. 10, 1824
Cooper, William	1		Matagorda	July 24, 1824
Cooper, William	1½		Waller	Aug. 10, 1824
		2	Austin	Aug. 10, 1824
Crier, John	1		Matagorda	June 6, 1827
Crownover, John	1		Wharton & Matagorda	Aug. 3, 1824
		1	Austin	Aug. 3, 1824
Cummings, James	1		Brazoria	Aug. 16, 1824
	5		(Forfeited)	Aug. 16, 1824
Cummings, John	1		Brazoria	July 21, 1824
Cummings, Rebecca	1		Brazoria	July 21, 1824
		2	Waller	July 21, 1824
Cummings, William	1		Brazoria	July 21, 1824

Name	Amount of Land sitios	labores	Present Location	Date of Title
Cummins, James	1		Colorado	July 7, 1824
	5		Austin	July 7, 1824
		1	Colorado	July 7, 1824
Curtis, Hinton	1		Matagorda	Aug. 10, 1824
Curtis, James Jr.	1		Brazos	Aug. 19, 1824
Curtis, James Sr.	1		Burleson	Aug. 3, 1824
Davidson, Samuel	1		Brazos	July 21, 1824
Davis, Thomas	1		Austin	July 29, 1824
Deckrow, D.	1		Matagorda	July 24, 1824
Demos, Charles	1		Matagorda	Aug. 3, 1824
Demos, Peter	1		Matagorda	
Dewees, Wm. B.			(Partner of James Cook)	
Dickinson, John	1		Galveston & Harris	Aug. 19, 1824
Dillard, Nicholas	1		Brazoria	Aug. 16, 1824
Duke, Thomas M.	1		Matagorda	July 24, 1824
Duty, George	1		Fayette	July 19, 1824
Duty, Joseph	1		Colorado	July 19, 1824
Dyer, Clement C.	1		Colorado	Aug. 10, 1824
		1½	Waller	Aug. 24, 1824
Earle, Thos.	1		Harris	July 7, 1824
		1	Harris	July 7, 1824
Edwards, G. E.	1		Wharton	Aug. 19, 1824
Elam, John	1		(Forfeited)	Aug. 7, 1824
Elder, Robert		1	Waller	Aug. 24, 1824
Falenash, Charles	1		Burleson	Aug. 19, 1824
Fenton, David	1		Matagorda	July 29, 1824
Fields, John F.		1	Brazoria	Aug. 24, 1824
Fisher, James	1		Burleson	July 19, 1824
Fitzgerald, David	1		Fort Bend	July 10, 1824
Flanakin, Isaiah		2	Austin	July 19, 1824
Flowers, Elisha	1		Matagorda	July 19, 1824
		1	Colorado	July 19, 1824
Foster, Isaac	1		Matagorda	Aug. 10, 1824

Name	Amount of Land		Present Location	Date of Title
	sitios	labores		
Foster, John	2½		Fort Bend	July 15, 1824
		3	Fort Bend	July 15, 1824
Foster, Randolph	1		Waller & Fort Bend	July 16, 1824
Frazier, James	1		Austin & Fort Bend	July 24, 1824
Fulshear, Charles	1		Fort Bend	July 16, 1824
Garret, Charles	1		Brazoria	July 15, 1824
		1	Waller	July 15, 1824
Gates, Samuel	½		Washington	July 8, 1824
	½		Washington	July 8, 1824
Gates, William	1		Washington	July 16, 1824
	1		Washington	July 16, 1824
George, Freeman	1		Matagorda	July 7, 1824
		1	Waller	July 7, 1824
Gilbert, Preston		1	Waller	July 7, 1824
Gilbert, Sarah	1		Wharton & Fort Bend	May 11, 1827
Gilleland, Daniel		1	Austin	Aug. 3, 1824
Gorbet, Chester S.	1		Brazoria	July 19, 1824
Gouldrich, Michael		1	Galveston	Aug. 24, 1824
Gray, Thos.	1		Brazoria	Aug. 16, 1824
		1	Colorado	Aug. 16, 1824
Groce, Jared E.	5		Brazoria	July 29, 1824
	2		Waller	July 29, 1824
	3		Grimes	July 29, 1824
Guthrie, Robert	1		Jackson	July 19, 1824
Haddan, John	1		Colorado	July 29, 1824
Hady, Samuel C.	1		Waller	Aug. 19, 1824
Hall, Geo. B.			(Partner of Samuel T. Angier)	
Hall, John W.	2		Brazoria	July 10, 1824
		2	Waller	July 10, 1824
Hall, W. J.	1		Fort Bend	July 10, 1824
Hamilton, David	1		Wharton	May 9, 1827
Harris, Abner	1		(Partner of William Baratt)	
Harris, David	1		Harris	Aug. 19, 182⁴
Harris, John R.	1		Harris	Aug. 16, 182⁴

Name	Amount of Land		Present Location	Date of Title
	sitios	*labores*		
Harris, William			(Partner of David Carpenter)	
Harris, William	1		Brazoria	July 10, 1824
Harris, William J.		1	Harris	July 21, 1824
Harrison, George	1		Brazoria	Aug. 16, 1824
Harvey, William	1		Austin	July 20, 1824
Haynes, Thomas S.	1		Brazos	Aug. 16, 1824
Hensley, James	1		Brazoria	Aug. 3, 1824
		1	Austin	Aug. 3, 1824
Hodge, Alexander	1		Fort Bend	April 12, 1828
Holland, Francis	1		Grimes	Aug. 10, 1824
Holland, William	1		Grimes	Aug. 10, 1824
Holliman, Kinchen	1		(Forfeited)	Aug. 10, 1824
Hope, James	1		Brazos	July 10, 1824
	¼		Brazos	July 10, 1824
		2		July 10, 1824
Hudson, C. S.	1		Wharton	July 29, 1824
Huff, John	1		Wharton	July 10, 1824
Huff, George	1½		Wharton & Fort Bend	Aug. 19, 1824
Hughes, Isaac			(Partner of John Cooke)	(Forfeited)
Hunter, Eli	1		Wharton	July 24, 1824
Hunter, Johnson	1		Harris	Aug. 10, 1824
Iiams, John	1		Chambers	Aug. 7, 1824
Ingram, Ira		1	Waller	Aug. 24, 1824
Ingram, Seth	2		Wharton	July 29, 1824
		1	Austin	July 29, 1824
Irons, John	1		Waller	July 16, 1824
Isaacks, Samuel	1		Fort Bend	July 16, 1824
Jackson, Alexander	2		Wharton	July 16, 1824
Jackson, Humphrey	1		Harris	Aug. 16, 1824
		1	Harris	Aug. 16, 1824
Jackson, Isaac	1		Grimes	Aug. 7, 1824
Jamison, Thomas	1		Matagorda & Brazoria	July 24, 1824
Johnson, Henry W.			(Partner of Thos. H. Borden)	

Name	Amount of Land		Present Location	Date of Title
	sitios	labores		
Jones, Henry	1		Fort Bend	July 8, 1824
Jones, J. W.	1		Wharton	Aug. 10, 1824
		1	Fort Bend	Aug. 10, 1824
Jones, Oliver	1		Brazoria	Aug. 10, 1824
		1	Austin	Aug. 10, 1824
Jones, R.	½		Wharton	July 15, 1824
	½	1	Fort Bend	July 15, 1824
		1	Fort Bend	July 15, 1824
Keep, Imla	1		Brazoria	July 24, 1824
Keller, John C.	1		Matagorda	June 4, 1827
Kelly, John		2	Brazos	July 19, 1824
Kennedy, Sam'l	1		Fort Bend	July 7, 1824
		1	Austin	July 7, 1824
Kennon, Alfred	1		Burleson	July 19, 1824
Kerr, James	1		Jackson	May 6, 1827
Kerr, Peter				
Kerr, William	1		Washington	Aug. 10, 1824
Kincheloe, William	1		Wharton	July 8, 1824
	1		Wharton	July 8, 1824
Kingston, William	1		Matagorda	May 8, 1827
Knight, James	1		Fort Bend	July 15, 1824
		1	Fort Bend	July 15, 1824
Kuykendall, Abner	1		Fort Bend	July 7, 1824
	½		Washington	July 7, 1824
		2	Austin	July 7, 1824
Kuykendall, Brazilla	1		Austin	Aug. 7, 1824
Kuykendall, Joseph	1		Fort Bend	July 8, 1824
Kuykendall, Robert	1		Wharton	
	1		Wharton	
League, Hosea H.	1		Matagorda	May 25, 1827
Leakey, Joel	1		Washington & Austin	May 28, 1827
Linsey, Benjamin	1		(Forfeited)	Aug. 19, 1824
Little, John	1		Austin	May 21, 1828
		1	Fort Bend	May 21, 1828
Little, William	1		Fort Bend	July 10, 1824
		1	Fort Bend	July 10, 1824

Name	Amount of Land		Present Location	Date of Title
	sitios	labores		
Long, Jane H.	1		Fort Bend	April 30, 1827
		1	Waller	May 1, 1827
Lynch, James	1		Washington	July 16, 1824
Lynch, Nathaneal	1		Harris	Aug. 19, 1824
McCroskey, John	1		Brazoria	Aug. 16, 1824
		1	Austin	Aug. 16, 1824
McCormick, Arthur	1		Harris	Aug. 10, 1824
McCormick, David	1		Brazoria	July 21, 1824
McCormick, John			(Partner of James Frazier)	
McCoy, Thomas			(Partner of Daniel Deckrow)	
McFarlan, Aechilles	1		Brazoria	July 10, 1824
		1½	Waller	July 10, 1824
McFarlan, John	1¼		Waller	Aug. 10, 1824
		1	Waller	Aug. 10, 1824
McKenney, Thos. F.	1		Brazos	Aug. 16, 1824
McKinsey, Hugh	1		Wharton & Matagorda	Aug. 3, 1824
McClain, A. W.				
McNair, James	1		Colorado	July 24, 1824
McNeel, Daniel	1		Brazoria	Aug. 3, 1824
McNeel, George W.				
McNeel, John G.	½		Brazoria	Aug. 10, 1824
McNeel, John	1		Brazoria	Aug. 3, 1824
McNeel, Pleasant D.	1		Brazoria	Aug. 7, 1824
McNeel, Sterling	1		Brazoria	Aug. 19, 1824
McNutt, Elizabeth	1		Jackson	July 21, 1824
McWilliams, William	1		Burleson	July 19, 1824
Marsh, Shubael	1		Brazoria	July 8, 1824
Martin, Wily	1		Brazoria	July 29, 1824
Mathis, William	1		Brazos	July 19, 1824
Milburn, David H.			(Partner of Thomas Davis)	
Miller, Samuel	1		Washington	Aug. 19, 1824
Miller, Samuel R.	1		Washington	Aug. 19, 1824
Miller, Simon	1		Fort Bend	Aug. 7, 1824
Millican, James D.	1		Brazos	July 16, 1824

Name	Amount of Land sitios labores		Present Location	Date of Title
Millican, Robert	2½		Brazos	July 16, 1824
Millican, William	1		Brazos	July 16, 1824
Minus, Joseph	1		Brazoria	Aug. 19, 1824
Mitchell, Asa	1		Brazoria	July 7, 1824
	½		Brazoria	July 7, 1824
		1	Brazoria	Aug. 24, 1824
Monks, John L.	1		(Forfeited)	
Moore, John H.			(Partner of Thomas Gray)	
Moore, Luke	1		Harris	Aug. 3, 1824
Morrison, Moses			(Partner of William Cooper)	
Morton, William	1½		Fort Bend	July 15, 1824
		1	Fort Bend	July 15, 1824
Mouser, David	1		Waller	Aug. 19, 1824
Nelson, James	1		Colorado	Aug. 7, 1824
Newman, Joseph	1		Wharton	Aug. 10, 1824
		1	Austin	Aug. 10, 1824
Nuckols, M. B.	1		Matagorda & Brazoria	Aug. 3, 1824
		1	Brazoria	Aug. 3, 1824
Orrick, James		1	Austin	Aug. 10, 1824
Osborn, Nathan	1		Colorado	July 24, 1824
Parks, Wm.				
Parker, Joshua	1		Wharton	July 24, 1824
Parker, William	1		Brazoria	July 8, 1824
		1	Waller	July 8, 1824
Pennington, Isaac	1		Fort Bend	Aug. 3, 1824
Pentecost, George S.	1		Matagorda	Aug. 19, 1824
Pettus, Freeman	1		Colorado & Fayette	Aug. 3, 1824
	1		Matagorda & Brazoria	Aug. 3, 1824
		1	Colorado	Aug. 3, 1824
Pettus, William	1		Wharton	July 10, 1824
	1		Fort Bend	July 10, 1824
		1	Waller	July 10, 1824
Petty, John	1		Fayette	Aug. 10, 1824
Peyton, J. C.	1		Matagorda	May 25, 1827
Phelps, James A. E.	1		Brazoria	Aug. 16, 1824
		2	Brazoria	Aug. 16, 1824

Name	Amount of Land		Present Location	Date of Title
	sitios	*labores*		
Philips, I. B.	1		Wharton	May 9, 1827
Philips, Zeno	1		Brazoria	July 19, 1824
Picket, Pamelia	1		Matagorda	July 21, 1824
		1	Austin	July 21, 1824
Polley, Joseph H.			(Partner of Samuel Chance)	
Polley, Joseph H.	1		Fort Bend	Aug. 16, 1824
Powell, Peter			(Partner of William Kingston)	
Prater, William	1		Brazoria	July 19, 1824
		1	Austin	July 19, 1824
Pruitt, Pleasant	1		Matagorda	July 24, 1824
Pryor, William		1	Waller	Aug. 24, 1824
Rabb, Andrew	1½		Wharton	Aug. 10, 1824
Rabb, John	1		Fort Bend	July 8, 1824
		2	Austin	July 8, 1824
Rabb, Thomas J.	1		Wharton	July 24, 1824
Rabb, William	3		Fayette	July 19, 1824
	2		Matagorda	July 19, 1824
		2	Fayette	Aug. 24, 1824
Raleigh, William	1		Burleson	Aug. 16, 1824
Ramey, L.	1		Matagorda	May 23, 1827
Randon, David			(Partner of Isaac Pennington)	
Randon, John	1		Fort Bend	Aug. 19, 1824
Rankin, Frederic H.	1		Harris	July 7, 1824
		1	Harris	July 7, 1824
Rawls, Amos	1		Matagorda	July 24, 1824
Rawls, Benjamin	1		Matagorda	Aug. 3, 1824
Rawls, Daniel	1¼		Matagorda	July 24, 1824
Richardson, Stephen	1		Brazoria	July 10, 1824
Roark, Elijah	1		Fort Bend	July 10, 1824
		1	Waller	July 10, 1824
Robbins, Earle		1	Austin	July 19, 1824
Robbins, William	1		Brazoria	July 19, 1824
		1	Austin	July 19, 1824

Name	Amount of Land		Present Location	Date of Title
	sitios	labores		
Roberts, Andrew	1		Fort Bend	May 10, 1827
Roberts, Noel F.	1¼		Fort Bend	July 15, 1824
Roberts, William	1		Brazoria	July 8, 1824
Robertson, Edward	1		Fort Bend	Mar. 31, 1828
Robinson, A.	1½		Brazoria	July 8, 1824
	½		Washington	July 8, 1824
		1	Waller	July 8, 1824
Robinson, Geo.	1		Brazoria	July 8, 1824
Ross, James	1		Colorado	July 19, 1824
San Pierre, Joseph		1	Fort Bend	Aug. 24, 1824
Scobey, Robert	1		Wharton	Aug. 3, 1824
Scott, James	1		Fort Bend	Aug. 7, 1824
Scott, Wm.	1		Harris	Aug. 19, 1824
	1		Harris	Aug. 19, 1824
		1	Harris	Aug. 19, 1824
Selkirk, William	1		Matagorda	Aug. 10, 1824
Shelby, David			(Partner of John McCormick)	
Shipman, Daniel			(Partner of Isaac N. Charles)	
Shipman, Moses	1		Fort Bend	July 19, 1824
		1	Austin	July 19, 1824
Sims, Bartlet	1		Wharton	Aug. 7, 1824
Singleton, G. W.	1		Wharton	May 14, 1827
Singleton, Philip	1		Burleson & Washington	Aug. 19, 1824
Smith, Christian	1		Harris & Chambers	July 19, 1824
Smith, Cornelius	1		Brazoria	Aug. 10, 1824
Smith, John			(Partner of Hugh McKinsey)	
Smeathers, William	1		Austin	July 16, 1824
Snider, Gabriel S.	1		Colorado	Aug. 7, 1824
Sojourner, Albert L.			(Partner of Pumphrey Burnet)	
Spencer, Nancy	1		Fort Bend	Aug. 19, 1824
Stafford, Adam		1	Waller	Aug. 24, 1824

Name	Amount of Land		Present Location	Date of Title
	sitios	labores		
Stafford, William	1½		Fort Bend	Aug. 16, 1824
		1	Waller	Aug. 16, 1824
Stevens, Thomas	1		Waller	Aug. 7, 1824
Stout, Owen H.			(Partner of Benjamin Rawls)	
Strange, James		1	Harris	Aug. 24, 1824
Sutherland, Walter	1		Brazos	Aug. 10, 1824
Talley, David	1		Brazoria	Aug. 16, 1824
		1	Austin	Aug. 16, 1824
Taylor, John I.	1		Harris	Aug. 10, 1824
Teel, George	1		Fort Bend	Aug. 3, 1824
Thomas, Ezekiel	1		Harris	Aug. 19, 1824
Thomas, Jacob		1	Waller	Aug. 24, 1824
Thompson, Jesse	1		Brazoria	Aug. 7, 1824
Tone, Thomas J.			(Partner of Thomas Jamison)	
Tong, James F.	1		Brazoria	Aug. 19, 1824
Toy, Samuel	1		Austin	May 7, 1827
Trobough, John			(Partner of Patrick Brias)	
Tumlinson, Elizabeth	1		Colorado	Aug. 16, 1824
		1	Colorado	Aug. 16, 1824
Tumlinson, James	1		Colorado	Aug. 19, 1824
	½		Wharton	Aug. 19, 1824
		1	Colorado	Aug. 19, 1824
Vandorn, Isaac			(Partner of Daniel E. Baylis)	
Varner, Martin	1		Brazoria	July 8, 1824
		1	Waller	July 8, 1824
Vince, Allen			(Partner of M. A. Calliham)	
Vince, Richard				Aug. 16, 1824
Vince, Robt.	1		Harris	Aug. 21, 1824
Vince, Wm.	1		Harris	July 21, 1824
Walker, James	1		Washington	July 21, 1824
Walker, Thomas			(Partner of Thomas H. Borden)	
Wallice, Caleb	1		Grimes	May 14, 1828
Wells, Francis F.	1		Jackson	July 21, 1824
		1	Brazoria	July 21, 1824

Name	Amount of Land		Present Location	Date of Title
	sitios	*labores*		
Westall, Thomas	1		Wharton	July 19, 1824
	1		Fort Bend	July 19, 1824
		2	Austin	July 19, 1824
White, Amy	1		Harris	Aug. 16, 1824
White, Joseph	1		Brazoria	Aug. 16, 1824
White, Reuben	1		Harris	Aug. 19, 1824
White, Walter C.			(Partner of James Knight)	
White, William C.	1		Austin	Aug. 19, 1824
Whitesides, Boland				Aug. 16, 1824
Whitesides, Henry	1		Brazos & Grimes	Aug. 10, 1824
Whitesides, James	1		Grimes & Brazos	July 16, 1824
		1	Waller	July 16, 1824
Whitesides, William	1		Waller	July 19, 1824
Whiting, Nath'l			(Partner of Nathan Osborn)	
Whitlock, William	1		Harris	Aug. 16, 1824
Wightman, Elias D.	1		Matagorda	May 25, 1827
Wilkins, Jane	1		Fort Bend	May 26, 1827
Williams, George I.	1		Matagorda	Aug. 19, 1824
Williams, Henry			(Partner of John J. Bowman)	
Williams, John			(Partner of Mills M. Battle)	
Williams, John		1	Waller	Aug. 24, 1824
Williams, John R.	1		(Forfeited)	July 29, 1824
		1	(Forfeited)	July 29, 1824
Williams, Robt. H.	1		Matagorda	Aug. 19, 1824
Williams, Samuel M.	1		Brazoria	Aug. 10, 1824
	1		Brazoria	Aug. 10, 1824
		1	Waller	Aug. 10, 1824
		1	Austin	Aug. 10, 1824
		1	Brazoria	Aug. 10, 1824
Williams, Solomon	1		Matagorda	Aug. 7, 1824
		1	Waller	Aug. 7, 1824
Williams, Thomas	1		Matagorda	Aug. 16, 1824
Woods, Zadock	1		Matagorda	May 15, 1827

Mass

Maps

The maps in this section show the land of Stephen F. Austin's first contract. The county maps give the approximate location of the individual grants. The Old Three Hundred settlers had the option to apply as a stockraiser/rancher for a *sitio* (4,428 acres) or as a farmer for a *labor* (177 acres). Many opted for both. The individual *labores* are not shown on the maps due to space consideration. In the grantee lists accompanying the maps, the legend (l) stands for *labor* and (s) for *sitio*.

The maps were drawn by Wolfram M. Von-Maszewski based on information from the Archives and Records of the Texas General Land Office, Austin, Texas.

Land Commissioner de Bastrop and Empresario Austin dispensing grant certificates.

Boundary of Stephen F. Austin's First Contract

—Map by W. M. Von Maszewski

Old Three Hundred grantees of a *sitio* (s) or a *labor* (l) in Austin County

1. Allen, Martin . . . (l)
2. Boatwright, Thomas . . . (s)
3. Bright, David . . . (l)
4. Cartwright, Thomas . . . (l)
5. Castleman, Sylvenus . . . (l)
6. Chriesman, Horatio . . . (l)
7. Cooper, William . . . (l)
8. Crownover, John . . . (l)
9. Cummins, James . . . (s)
10. Davis, Thomas & David Milburn . . . (s)
11. Flanakin, Isaiah . . . (l)
12. Frazier, James, David Shelby, & John McCormick . . . (s)
13. Gilleland, Daniel . . . (l)
14. Harvey, William . . . (s)
15. Hensley, James . . . (l)
16. Ingram, Seth . . . (l)
17. Jones, Oliver . . . (l)
18. Kennedy, Samuel . . . (l)
19. Kuykendall, Abner . . . (l)
20. Kuykendall, Barzilla . . . (l)
21. Little, John . . . (l)
22. McCrosky, John & James Frazier Shelby . . . (l)
23. Newman, Joseph . . . (l)
24. Orrick, James . . . (l)
25. Picket, Pamelia . . . (l)
26. Prater, William . . . (l)
27. Rabb, John . . . (l)
28. Robbins, Earle . . . (l)
29. Robbins, William . . . (l)
30. Shipman, Moses . . . (l)
31. Smeathers, William . . . (s)
32. Talley, David . . . (l)
33. Toy, Samuel [cannot locate] . . . (s)
34. Westall, Thomas . . . (l)
35. White, William C. . . . (s)
36. Williams, Samuel M. . . . (l)

The majority of *labores* in Austin County were north of the town of San Felipe (#38) and south of the town of San Felipe (#39). The *labores* (#40) in present Waller County were east of the Brazos River directly across the town of San Felipe.

Austin County

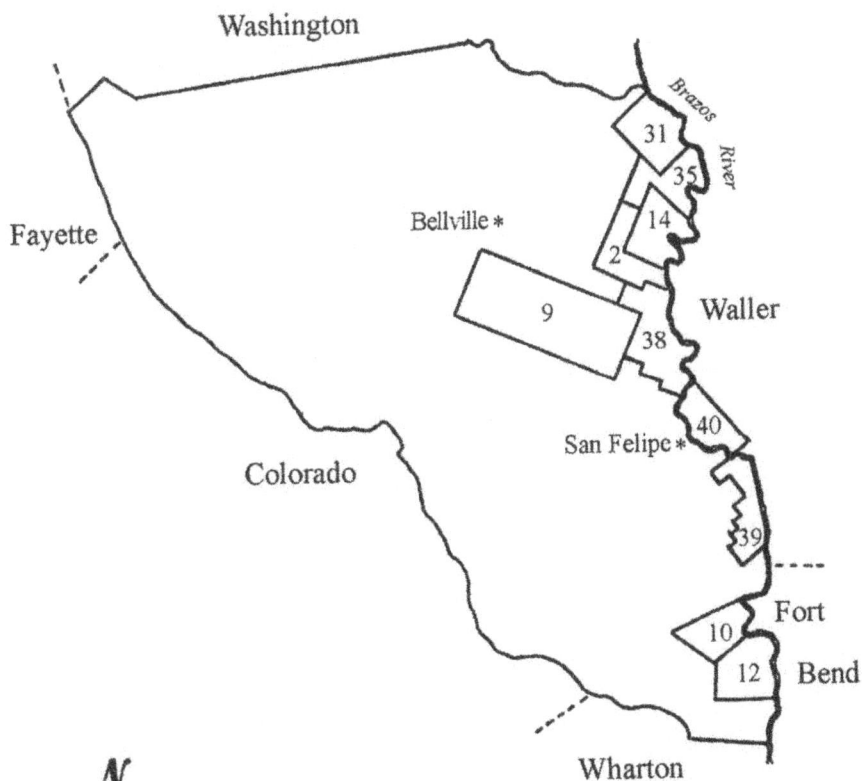

Washington

Fayette

Bellville *

Brazos River

31

35

14

2

9

38

Waller

Colorado

San Felipe *

40

39

Fort

10

12

Bend

Wharton

N
W · E
S

WMVM

Old Three Hundred grantees of a *sitio* (s) or a *labor* (l) in Brazoria County

1. Alley, Thomas & William ... (s)
2. Alsbury, Charles G., Harvey & Horace [in Fort Bend & Brazoria] ... (s)
3. Angier, Samuel T., George B. Hall, & Thomas W. Bradley. ... (s; l)
4. Austin, John ... (l)
5. Austin, J. E. B. ("Santiago"). ... (s; l)
6. Austin, Stephen F. ("Estavan"). ... (s; l)
7. Baily, James B. ... (s)
8. Bell, Josiah H. ... (s)
9. Bell, Thomas B. ... (s)
10. Biggam, Fras ... (s)
11. Borden, Thomas, Henry Johnson, & Thomas Walker ... (s)
12. Bradley, Edward R. ... (s)
13. Bradley, John ... (s)
14. Breen, Charles ... (s)
15. Calvit, Alexr. ... (s; l)
16. Carson, William C. ... (s)
17. Carter, Saml. ... (s)
18. Chance, Samuel ... (s)
19. Charles, Isaac N. & Daniel Shipman ... (s)
20. Clarke, Antony R. ... (l)
21. Coles, Jno. P. ... (s)
22. Cummings, James ... (s)
23. Cummings, John ... (s)
24. Cummings, Rebecca ... (s)
25. Cummings, William ... (s)
26. Dillard, Nicholas ... (s)
27. Fields, John F. ... (l)
28. Garret, Charles ... (s)
29. Gorbet, Chester S. ... (s)
30. Gray, Thos. & John Moore ... (s)
31. Groce, Jared E. ... (s)
32. Hall, John W. ... (s)
33. Harris, William ... (s)
34. Harrison, George ... (s)
35. Hensley, James ... (s)
36. Jamison, Thomas ... (s)
37. Jones, Oliver ... (s)
38. Keep, Imla ... (s)
39. McCroskey, John ... (s)
40. McCormick, David ... (s)
41. McFarlan, Aechilles ... (s)
42. McNeel, Daniel ... (s)
43. McNeel, George W. ... (s)
44. McNeel, John G. ... (s)
45. McNeel, John ... (s)
46. McNeel, Pleasant D. ... (s)
47. McNeel, Sterling ... (s)
48. Marsh, Shubael ... (s)
49. Martin, Wily ... (s)
50. Mims, Joseph ... (s)
51. Mitchell, Asa. ... (s; l)
52. Nuckols, M. B. ... (l)
53. Parker, William. ... (s)
54. Phelps, James A. E.. ... (s; l)
55. Philips, Zeno ... (s)
56. Prater, William ... (s)
57. Richardson, Stephen ... (s)
58. Robbins, William ... (s)
59. Roberts, William ... (s)
60. Robinson, A. ... (s)
61. Robinson, Geo. ... (s)
62. Smith, Cornelius ... (s)
63. Talley, David ... (s)
64. Thompson, Jesse ... (s)
65. Tong, James F. ... (s)
66. Varner, Martin ... (s)
67. Wells, Francis F. ... (l)
68. White, Joseph ... (s)
69. Williams, Samuel M.. ... (s; l)

Brazoria County

Old Three Hundred grantees of a *sitio* (s) or a *labor* (l) in Brazos County

1. Alley, Rawson . . . (s)
2. Andrews, John . . . (s)
3. Beason, Benjamin . . . (s)
4. Burnam, Jesse . . . (l)
5. Cartwright, Thomas . . . (s)
6. Cook, James & William Dewees . . . (s)
7. Cummins, James . . . (s; l)
8. Duty, Joseph . . . (s)
9. Dyer, Clement C. . . . (s)
10. Flowers, Elisha . . . (s)
11. Gilbert, Preston . . . (s)
12. Gray, Thomas . . . (s)
13. Haddon, John . . . (s)
14. McNair, James & A. W. McCain . . . (s)
15. Nelson, James . . . (s)
16. Osborn, Nathan & Nathaniel Whiting . . . (s)
17. Pettus, Freeman . . . (s; l)
18. Ross, James . . . (s)
19. Snider, Gabriel S. . . . (s)
20. Tumlinson, Elizabeth . . . (s; l)
21. Tumlinson, James . . . (s; l)

Brazos County

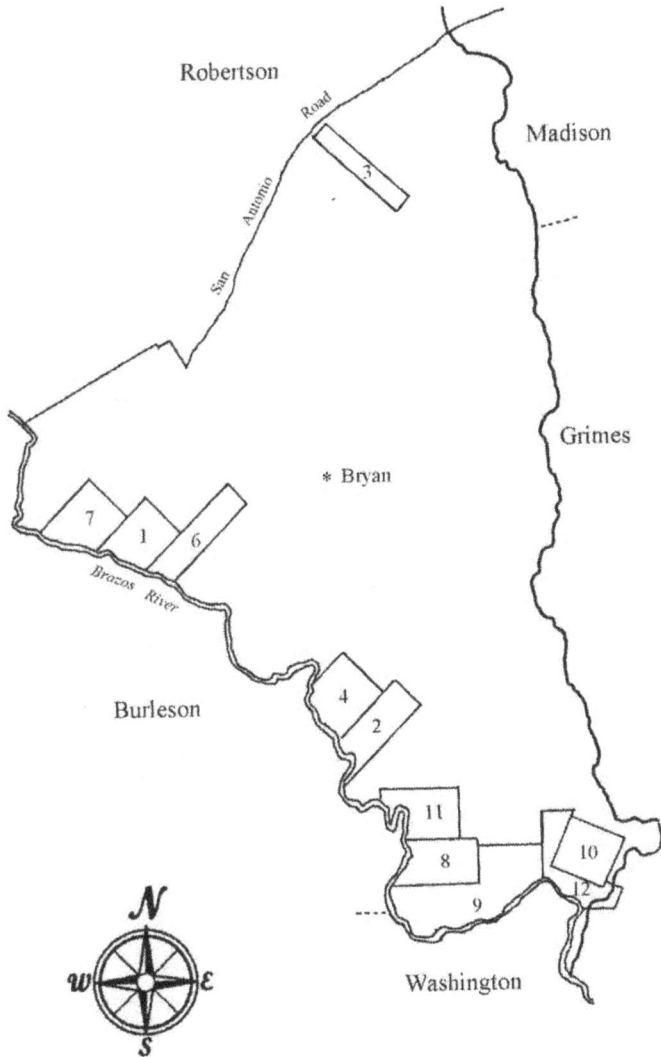

Robertson

Madison

San Antonio Road

3

Grimes

* Bryan

7

1

6

Brazos River

Burleson

4

2

11

8

10

9

12

N

W E

S

WMVM

Washington

Old Three Hundred grantees of a *sitio* (s) or a *labor* (l)
in Burleson County

1. Coles, Jno. P. . . . (s)
2. Curtis, James, Sr. . . . (s)
3. Falenash, Charles . . . (s)
4. Fisher, James . . . (s)
5. Kennon, Alfred . . . (s)
6. McWilliams, William . . . (s)
7. Raleigh, William . . . (s)
8. Singleton, Philip . . . (s)

Burleson County

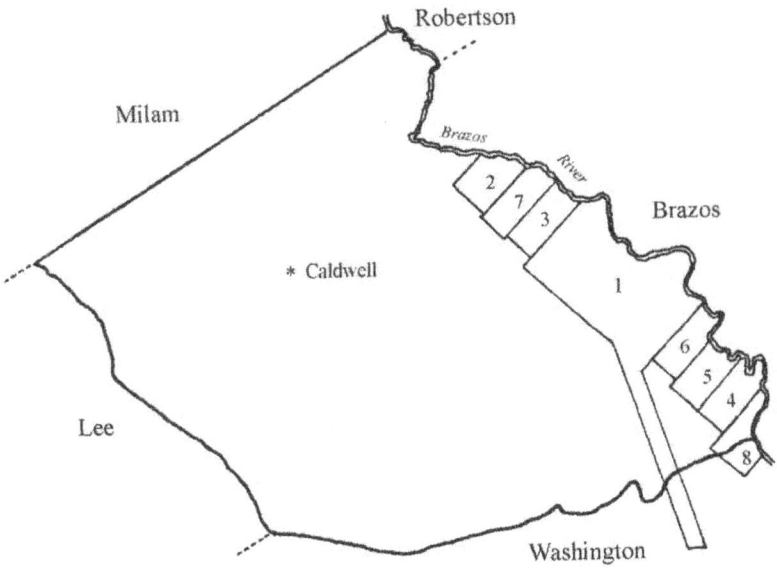

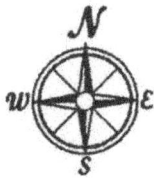

Robertson

Milam

Brazos

2

7

3

River

Brazos

* Caldwell

1

6

5

4

Lee

8

Washington

N

W E

S

WMVM

Old Three Hundred grantees of a *sitio* (s) or a *labor* (l)
in Colorado County

1. Alley, Rawson . . . (s)
2. Andrews, John . . . (s)
3. Beason, Benjamin . . . (s)
4. Burnam, Jesse . . . (l)
5. Cartwright, Thomas . . . (s)
6. Cook, James & William Dewees . . . (s)
7. Cummins, James . . . (s; l)
8. Duty, Joseph . . . (s)
9. Dyer, Clement C. . . . (s)
10. Flowers, Elisha . . . (l)
11. Gilbert, Preston . . . (s)
12. Gray, Thomas . . . (l)
13. Haddon, John . . . (s)
14. McNair, James & A. W. McCain . . . (s)
15. Nelson, James . . . (s)
16. Osborn, Nathan & Nathaniel Whiting . . . (s)
17. Pettus, Freeman . . . (s; l)
18. Ross, James . . . (s)
19. Snider, Gabriel S. . . . (s)
20. Tumlinson, Elizabeth . . . (s; l)
21. Tumlinson, James . . . (s; l)

Colorado County

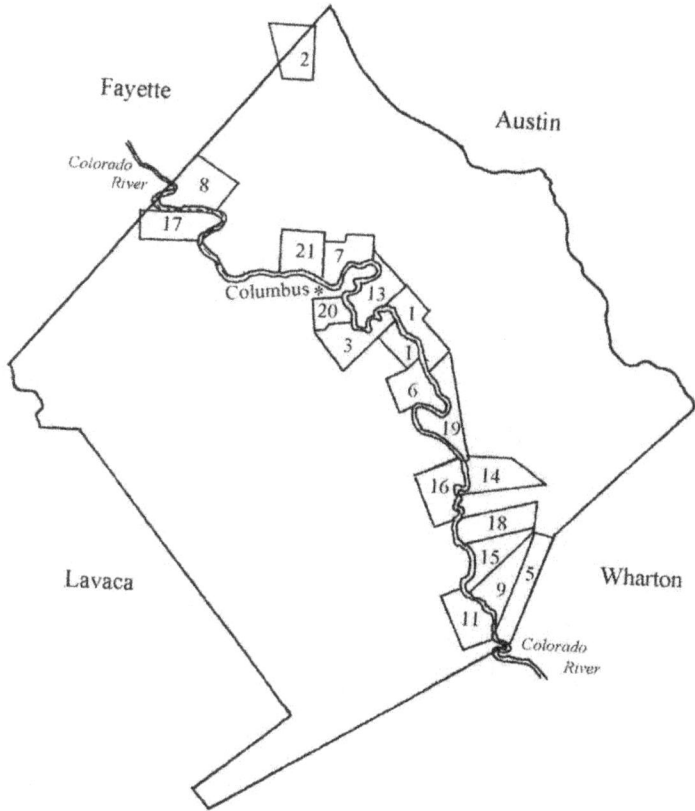

Fayette

Austin

Colorado River

8

17

2

21 7

Columbus *

13

20

3

1

1

6

19

16

14

18

15

9 5

11

Lavaca

Wharton

Colorado River

N

W E

S

WMVM

Old Three Hundred grantees of a *sitio* (s) or a *labor* (l) in Fayette County

1. Alley, John . . . (s)
2. Anderson, S. A. . . . (s)
3. Andrews, John . . . (s)
4. Burnam, Jesse . . . (s)
5. Castleman, Sylvenus . . . (s)
6. Duty, George . . . (s)
7. Pettus, Freeman . . . (s)
8. Petty, John . . . (s)
9. Rabb, William . . . (s; l)

Fayette County

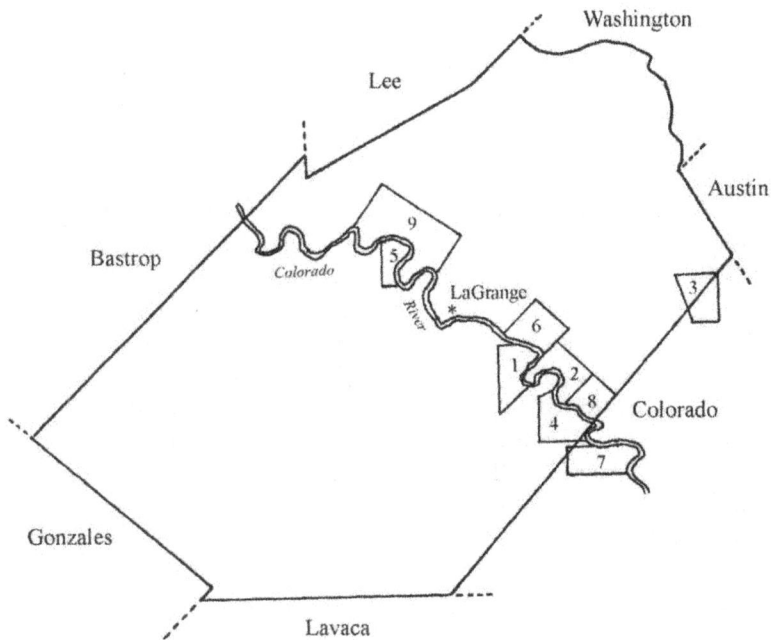

Washington

Lee

Austin

Bastrop

9
5
Colorado
LaGrange
*
River
6
3
1
2
8
4
Colorado
7

Gonzales

Lavaca

N
W · E
S

WMVM

Old Three Hundred grantees of a *sitio* (s) or a *labor* (l)
in Fort Bend County

1. Allcorn, Elijah . . . (s)
2. Alsbury, Thomas . . . (s)
3. Andrews, William . . . (s; l)
4. Baratt, William &
   Abner Harris . . . (s)
5. Barnett, Thomas . . . (s)
6. Battle, Mills M., John Williams,
   & M. Berry . . . (s)
7. Beard, James . . . (s)
8. Belknap, Charles &
   George Brown . . . (s)
9. Bright, David . . . (s)
10. Cartwright, Jesse H. . . . (s)
11. Chriesman, Horatio . . . (s)
12. Fitzgerald, David . . . (s)
13. Foster, John . . . (s; l)
14. Foster, Randolph . . . (s)
15. Frazier, James &
    John McCormick . . . (s)
16. Fulshear, Churchill . . . (s)
17. Gilbert, Sarah [located in
    Wharton & Fort Bend] . . . (s)
18. Hall, W. J. . . . (s)
19. Hodge, Alexander . . . (s)
20. Huff, George . . . (s)
21. Isaacks, Samuel . . . (s)
22. Jones, Henry . . . (s)
23. Jones, J. W. . . . (l)
24. Jones, R. . . . (s; l)
25. Kennedy, Sam'l . . . (s)
26. Knight, James &
    Walter C. White . . . (s; l)
27. Kuykendall, Abner . . . (s)
28. Kuykendall, Joseph . . . (s)
29. Little, John . . . (l)
30. Little, William . . . (s; l)
31. Long, Jane H. . . . (s)
32. Miller, Simon . . . (s)
33. Morton, William . . . (s; l)
34. Pennington, Isaac &
    David Randon . . . (s)
35. Pettus, William . . . (s)
36. Polley, Joseph H. . . . (s)
37. Rabb, John . . . (s)
38. Randon, J. . . . (s)
39. Roark, Elijah . . . (s)
40. Roberts, Andrew . . . (s)
41. Roberts, Noel F. . . . (s)
42. Robertson, Edward . . . (s)
43. San Pierre, Joseph . . . (l)
44. Scott, James . . . (s)
45. Shipman, Moses . . . (s)
46. Spencer, Nancy . . . (s)
47. Stafford, William . . . (s)
48. Teel, George . . . (s)
49. Westall, Thomas . . . (s)
50. Wilkins, Jane . . . (s)
51. Fort League:
    Jones, J. W.
    Jones, Randall
    Knight, James & W. C. White
    Little, John
    Little, William
    Morton, William

Fort Bend County

Waller

Harris

Austin

14

49 41 38
40   16
   34
15   Brazos
      13
46   River   3 21 26 24
              33 50 10
                  6 19
            51
Richmond   31 28
                27 22
                        30
                        11
                        25
                        37
                        36
                        4
                        42
                        2

8

47

1

9

39
45
5
12
18
35

San Bernard River

17
20
48
32
44
7

Wharton

Brazoria

N
W   E
S

WMVM

Old Three Hundred grantees of a *sitio* (s) or a *labor* (l)
in Grimes County

1. Groce, Jared E. . . . (s)
2. Holland, Frances . . . (s)
3. Holland, William . . . (s)
4. Jackson, Isaac . . . (s)
5. Wallace, Caleb . . . (s)
6. Whitesides, James . . . (s)

Grimes County

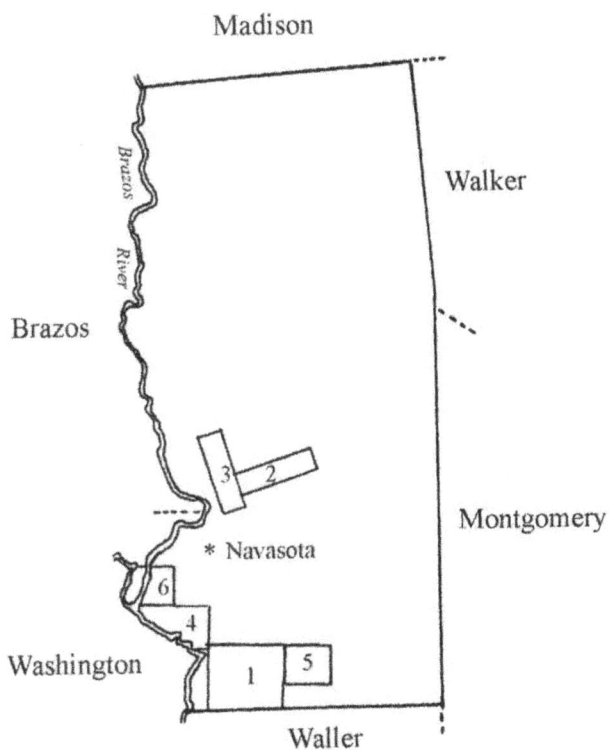

Madison

Brazos River

Walker

Brazos

3 2

Montgomery

* Navasota

6

4

Washington

1 5

Waller

WMVM

Old Three Hundred grantees of a *sitio* (s) or a *labor* (l)
in Harris, Chambers, and Galveston counties

Harris County:

1. Austin, John . . . (s)
2. Brias/Reels, Patrick . . . (s)
3. Brinson, Enoch . . . (s)
4. Brown, John . . . (s)
5. Calliham, Moses A. & Allen Vince . . . (s)
6. Carpenter, David & William Harris . . . (s)
7. Cook, Jno. . . . (l)
8. Earle, Thos. . . . (s; l)
9. Harris, David . . . (s)
10. Harris, John R. . . . (s)
11. Harris, William J.. . . . (l)
12. Hunter, Johnson . . . (s)
13. Jackson, Humphrey . . . (s; l)
14. Lynch, Nathaniel . . . (s)
15. McCormick, Arthur . . . (s)
16. Moore, Luke . . . (s)
17. Rankin, Frederic H. . . . (s; l)
18. Scott, William . . . (s; l)
19. Smith, Christian . . . (s)
20. Strange, James. . . . (l)
21. Taylor, John I. . . . (s)
22. Thomas, Ezekiel . . . (s)
23. Vince, Robert . . . (s)
24. Vince, William . . . (s)
25. White, Amy . . . (s)
26. White, Reuben . . . (s)
27. Whitlock, William . . . (s)

Chambers County:

28. Bloodgood, William . . . (s)
29. Iiams, John . . . (s)

Galveston County:

30. Dickinson, John . . . (s)
31. Gouldrich, Michael. . . . (l)

Harris, Chambers, Galveston Counties

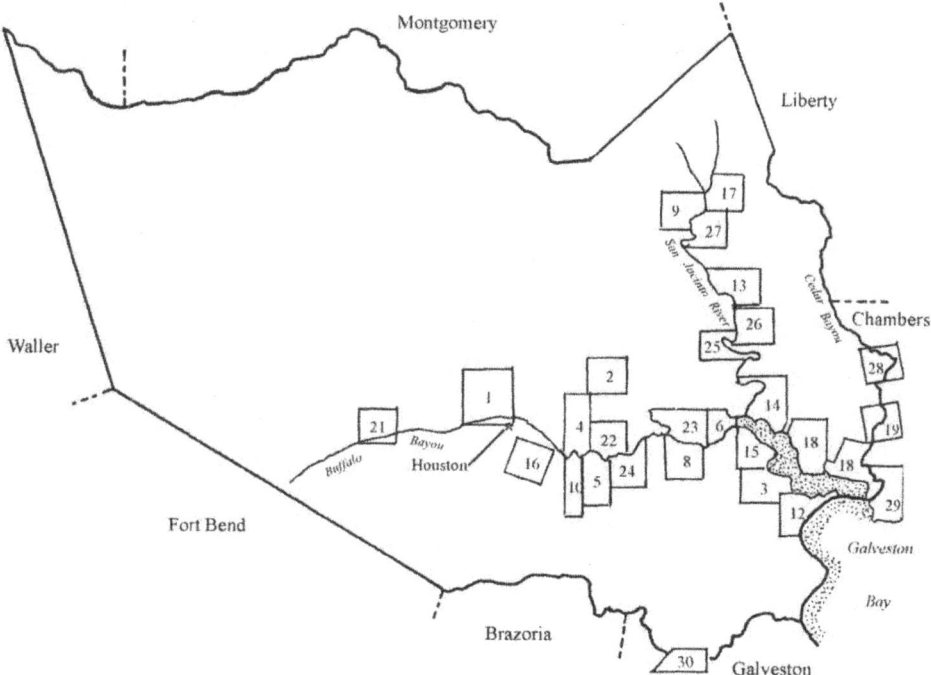

Montgomery

Liberty

Waller

Chambers

San Jacinto River

17

9

27

13

26

25

28

2

1

Bayou

21

Buffalo

Houston

16

4

22

24

8

23

6

15

14

18

19

18

5

10

3

29

12

Fort Bend

Galveston

Galveston Bay

Brazoria

30

Galveston

N

W **E**

S

WMVM

Old Three Hundred grantees of a *sitio* (s) or a *labor* (l)
in Jackson and Lavaca counties

Jackson County:

1. Alley, John . . . (s)
2. Bridges, William B. . . . (s)
3. Guthrie, Robert . . . (s)
4. Kerr, James . . . (s)
5. McNutt, Elizabeth . . . (s)
6. Wells, Francis F. . . . (s)

Lavaca County:

1. Cartwright, Jesse H. . . . (l)

Jackson and Lavaca Counties

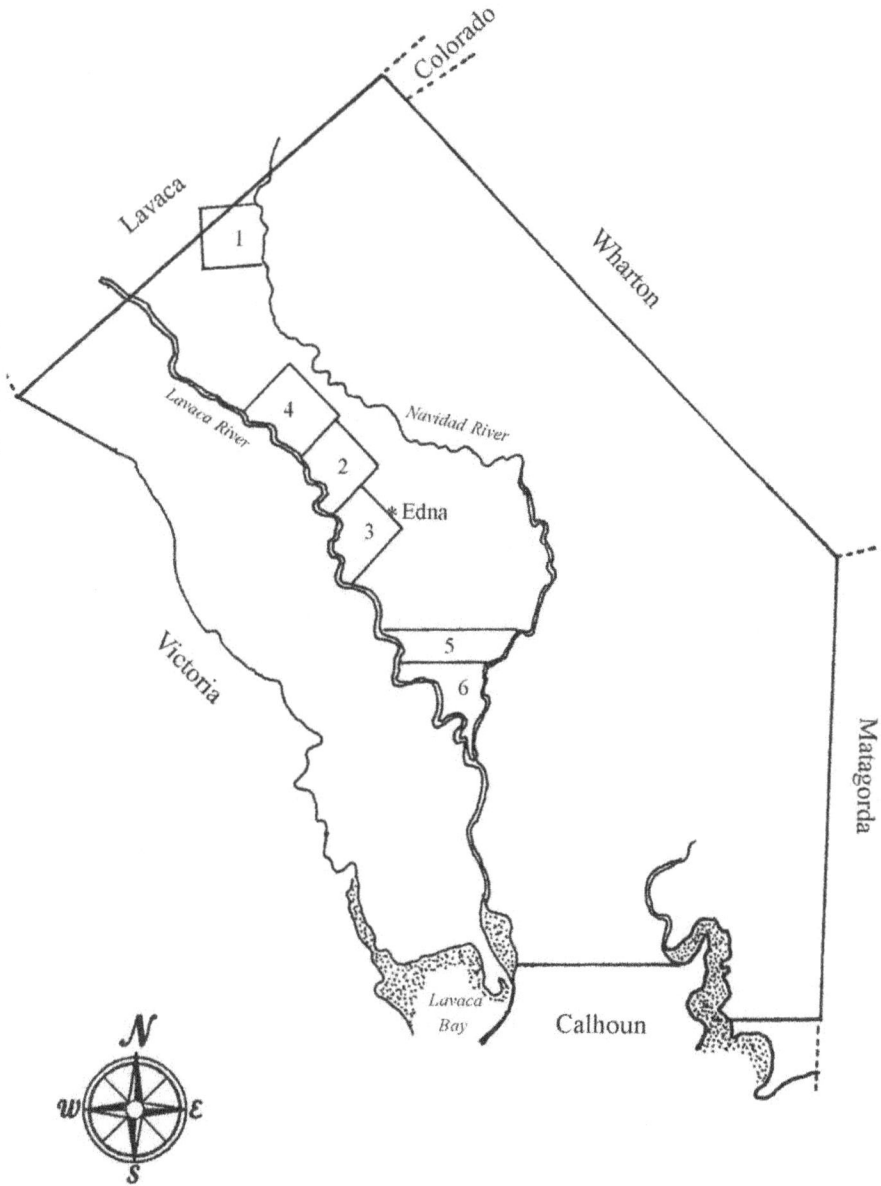

Colorado

Lavaca

Wharton

1

Lavaca River

4

Navidad River

2

3

*Edna

5

6

Victoria

Matagorda

N

W E

S

Lavaca
Bay

Calhoun

WMVM

Old Three Hundred grantees of a *sitio* (s) or a *labor* (l)
in Matagorda County

1. Balis/Bayliss, Daniel E. &
   Isaac Vandorn . . . (s)
2. Battle, M. M., Manders Berry,
   & John Williams . . . (s)
3. Betts, Jacob . . . (s)
4. Bostick, Caleb R. &
   Robert Brotherton . . . (s)
5. Bowman, John T. &
   Henry Williams . . . (s)
6. Buckner, Aylett C. . . . (s; l)
7. Burnet, Pumphrey &
   Albert S. Sojourner . . . (s)
8. Cooper, William &
   Moses Morrison . . . (s)
9. Crier, John . . . (s)
10. Crownover, John . . . (s)
11. Curtis, Hinton . . . (s)
12. Deckrow, D. &
    Thomas McCoy . . . (s)
13. Demos. Charles . . . (s)
14. Demos, Peter . . . (s)
15. Duke, Thomas M. . . . (s)
16. Fenton, David . . . (s)
17. Flowers, Elisha . . . (s)
18. Foster, Isaac . . . (s)
19. George, Freeman . . . (s)
20. Jamison, Thomas &
    Thomas Tone . . . (s)
21. Keller, John C. . . . (s)
22. Kingston, William &
    Peter Powell . . . (s)
23. League, Hosea H. . . . (s)
24. McKinsey, Hugh &
    John Smith . . . (s)
25. Nuckols, M. B. . . . (s)
26. Pentecost, George S. . . . (s)
27. Pettus, Freeman . . . (s)
28. Peyton, J. C. . . . (s)
29. Picket, Pamelia . . . (s)
30. Pruitt, Pleasant . . . (s)
31. Rabb, William . . . (s)
32. Ramey, L. . . . (s)
33. Rawls, Amos . . . (s)
34. Rawls, Benj. &
    Owen H. Stout . . . (s)
35. Rawls, Daniel . . . (s)
36. Selkirk, William . . . (s)
37. Wightman, Elias D. . . . (s)
38. Williams, George I. . . . (s)
39. Williams, Robert H. . . . (s)
40. Williams, Solomon . . . (s)
41. Williams, Thomas . . . (s)
42. Woods, Zadock . . . (s)

Matagorda County

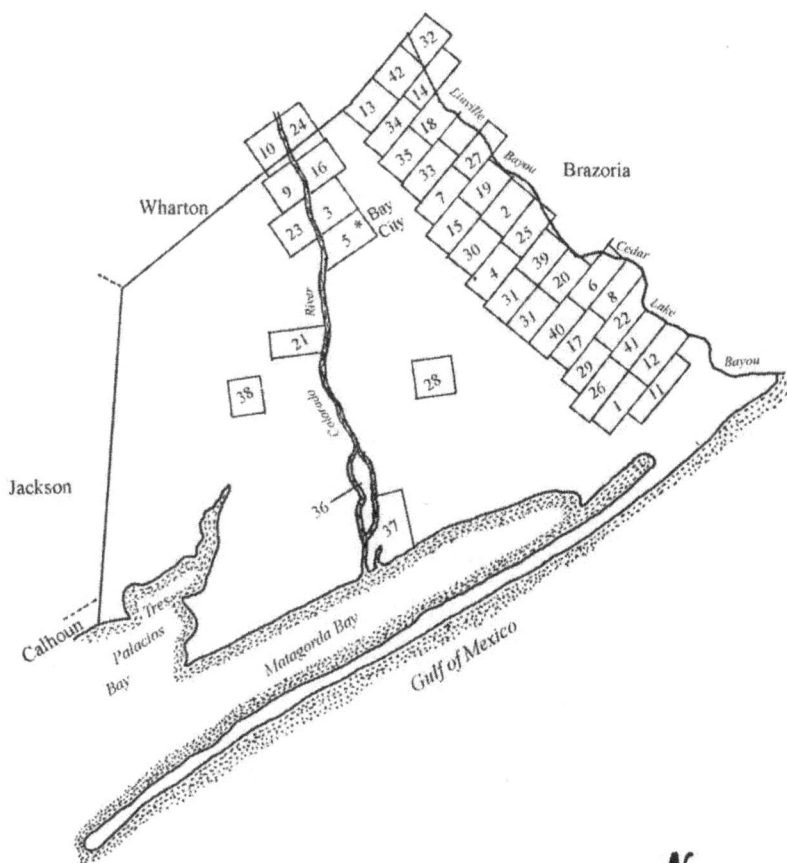

Old Three Hundred grantees of a *sitio* (s) or a *labor* (l)
in Waller County

1. Allcorn, Elijah . . . (l)
2. Alsbury, Thomas . . . (l)
3. Andrews, John . . . (l)
4. Best, Isaac . . . (s)
5. Biggam, Fras . . . (l)
6. Brown, John . . . (l)
7. Calvit, Alexr. . . . (l)
8. Coats, Merit M. . . . (s)
9. Cooper, William . . . (s)
10. Cummins, Rebecca . . . (l)
11. Dyer, C. C. . . . (l)
12. Elder, Robert . . . (l)
13. Foster, Randolph . . . (s)
14. Garret, Charles . . . (l)
15. George, Freeman . . . (l)
16. Groce, Jared . . . (s)
17. Hady, Samuel . . . (s)
18. Hall, John W. . . . (l)
19. Ingram, Ira . . . (l)
20. Irons, John . . . (s)
21. Long, Jane H. . . . (l)
22. McFarlan, Aechilles . . . (l)
23. McFarlan, John . . . (s; l)
24. Mouser, David . . . (s)
25. Parker, William . . . (l)
26. Pettus, William . . . (l)
27. Pryor, William . . . (l)
28. Roark, Elijah . . . (l)
29. Robinson, A. . . . (l)
30. Stafford, Adam . . . (l)
31. Stafford, William . . . (l)
32. Stevens, Thomas . . . (s)
33. Thomas, Jacob . . . (l)
34. Varner, Martin . . . (l)
35. Whitesides, James . . . (l)
36. Whitesides, William . . . (s)
37. Williams, John . . . (l)
38. Williams, Samuel M. . . . (l)
39. Williams, Solomon . . . (l)

The majority of *labores* in present Waller County (#40) were concentrated along the Brazos River, across from the town of San Felipe, so were the *labores* across the river in present Austin County to the north (#41) and the south of the town of San Felipe (#42).

Waller County

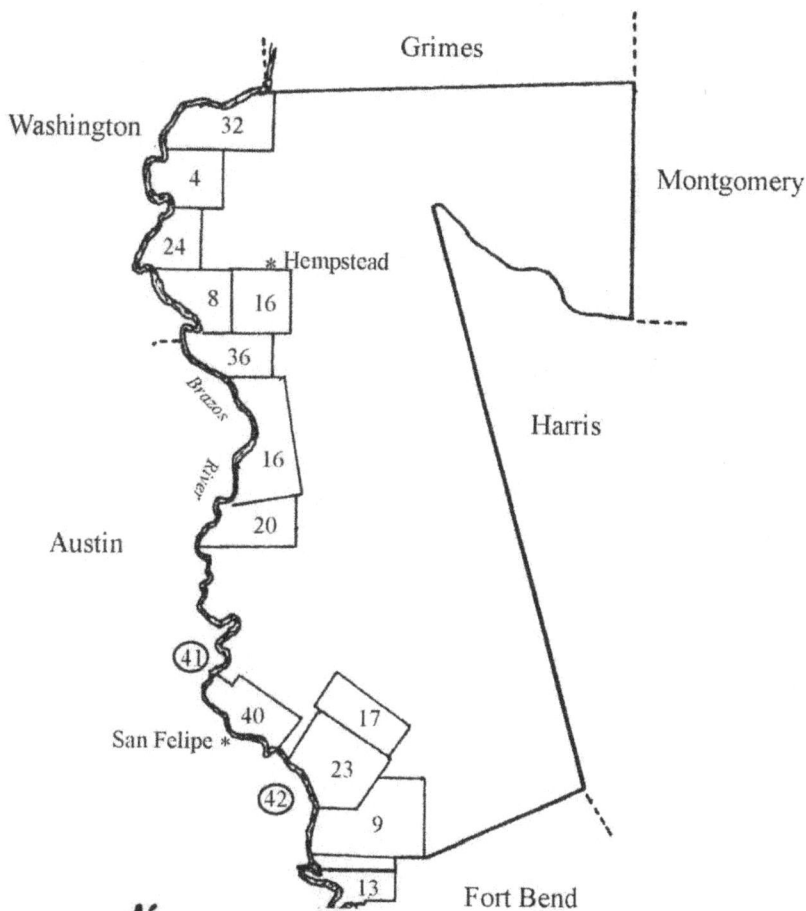

Grimes

Washington

32

4

24

* Hempstead

8

16

36

Brazos

River

16

20

Austin

41

40

17

San Felipe *

23

42

9

13

Fort Bend

Harris

Montgomery

N

W E

S

WMVM

Old Three Hundred grantees of a *sitio* (s) or a *labor* (l)
in Washington County

1. Allcorn, Elijah . . . (s)
2. Brown, William S. . . . (s)
3. Byrd, Micajah . . . (s)
4. Coles, Jno. P. . . . (s)
5. Gates, Samuel . . . (s)
6. Gates, William . . . (s)
7. Kerr, Willian . . . (s)
8. Kuykendall, A. . . . (s)
9. Lynch, James . . . (s)
10. Miller, Samuel . . . (s)
11. Miller, Samuel R. . . . (s)
12. Robinson, A. . . . (s)
13. Walker, James . . . (s)

Washington County

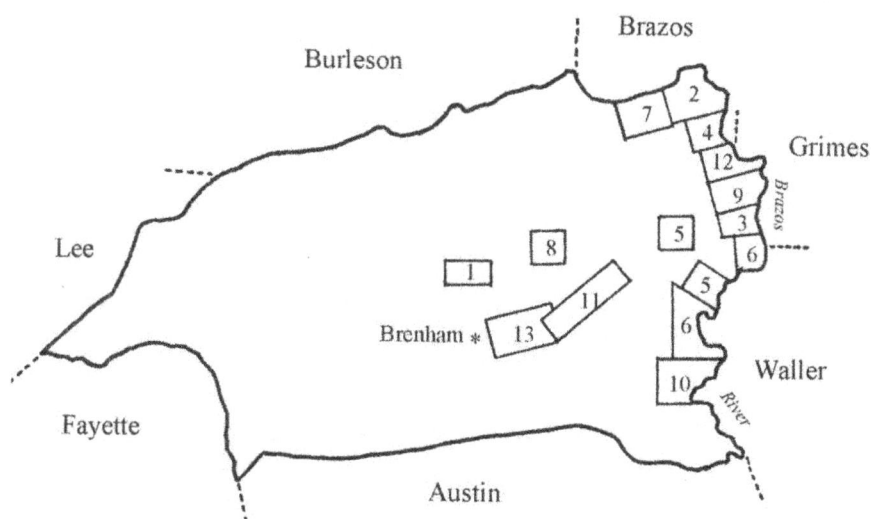

Brazos

Burleson

Grimes

7 2

4

12

9

5   3

6

Lee

8

1

5

11

6

Brenham *

13

10

Waller

Fayette

Austin

River

N

W   E

S

WMVM

Old Three Hundred grantees of a *sitio* (s) or a *labor* (l) in Wharton County

1. Allen, Martin . . . (s)
2. Austin, Estevan . . . (s)
3. Biggam, Fras . . . (s)
4. Castleman, Sylvenus . . . (s)
5. Clark, John C. . . . (s)
6. Crownover, John . . . (s)
7. Edwards, G. E. . . . (s)
8. Gilbert, Sarah . . . (s)
9. Hamilton, David . . . (s)
10. Hudson, C. S. . . . (s)
11. Huff, John . . . (s)
12. Huff, George . . . (s)
13. Hunter, Eli . . . (s)
14. Ingram, Seth . . . (s)
15. Jackson, Alexander . . . (s)
16. Jones, J. W. . . . (s)
17. Jones, R. . . . (s)
18. Kincheloe, William . . . (s)
19. Kuykendall, Robert . . . (s)
20. McKinsey, Hugh & John Smith . . . (s)
21. Newman, Joseph . . . (s)
22. Parker, Joshua . . . (s)
23. Pettus, William . . . (s)
24. Philips, I. B. . . . (s)
25. Rabb, Andrew . . . (s)
26. Rabb, Thomas J. . . . (s)
27. Scobey, Robert . . . (s)
28. Sims, Bartlet . . . (s)
29. Singleton, G. W. . . . (s)
30. Tumlinson, James . . . (s)
31. Westall, Thomas . . . (s)

Wharton County

Austin

San

Bernard

River

Colorado

Fort Bend

26

25

21

16

Colorado

River

5

19

2

2

18

2

15

29

24

9

8

1

28

12

17

30

13

22

11

Wharton

3

10

2

22

31

4

14

14

Brazoria

27

7

23

4

Jackson

6

20

Matagorda

N

W *E*

S

WMVM

Descendants of
Austin's
Old Three
Hundred

Each ancestor is listed in boldface,
followed by member name and number.
CODE: Supplement: S-1, S-2, S-3, etc.

ALCORN, ELIJAH
259	Alcorn, Audrey "Maxine"
799	Jackson, Charles Leonard
801	Keller, Carrie Lanette Jackson
802	Keller, Kelly Kyle
480	Konarik, Evelyn "June" Dworsky
439	Konarik, Larry Edwin
803	Kuhn, Holly Nannette Jackson
834	McLure, Sammy Ray
761	Rabel, Betty Joyce Bruno
820	Riley, Delbert Louis
443	Thomas, Jessie "Vera" Maddox

ALLEN, MARTIN
431	Allen, Arthur Charles, Jr.
744	Allen, Denny Ryan
453	Allen, Donald Sam
451	Allen, Donald Steven
595	Allen, Janette Louise
469	Allen, Troy Steven
444	Anderson, Kay Frances Allen
445	Anderson, Sheri Annette
66	Belt, Daryl Duckett
57	Belt, Walter Edwin, Jr.
152	Belt, Walter Edwin, III
68	Belt, William Jackson
15	Benton, Orville Russell
769	Bolte, Jan Ellen Rumsey Wimmer
104	Byars, Lottie Fay O'Rear
103	Chiodo, Cleatis Marie O'Rear
73	Coleman, George Howard, Jr.
72	Coleman, Lucille Rumsey
754	Franke, Lillie La Nora Underwood
2	Harrison, Katherine Allen
331	Jensen-Deign, Symantha Byars
801	Keller, Carrie Lanette Jackson
802	Keller, Kelly Kyle
803	Kuhn, Holly Nannette Jackson
69	Landers, Becky Jean Belt

487	McCorcle, Gary Edwin
446	Michulka, Jennifer Marie Allen
447	Michulka, Jonathan Miles
448	Penney, Laura Kay Michulka
756	Ruckman, Dorothea Ann Underwood
177	Rumsey, Wallace Lloyd
511	Strauss, William Frederick
4	Stucky, Dixie Dee Benton
510	Waggoner, Mary Helen Strauss
278	Woliver, Clarence Hugh, Jr., Col. Ret.
399	Woliver, David Allen
398	Woliver, Walter Hugh

ALSBURY, THOMAS, JR.
| 434 | Miller, Katherine Pearl Lentz |
| 374 | Whitaker, Delbert Walter |

ANDREWS, WILLIAM
188	Ballmer, Jonette Henson
83-S 1	Duncan, Rebecca Hargrove
58-S 2	Foster, Sam Weston, Jr.
67-S 1	Lubojacky, Stephen Hampton
244	Russell, Martha Jo Ballmer
234	Russell, Shelly Arlene

ANGIER, SAMUEL TUBBS
| 221 | Patton, James Donald |
| 220 | Patton, Nolia "Eugenia" Angier |

BAILEY, JAMES BRITTON
| 196-S 1 | Everts, George Bert |
| 400 | Kolber, Jeriann Whitcomb |

BARNETT, THOMAS
| 38 | Fuste, Annadeil Elliott Icet |

BARRET, WILLIAM
60	Hadley, Arthur Richard
59	Hadley, Audrey Merle Barrett
61	Hadley, William Melvin
328	Moore, Joyce Elaine Speer
62	Morgan, Deurene Oates
63	Morgan, Tracy Diane
329	O'Connell, JoAnn Speer
102	Speer, Louie Belle Barrett
64	Wray, Dana Michele

BEASON, BENJAMIN

243	Etheridge, Bernice Elizabeth Perry
484	Etheridge, Jodick Perry
251	Moeller, Joann Cecilia Perry
242	Wooten, Nancy Jane Perry
483	Wooten, Sarah Jane

BEST, ISAAC

277	Bader, Eddie "Wayne"
750	Blake, Charles Vernon
777	Blake, Kimberly Ann
804	Clow, Julia Frances Woodruff
819	Crouch, Anjuli Belle
818	Crouch, Charles Nelson
817	Crouch, Lisa Frances Wade
797	Crouch, William James
815	Drake, Sylvia Laureen Wade
743	Gann, Thomas H.
476	Hamilton, Odelle
800	Parker, Lois Mildred Dickerson
650	Spivey, Bessie Mae Westmoreland
793	Wade, Nelsyn Ernest
794	Wade, Timothy Caleb
798	Wade, William Alan
653	Westmoreland, Ocie Lee

BOATRIGHT, THOMAS

841	Carter, Beverly Gayle
555	Carter, Frankie Leland
842	Carter Gregory Alan
814	Carter, James Paul
840	Carter, Manny Monroe
743	Gann, Thomas Huey
461	McKelroy, Cecilia "Joy" Boatright
587	Scott, Sherrye "Eileen" Boatright
588	Scott, Shelby Erin

BRADLEY, EDWARD R.

274	Peters, Doris Letitia Harrison
476	Miller, Sylvia Seale
455	Waites, Jacquelyn Maurice Thompson

BREEN, CHARLES C.

| 417 | Corbin, Lillian Frances Smith |
| 380 | Jacobs, Julie Ann |

353	Jacobs, Louis Leo, Jr.
687	Jacobs, Louis Leo, III
336	Johnson, Sherrell Louise Smith
686	Maskas, Auba Sue Jacobs
632	Pool, Thomas Calton Smith
350	Puett, Sarah B. Jacobs
368	Smith, Thomas Calton
379	Sylvest, Sally Irene Jacobs
369	Taylor, Linda Gay Jacobs

BRIDGES, WILLIAM B.

342	McElhinney, Violet Ranne

BRIGHT, DAVID

23-S 1	Johnson, Donna Louise McCrosky

BROOKS, BLUFORD

631	Derksen, Richard Douglas

BURNAM, JESSE

28	Higginbotham, Sarah Russell Moss
26	Moss, Julia Nail
27	Moss, Janice Jordan

BYRD, MICAJAH

75	Howard, John Steven
762	Koch, Gwen Millicent Sorsby
316	Mock, Vivian Lin Pollard
263	Pollard, James Tris
151	Schmitz, Kathleen Howard
205	Sorsby, Kirk Morrow
191	Sorsby, William Frederick, Sr.

CALVIT, ALEXANDER

643	Lester, Mary Elizabeth Wheeler
266	Williams, Mary Elizabeth

CARTWRIGHT, THOMAS

13	Willhoite, Martha Lovellette

CASTLEMAN, SYLVANUS

132	Faul, Kathy Vee Woodham
557	Hereford, Charles Ray
699	Hereford, Gerri Lyn
711	Reed, Elizabeth Quirl
752	Schwebel, Patricia Weems Chesney

COLES, JOHN PRINCE

729	Appel, Mary Lou Gibson

755	Coles, Luanne Appel
825	Phillips, Mellinda Ramsey
824	Ramsey, Martha Elliott

CRIER, JOHN
696	Bailey, Karen Rose Thompson
229	Haecker, Mary Elizabeth Thompson
230	Haecker, Frank August, III
231	Hamilton, Lora Jane Thompson

CROWNOVER, JOHN
| 711-S 1 | Reed, Mary Elizabeth Quirl |

CUMINGS, REBEKAH RUSSELL
100	Cumings, Edward Nesbitt
429	Cumings, Kenneth
36	Cumings, Louis William, III, Rev.
18	Cumings, Timothy Austin
37	Cumings-Jordan, Christina Marie

CUMINGS, WILLIAM
| 5 | Hill, Guy Susan Cumings |

CUMMINS, JAMES
28-S 1	Higginbothem, Sarah R. Moss
23-S 3	Johnson, Donna Louise McCrosky
27-S 1	Moss, Janice Jorden
26-S 1	Moss, Julia Nail

CURTIS, JAMES, SR.
17	Callies, Georgia "Sue" Donovan
851	Chastain, Linda J.
16	Donovan, Dorothy D. Davis
325	Donovan, Eugene Patrick, III
326	Donovan, John Lyle Scott
852	Jacobs, Betty J.
185	Pettit, Helen Grace Grover
318	Reid, Charles Lee
21-S 1	Thomas, Corine Crossland

DeMOSS, CHARLES
425	DeMoss, Charles Fannin, III
779	Hunter, James Franklin
138	Sanders, Allen "Hardy"

DeMOSS, PETER
| 795 | Pope, Jack McCoy |
| 789 | Wynne, Ashley Diane Pope |

DUTY, JOSEPH
   65   McWhorter, Agnes McAnaney

DYER, CLEMENT C.
   294   Weatherly, Hazel "Inez" Heard

EDWARDS, GUSTAVUS EIXON
   806   Gustafson, Judith Ellon Stanford
   774   Herzer, Anna Beth Stanford
   807   Herzer-McKee, Ann Elizabeth
   805   Herzer, John Clifford

FISHER, JAMES
   709   Schoonover, Tony Ray

FITZGERALD, DAVID
   689   Bennett, Rebecca Ann Fenn
   665   Fenn, Jennifer Renee
   690   Fenn, Joanne Elizabeth
   664   Fenn, John Rutherford
   661   Fenn, John Rutherford, Jr.
   655   Fenn, Joseph Johnson, III
   673   Fenn, William Edward
   663   Joice, Susan Marie Fenn
   662   Neisig, Laura Kay Fenn
   666   Stamey, Mary "Elizabeth" Fenn

FLOWERS, ELISHA
   714   Miller, James Glenn, Jr.

FOSTER, JOHN
   607   Bowen, Michael James
   608   Bowen, Rick Allen
   630   Kelly, Mae Agnes Baker
   649   Mayes, Edward Eugene
   648   Menasco, Judy Eileen Mayes
   702   Parker, Ethan Gordon
   703   Parker, Jon Curtis
   704   Parker, Jon Ryan
   606   Paxson, Betty "Jo" Purvis
   614   Roberts, Dorothy Ernestine Foster
   463   Tharp, Dorothy Ruth Baker
   491   Utter, Bettie Mae Perkins
   462   Warnock, Barbara Ann Baker
   737   Zuckero, Victor Allen
   343   Zvolanek. Nadine Foster

FOSTER, RANDOLPH
50	Cowgill, Barbara Jean
48	Cowgill, Ralph Frederick "Fred"
47	Cowgill, Winnie Rhea Wroten
52	Edenfeld, Katrina Marie
51	Edenfeld, Susan E. Cowgill
58	Foster, Sam Weston, Jr.
49	Paulson, Carolyn Elaine Cowgill

FULSHEAR, CHURCHILL, Sr.
371	Inman, A. "Elizabeth" Johnson
473	Kipp, Jeffrey Layne
113	Kipp, John Emmette "Dick"
471	Kipp, Kenneth Wayne
472	Kipp, Michael Wayne

GATES, WILLIAM
118	Armstrong, Elizabeth Lacewell
147	Brooks, Thomas Sidney
173	Callaway, Oswald Elvan
280	Flores, Ricardo Nicolas
281	Holmes, Barbara Elizabeth Striegler
174	Johnston, Besta Callaway
279	Konkle, Margaret Amabel Flores
311	Konkle, Molly Esther
627	McCune, Frank Bates
292	McDavid, Carolyn Gates
189	Patton, Brett Lee
19	Truitt, Barton "Brent"
9	Truitt, Cynthia Lynn
8	Truitt, Dorothy L. Butler
10	Truitt, Robert Ralph, Jr.
20	Truitt, Stephen Patrick
282	Warford, Star Irene Striegler

GEORGE, FREEMAN
391	Hardy, Marshel Warren
625	McCullough, Jack Dennis, Jr.

GILBERT, SARAH
758	Bailey, Vivian Ann Smith
698	Ratcliff, Carla Hillman

GILLELAND, DANIEL
708	Abbe, Roberta Byrom
757	Davis, Chersie Delores Selfridge

475	Duncan, Faye Oma Darby
600	Fenton, Norma Carolyn Anders
208	Hale, Jamie Shawn
206	Hale, Manza Lewis, Sr.
207	Hale, Manza Lewis, Jr.
810	Holdridge, Billie Sue Cathey
846	Liles, Jakob Parker — **Junior Member**
252	Longmire, Lowell Kenneth
432	Scroggins, Lawrence Reginol
319	Scroggins, Lawrence "Richard"
745	Selfridge, Howard Dale
209	Shaw, Vanna Leigh Hale
767	Thompson, Kevin Paul

GORBET, CHESTER SPALDING

341	Maddox, David Thomas
276	Maddox, Frederick Andrew
297	Maddox, Larry Allen
210	Schorr, Hattie Norene Gorbet

GROCE, JARED ELLISON, II

467	Bennatte, Joe Michael
211	Groce, Mary Bethany
3	Kipp, Cheryl "Sissie" Bennette

HADDEN/HADDON, JOHN

775	Fontaine, Dianna Paige Sparks

HADDY, SAMUEL C.

426	Bowers, Johnanna Laxson
377	Boyd, Joanna "Jody" Vaughn Calvin
373	Calvin, Dea Bailey, Jr.
365	Calvin, Novella Vaughn
427	Hodge, Wilma Eunice Laxson
428	Jones, Nellie Velma Laxson
430	Laxson, John Henry, III
364	Marble, Ida "Carolyn" Calvin
375	Marble, Sanford Calvin
376	Marble, Stephen Theodore
378	Marble, Stuart Laxson
372	Thornton, Georgina Vaughan

HALL, GEORGE BRAXTON

482	Hall, Jody
479	Hall, Larry Joe
481	Jackson, Becki Laree Hall

HARRISON, GEORGE
324   Griffin, Zuleika Elizabeth Stanger

HODGE, ALEXANDER
283   Boyce, Billie "Jean" Butts
489   Burwell, Brownie Alice Neason
30   Crain, Marguerite Starr
384   Eason, Inez Sutherlin
289   Green, Angela Denice Spence
385   Rideout, Frances Sutherlin
25   Shaddix, Laverne Secrest
288   Spence, Patricia Ann Franks
490   Whitley, Lara Ann
416   Worrell, Frances Geraldine Kegans
287   Zschiesche, Mildred Rae Reed

HOLLAND, FRANCIS
617   Tate, Dorothy Nell Shepperd

HOLLAND, WILLIAM
602   Floyed, Brenda Arlene
603   Floyed, Homer Scott
604   Floyed, Todd Louis
601   Floyed, Virginia Louise Williams
611   Goodman, Terry Dell Hudson
613   Hudson, Michael Royce
612   Hudson, William Russell
615   Hurt, Bradley Royce
610   Hurt, Lynda Lynn Hudson
609   Tuck, Barbara Ann Williams Hudson

HOPE, JAMES
599   Cooley, Carolyn Lindley
390   Hightower, Colleen Ward

HUFF, GEORGE
442   Klussmann, Florine Clegg Robinson
440   Robinson, Joyce Gray Clegg
441   Snipes, Frances Alla Robinson

HUNTER, JOHNSON CALHOUN
293   Beyer, Julie Christine Johnston
337   Burnham, Suzanne L. Schoener
222   Dudley, Frances L. "Sita" Hood
314   Eddington, Robert Cagle
200   Hood, Doris Lenore Williford
240   Izzo, Dianne L. Schoener

347	Johnston, Harris Greg, Jr.
312	Johnston, Louis Earl
253	Johnston, Robert Thomas
245	Robertson, Eunice Earl Williford
197	Schoener, Dorothy L. Williford

ISAACS, SAMUEL
478	Gassett, Dorothy Reid Mathews
681	Inselmann, Mary Margaret Isaacs
55	Massingill, Tensie "Juanita" Taylor
264	Moczygemba, Betty Jane Isaacs
401	Verette, Mary Jane Moczygemba

JACKSON, ALEXANDER
707	Plageman, Laura Christine
706	Plageman, William Henry, Jr.
773	Plageman, Elizabeth Kimberly

JACKSON, ISAAC
388	Dotson, Desda "Diane"
383	Dotson, Joy Mellie Gooch
387	Hume, Gladys Mozelle Gooch
562	Nussman, Loretta Ann Inman

JONES, HENRY
403	Cline, Adoris "June" Nichols
162	Davis, Sydney Warren, Jr.
412	Feeny, Curtis Frederick
392	Feeny, Virginia Lee Nichols
409	Nichols, Curtis Stanley
402	Nichols, Elmer Lee
406	Nichols, James Curtis
161	Reading, Antoinette Davis

JONES, JAMES WALES
267	Antal, Laurie Ann Lee
722	Baugh, Eric Douglass
298	Bowen, Carol Jo Clark Baugh
34	Boyd, Melinda Lou Lee
190	Brawley, Harriett Elinda Jones
195	Carroll, Carl Bruce
183	Carroll, John Edward
168	Carroll, Katie Jones
184	Carroll, Nanci Lynn
269	Carroll, Sandra Annette
526	Ericson, Gertrude Francis Richardson

120	Hendershot, Patsy E. Jones
198	Hoff, Cynthia Sue Lee
268	Howell, Harry Newton, Jr.
130	Lee, Molly Rebecca Brawley
270	Weimer, Audrea Kay Carroll

JONES, RANDALL
83	Duncan, Rebecca Hargrove
101	Duntley, Sharon Ambrose
58-S 1	Foster, Sam Weston, Jr.
93	Thompson, Mary Jane Ford

KELLY, JOHN
| 647-S 1 | Wilson, Joe Darrell |

KINCHELOE, WILLIAM
| 700 | Harris, Louise Green |
| 774-S 1 | Herzer, Anna Beth Stanford |

KUYKENDALL, ABNER
370	Baggett, Jewell Sparks
345	Boyd, Gertrude Patrick
465	Coburn, Gail Erin Willson
616	Coburn, Kirk Brand
529	Drosihn, Eric Lee
642	Kuykendall, Albert Orien
827	Kuykendall, Gyanne
826	Kuykendall, Sidney Martin
346	Nichols, Bettye V. Patrick
381	Seaver, Sydney Dawn Holleman
92	Williams, Inez Kuykendall Napier
466	Willson, Don Eric
582	Willson, Gary Evan
565	Wyatt, Colin Frederick

KUYKENDALL, BARZILLAI
| 290 | Patrick, Orrell Lee, Col. Ret. |
| 320 | Patrick, Orrell Lee, Jr. |

KUYKENDALL, ROBERT H.
| 23-S 4 | Johnson, Donna L. McCrosky |
| 205 | Kuykendall, Marshall Early |

LEAKEY, JOEL
178	Armstrong, Evelyn Tompkins
338	Clark, Nelwyn Ruth Lakey
80	Foiles, Ruth Oleta Thompson

652	Giffin, Christopher Shane
811	Harris, Carolyn Rae Cook
780	Rachel, Mildred Louise Talley
31	Schuder, Vernon Marie Cleveland
82	Strickland, Tommie Jean Roach
784	Stubbs, Kenneth Franklin
785	Stubbs, Louis Dale
786	Stubbs, Mark Alan
781	Womack, Charissa Lynne Stubbs
782	Womack, Stephanie Dianne
783	Womack, Steven Eric

LITTLE, WILLIAM

181	Morgan, V. Lynne Scarborough
182	Murchison, Marie Scarborough
351	Scarborough, Alfred Young, Jr.
180	Scarborough, Bernard "Davis"
160	Scarborough, Virginia Wessendorff Davis

LYNCH, NATHANIEL

131	Keels, Flossie Stanley
155	Ray, Marjorie M. Stanley

MARSH, SHUBAEL

357	Coonly, Genevieve S. Hicks
356	Richey, Jean Elizabeth Hicks

McCORMICK, ARTHUR

534	Gaume, June McCormick

McCROSKY, JOHN

23	Johnson, Donna L. McCrosky
22	McCrosky, John "Voss"

McNEEL, DANIEL

305	Christian, Anna Lee McNeel
306	Christian, Lewis S., Jr.
250	Kyle, Kathleen Michelle McNeel
411	McNeel, John Marshall, III
366	McNeel, John "Marshall", VI
247	McNeel, Linea Ann, Dr.
367	McNeel, Michael "David"
246	McNeel, Synott Lance, Sr.
249	McNeel, Synott "Lance", Jr.
248	Rapp, Peggy Janice McNeel
768	Trippodo, Linda Sue Evers

McNEEL, JOHN
771   Noonan, Katherine Ann Thomas
772   Noonan, Patrick Murphy
770   Thomas, George Warren

MILLICAN, ROBERT
165   Curbello, Lon Felix, Jr.
679   Robinson, Mattilene Fay Brett
41   Rosson, Coleen Mozelle Snyder
42   Rosson, Joe Audie

MIMS, JOSEPH
739   Jones, Crawford Dow
847   Jones, Kellen McGovern — **Junior Member**
738   Jones, Mark Loring
735   Rhoads, Pamela Smith

MOORE, JOHN HENRY, SR.
145   Fisk, Gladys Aleen Wilie
355   Hale, M. Kathleen Fisk
23-S 2   Johnson, Donna L. McCrosky

MORTON, WILLIAM
442-S 1   Klussmann, Florine Clegg Robinson
440-S l   Robinson, Joyce Gray Clegg
441-S 1   Snipes, Frances Alla Robinson

MOUSER, DAVID
743-S l   Gann, Thomas Huey
650-S 1   Spivey, Bessie Mae Westmoreland
653-S 1   Westmoreland, Ocie Lee

NEWMAN, JOSEPH
746   Adams, Harriet Elaine Zirkle
838   Adams, Janna Renee
839   Adams, Rachelle Leigh
567   Anderson, Ada "Charlene" Bradford
541   Ball, Alvin Payne
146   Barron, Ferolee Joyce Newman
701   Bartley, N. Jeanne Seymore
684   Bewley, Vera Edith Wood
545-S 1   Bolen, Jeremy Andrew
544-S 1   Bolen, Kenny Lamar, Jr.
542   Bolen, Kenny Lamar, Sr.
546-S 1   Bolen, Nathaniel Paul
543-S 1   Bolen, Shelley Lee
578   Box, Cynthia "Diane" Weber

844	Box, Joel Craig
15	Braucht, Gladys Evelyn Newman
629-S 1	Brewer, Lynda Lois Hill
586	Butts, Craig Johnson
598	Butts, Danette Faye
585	Butts, Perry Kyle
548	Coker, Frances Dunn
574	Creek, Howard Eugene
533-S 1	Creek, Wayne Eugene
579	Davis, Rebecca Diane Box, Dr.
549	Dubose, Keith Dunn
449	Dubose, Mildred Evelyn Dunn
547	Dunn, Julia Matthew
577	Ferrill, Jimmie Yvonne Parker
522	Fink, Norma Jean Billings
626-S 1	Hausermann, Gayla Lynne Hill
561	Hull, Billie Jean Caruthers
837	Leinen, James Robert
718	Mauer, Brian Keith
697	Mauer, David Ray
715	Mauer, David Ray, Jr.
717	Mauer, Heather Christine
716	Mauer, Randall Keith
539-S 1	Moore, Carol Kuester
116	Newman, Coleman Conway
143	Newman, Nicholas Conway
239	Newman, William Green
156	Newman, William "Ivan", Dr.
531-S 1	Rickey, Dorothy Matthew
724	Riedlinger, April Denise Wood
836	Ruecker, Margaret Ann Chapman
705	Seymore, Edna Maxine Wood
692	Sharpe, Kimberly Michelle Wood
605	Sievers, Uvalda Jo Kubala
688	Smith, Cynthia Marie
685	Stevens, Daniel Wayne
525	Turner, Patty Newman
674	Walker, Sandra Maxine Bewley
583	Wallace, Mamie Ethelyn Parker
494-S 1	Wauer, Betty Newman
580	Weber, Robbie J. Hattenbach
731-S 1	Weddle, Jay Edward

730-S 1	Weddle, Jodie Lyn
732-S 1	Weddle, Jon Perry
520-S 1	Weddle, Joseph Edward
519-S 1	Weddle, William Leland
778	White, Pamela Jean
228	Wood, Arthur Vernon
725	Wood, Brian Hollis
313	Wood, Gary Lynn
726	Wood, Kyle Patrick
727	Wood, Megan Elise
691	Wood, William Bruce

PENTECOST, GEORGE SAMUEL

359	Barrett, Wanda Ellen Brown
85	Beard, Amelia Josephine
86	Beard, Bonnie Ruth
457	Beard, David Ralph
84	Beard, Sidney Bertran
88	Beard, Sidney Bertran, III
89	Beard, Tommy Andrew
423	Bell, Kenneth Russell
422	Bell, Sally Joe Brumbelow
354	Bell, Verner Lee
219	Bhatti, Clarlyn Ruth Brown
150	Boring, Patricia Marlene Kennelly
109	Bowles, Carla Sue Goldsmith
317	Boyd, Thurmond Roger
216	Brown, Clarence McFarlane
217	Brown, Doran Lamar
360	Brown, Gary Wade
169	Brown, Glenn
358	Brown, James Wade
218	Brown, Joel Denton
382	Brown, Thurmond Arnold
424	Brumbelow, Patricia Glenn
421	Brumbelow, Russell Sage
395	Callender, Doyle Gene
454	Callender, John Kennelly
394	Callender, John Randall
408	Callender, Kyle Jenkins
393	Callender, Thelma Florene Kennelly
135	Carter, Annie Lorine Weakley
225	Coffin, Jessie Carolyn Kitchen

456	Filla, Austine Beard
590	Galpin, Marjorie Elizabeth Beard
108	Goldsmith, Duff Marshall
105	Goldsmith, Jo Evelyn Brumbelow
362	Guajardo, Linda Kay Kennelly
149	Haas, Rebecca Shirlene Kennelly
87	Junker, Rebecca Lee Beard
361	Kennelly, Andrew Jackson
349	Kennelly, Clyde Brown, Judge
153	Kennelly, Sallie Brown
148	Kennelly, Shirley Thurmond
223	Kitchen, Edda Mae Brown
227	Kitchen, Edward Jackson
224	Kitchen, George Allen
656	Kitchen, Sarah Caroline M.
538	Lewis, George Russell
407	Lindsay, Cambrey Dori
396	Lindsay, Connie Gail Callender
67-S 2	Lubojacky, Stephen Hampton
110	Miksch, Marian Gay Goldsmith
241	Moore, Iva Naomi Brown
796	Morgan, Kristin Dawn Beard
136	Powell, Charlotte Fay Weakley
262	Roberts, Dorothy "Sue" Boyd
226	Roberts, Tammy Lynn Coffin
171	Robinson, Diana P. Brown
106	Roehling, Sherry Ann Goldsmith
468	Rogers, Alton Gayle
474	Rogers, Gary Zeno
170	Saman, Glenda Kay Brown
581	Saman, Ronda Kay
107	Schneider, Donna Goldsmith
154	Skinner, Jessie Mae Kennelly
137	Weakley, Grace Truet Brumbelow
134	Weakley, Grace Truet Brumbelow

PETTUS, WILLIAM

321	Cohn, M. Lee Pettus
323	Pettus, June
291	White, Ruth Elizabeth "Beth"

PHELPS, JAMES AENEAS

235	Renaud, Aristide Frederick, Jr.

PICKET, PAMELA
751   Staton, Augustus Lee, III

POLLEY, JOSEPH HENRY
196   Everts, George Bert
233   Everts, Michael Lea

PRYOR, WILLIAM
734   Baker, Jana Sue Scott
66-S 1   Belt, Daryl Ducket
57-S 1   Belt, Walter Edwin, Jr.
152-S 1   Belt, Walter Edwin, III
68-S 1   Belt, William "Jackson"
568   Clanton, John Leonard
303   Ditta, Doris Elizabeth Belt
721-S 1   Ford, Joan Katherine Segars
39-S 1   Kerr, Rita Lee Roberts
69-S 1   Landers, Becky Jean Belt
275   Marosko, Mary Kathleen "Kitty" Belt
302   Marosko, Ronald Jon, Jr.
594   Roberts, Byron B.
493-S 1   Palmiter, Jana Lynn Roberts
816-S 1   Roberts, Brillani Lauran
488-S 1   Roberts, James Edgar, III
505-S 1   Roberts, James Edgar, IV
668   Roberts, Monty Sha
736   Scott, David Stuart
651   Scott, Jerry Lou Segars
765-S 1   Scott, Randel Brian
733   Scott, Stephen Clayton
309   Smith, Evelyn Mae Tubbs
285-S 1   Smith, Pamela Lynne Smith
284-S 1   Smith, Shirley W. Segars
286-S 1   Smith, Sue Ann
463-S 1   Tharp, Dorothy Ruth Baker
308   Vaughn, Betty Jo Huddleston
310   Ware, Evelyne Ann

RABB, JOHN
129   Rabb, Lillian Bell
560-S 1   Ranne, Edna "Frances" Rabb

RABB, THOMAS J.
114   Wegenhoft, Victor C., Col. Ret.

RABB, WILLIAM

701	Bartley, Norma Jean Seymore
545	Bolen, Jeremy Andrew
544	Bolen, Kenny Lamar, Jr.
542-S 1	Bolen, Kenny Lamar, Sr.
546	Bolen, Nathaniel Paul
542	Bolen, Shelly Lee
813	Bowles, John Laton
812	Bowles, Linda Kay Bewley
629	Brewer, Lynda Lois Hill
533	Creek, Wayne Eugene
641	Daniels, Mildred Mattie Vaughan
626	Hausermann, Gayla Lynne Hill
634	Hodge, Penelope Louise Petch
539-S 1	Moore, Carol Kuester
498	Nichols, Barry Stewart
496	Nichols, Bradford Eugene
497	Nichols, Charles Brent
495	Nichols, William Wade
633	Petch, Kathryn Meyer
635	Petch, William Grant
172	Philips, Irene Elsie Tutschke
552	Rabb, Jennifer Christine
563	Rabb, Russell Carl
550	Rabb, Sam Warren Jr.
553	Rabb, Sam Warren Sr.
551	Rabb, Scott Warren
554	Raines, Lorene Newman
560	Ranne, Edna "Frances" Rabb
214	Reedy, Felicity Ann Robinson
531	Rickey, Dorothy Matthew
213	Robinson, Mark Edward
705	Seymore, Edna Maxine Wood
504	Smith, Catherine Munson
575	Smith, Lula Bella Kirkland
573	Stringfellow, Kimberly Dianne Elzen
525-S 1	Turner, Patty Newman
494	Wauer, Betty Newman
731	Weddle, Jay Edward
730	Weddle, Jodie Lyn
732	Weddle, Jon Perry
520	Weddle, Joseph Edward

| 519 | Weddle, William Leland |
| 486 | Young, Jo Ann Munson |

ROARK, ELIJAH
460	Craft, Juanita Kay Stark Grogan
452	Drake, Daniel Dwight
272	Drake, Doris A. Ballard
418	Garito, Juliette Anne LeBaron
713	Gill, Marville Bruce
419	Odem, Joyce Ann Moore
435	Slagle, Karen Dianne Drake

ROBBINS, WILLIAM
55	Becker, Nanetta Key (Burkholder)
658	Joiner, Duwaine Keith
646	Joiner, Virginia Ann Pearse
12	Keatts, Orton Gobern "Alex"
654	Watson, Peggy Lee Smith

ROBERTS, ANDREW
| 822 | Speed, Melissa Carol |

ROBERTS, NOEL FRANCIS
734	Baker, Jana Sue Scott
721	Ford, Joan Katherine Segars
39	Kerr, Rita Lee Roberts
493	Palmiter, Jana Lynn Roberts
816	Roberts, Brillani Lauran
594	Roberts, Byron B.
488	Roberts, James Edgar, III
505	Roberts, James Edgar, IV
492	Roberts, Lee Roy
668	Roberts. Monty Sha
736	Scott, David Stuart
651	Scott, Jerry Lou Segers
765	Scott, Randel Brian
733	Scott, Stephen Clayton
285	Smith, Pamela Lynne Smith
284	Smith, Shirley Wilma Segars
286	Smith, Sue Ann

ROBERTS, WILLIAM
| 628 | Wilmeth, John Robert |
| 570-S 1 | Wright, LaNell Lee Moses |

ROBINSON, GEORGE
| 710 | Griffin, Carolyn Crenshaw |

SCOBEY, ROBERT
113-S 1   Kipp, John Emmette "Dick"

SCOTT, JAMES
127   Boaz, Wanda Josephine Smith
126   Durham, Willie Mae Scott
117   Halbert, Katherine "Esther" Smith

SCOTT, WILLIAM
584   Fisher, Ida Marie Davis

SELKIRK, WILLIAM
843   Triplett, Georganna Hastings

SHIPMAN, DANIEL
192-S 1   Cunningham, Helen Irma Shipman
193-S 1   Frost, Carolyn Frances Cunningham
194-S 1   Nichol, Susan J. Cunningham
647   Wilson, Joe Darrell

SHIPMAN, MOSES
192   Cunningham, Helen Irma Shipman
193   Frost, Carolyn Frances Cunningham
194   Nichol, Susan J. Cunningham
647-S 1   Wilson, Joe Darrell

SIMS, BARTLETT
258   Allen, Lelia Sue Suthers
128   Moore, Joyce Jeane Avery
254   Ramp, Al'Louise Suthers
255   Ramp, Susan Lynn
256   Sturgeon, Karlyn "Beth" Ramp
257   Suthers, Gwendoline Lenoir Robinson
21   Thomas, Corine Crossland

SINGLETON, GEORGE WASHINGTON
433   Fox, Vera "Dee" Morris Smith

SINGLETON, PHILIP
112   Anders, Donald Ray
119   Anders, James Wyatt
111   Anders, Victor Henry, Jr.
260   Caffall, Thomas Henry "Jack"
261   Caffall, Thomas Henry, III
572   Conner, Priscilla Marie Lambert
78   Domingue, Dorothy Oates
90   Evans, Ann Eulalie Oates
749   Johnson, Erwin Wayne

124	Kauffman, Ellen Kay Stedman
742	Lambert, Angela Rae
741	Lambert, Christopher James
740	Lambert, Jimmy Ray
597	Leskovjan, Marjorie Ann Thacker
636	Murdock, Ruth Marie Martin
720	Murdock, Dennis Hugh
79	Oates, Marion Arietta
33	Owens, Bertha Luella Oates
81	Owens, Ruby Leona Oates
53	Stedman, Shirley J. Hanagriff
123	Stedman, Wyatt Kendall
91	Stewart, Marguerite Faye Oates
596	Tanoos, Carol Ruth Thacker

SMITH, CHRISTIAN

140	Blanton, Rosedawn Wilbourn
527	Keith, Arleta Bowles
517	Luther, Marilyn Clair Roeller
518	Luther, Paul Thomas
142	May, Rose Mae Shannon
176	McBee, Charles Douglas, Jr.
528	Monahan, Douglas
141	Wilbourn, Evelyn M. Shannon

SMITH, CORNELIUS

| 139 | Henderson, Iantha "Maxine" Moses |
| 570 | Wright, LaNell Lee Moses |

SMITHERS/SMOTHERS/SMEATHERS, WILLIAM

764	Cassity, Chism Wayne
835	Cassity, Crockett Wayne
763	Cassity, Darlyn Marnell Lyne
759	Lyne, Betty Joyce Upchurch
591	Montgomery, Pricilla Ann Lucas
683	Robinson, Tina Janine Upchurch
589	Skrobarcek, Lillie Mae Cheney
675	Upchurch, Tara Jean
670	Upchurch, Travis J., Jr.
676	Upchurch, Travis Justin

STAFFORD, ADAM

| 215-S 1 | Campbell, Wincie Marie Chenault |
| 238-S 1 | Chenault, Marie Estell Clark |

STAFFORD, WILLIAM JOSEPH
845   Borden, Guy, Jr.
215   Campbell, Wincie Marie Chenault
238   Chenault, Marie Estell Clark
671   Hazelwood, Gail Borden Gumm
677   Hazelwood, Mary Elizabeth

TEEL, GEORGE WASHINGTON
693   Marshall, Sarah Jane
821   Sharp, Valerius Henry, Jr.

THOMAS, EZEKIEL
386   Francis, Blanche Nell Peters Tevis

THOMPSON, JESSE
334   Campbell, Linda Joy Wilkerson
831   Cook, Cornelia Thompson Bailey
833   Cook, David Loch
832   Cook George Thompson
125   Lubojacky, Jo Ann Bailey
 67   Lubojacky, Stephen Hampton
121   McDowell, Lisa Carol Lubojacky
163   Smith, Frances Cornelia Thompson
327   Van Ordstrand, Alice Virginia Thompson

TUMLINSON, ELIZABETH PLEMMONS
212   Autry, John Franklin
848   Barta, Myrtle Earlene Smithey
849   Barta, Wilma Lee Smithey
354   Bell, Verner Lee
645   Bell, Bert Lee
776   Bell, Herman Lee
158   Blakeway, Annette Tumlinson
657   Bolstad, Jane Alice Bell
508   Brown, James Michael
 24   Cammack, Ruth Estelle Reed
175   Dent, Margaret Gould
592   Edmondson, Della Louise Reichert
300   Haddon, Joyce Ann Reimschissel
307   Hall, Sally Patricia Carr
521   Hardy, Marjorie Mae Moss
115   Harkey, Joyce Annette Carr
 74   Hays, Nadine Frances Dees
620   Jeffries, Phyllis Ann Reichert
559   John, Elena Josephine

723	John, Philip James, Jr.
618	John, Zora Elizabeth Sheehy
719	King, Marilyn Sue Dyal
133	Kirkscey, Bena Ray Taylor
850	Light, Sandra Kay Barta
537	Lowther, Georgia Catherine Vann
187	McCauley, Constance Joy Stark
159	Meine, Vina Mae Tumlinson
464	Moore, Charlsie Mae English
485	Murdock, Sammie Lee
540	Pittman, Ellen Joyce Simpson
523	Pollard, Edwin Lloyd, Jr.
524	Pollard, Stephen Alan
621	Reichert, Brad Alan
619	Reichert, Lester Dee
622	Reichert, Ryan Scott
301	Reimschissel, Charlie Hugo, Jr.
470	Reimschissel, David Wayne
299	Reimschissel, Mary Louise Acord
179	Sucke, Mary Winthrop Warren
564	Upton, Michael Wayne
500	Upton, William Travis
506	Wheeless, Georgia Mae Winn
507	Winn, Charles Thomas

TUMLINSON, JAMES

335	Blackstone, Sandra Deanne Cain
348	Clayton, Sharron Dianne Cain

WALKER, JAMES, SR.

660	Blount, Robert Earl
450	Boothe, Ruby "Marie" Lindsey
624	Burton, Irene Elizabeth Walker
680	Burton, William Edward
201	Creel, Georgia Jane Grubb
295	Davis, Betty Sue Walker
830	Davis, Darren Ray
828	Davis, Rhonda Ann
265	Hale, June Panton
203	Holmes, Ada Eleanor Johnson
669	Johnson, Barbara Ann Blount
204	Johnson, Lloyd Seamon
499	Johnson, Norma Louise Lindsey
296	Love, Gladys Marie Walker

566	Miller, Irma Geraldine Brannan
199	Ramsey, Charlie Glen Johnson
728	Simpson, Don Ray
436	Simpson, Vera Oleta Lindsey
678	Smith, Sterling Henry
202	Smith, Zenda Ruth Johnson
271	Thacker, Marilyn Ruth Walker
459	True, Ina Mozelle Walker
659	Vavra, Martha "Lou" Simpson Davis
829	Watson, Leah Carol Davis
569	Wilkinson, Winona Ruth Moorhead
623	Wright, Floryne Elaine Walker

WALLACE, CALEB
808	Freeman, Joann Ivie
792	McClellan, Andrew Lindsay
787	McClellan, Betty Sue Ivie Weaver
823	Smith, Mary Jean
791	Weaver, Brenton Neil
790	Weaver, Howard Randal

WELLS, FRANCIS FLOURNOY
515	Byrd, David Harold, III
514	Byrd, Roberta Adele Brackenridge Menger
516	Caruth, Adele Leigh
513	Caruth, Owene Brackenridge Peeler Crutcher Menger
512	Menger, Johnowene Brackenridge Peeler Crutcher

WESTALL, THOMAS
766	Wells, Gaynell Tinsley

WHITE, AMY COMSTOCK
167	Bruce, Thomas Howard
166	Bruce, William Thomas, Jr.
46-S 1	Maxfield, Rose "Mary" Stiarwalt
144	Purdy, Catherine C. Bruce
40	White, Gifford E.

WHITE, WILLIAM C.
751	Staton, Augustus Lee, III

WHITESIDE/S, WILLIAM B.
788	Chojecki, Traci Caroline Pittard

WHITLOCK, WILLIAM
315	Blair, Mary Patricia "Pat" Maxfield
695	Martinez, Carole Stiarwalt

99   Maxfield, Mary Constance "Connie

46   Maxfield, Rose "Mary" Stiarwalt 3

97   Weibruch, Marilyn Joan Maxfield

WILLIAMS, SAMUEL MAY

322   Harghman, Walter Neill, Jr.

WILLIAMS, THOMAS

576   Amerine, Irva "Luella" Williams

570   Elliott, Mable Josephine Wilkerson

644   Evans, Nancy Louise Peltier

682   Hammond, Amy Katherina Williams

760   Hammond, William Charles, Jr.

672   Keegan, Ruby Mae Carr

639   Peltier, Barbara Ann Williams

532   Rusk, Betty Joe Ray

638   Seibert, Albert Frank, Jr.

637   Seibert, Cecelia Ruth Williams

712   Seibert, Eric Karl

640   Wilbeck, Dorothy Frances Williams

593   Williams, Bradford Irving, Jr.

WOODS, ZADOCK

558   Allred, Jane Lynne Deason

389   Baker, M. Lounell Wagoner

236   Bell, Neva Frances Harrell

11   Brantley, Harold Clayton, Sr.

97   Brinson, Karen E. Roach

414   Crowl, Leesa Ellen Hahn

410   Davies, Elizabeth Brantley Durha

536   Deason, Jay Warren

556   Deason, Jeff Timothy

535   Deason, Marian (Mary) Maxine Duderstadt

419   Durham, Andrew David

164   Durham, David Ross

404   Durham, Marshall Pershing, Jr.

405   Durham, Wendy Hanks

94   Durham, Zoie Avanell Brantley

363   Elgin, Laurinda Rae Hall Thomas

340   Frazier, Joel Edward

415   Hahn, Anson Justin

413   Hahn, Jack Burton

122   Hall-Little, Marianne Elizabeth Hall

35   Harrell, Hollis R.

70	Harrison, Virginia R. Niemeier
45	Harvey, Elizabeth Nuinez
232	Hatcher, Mary Joyce Mobley
557	Hereford, Charles Ray
503	Hill, Ann Glimp
34	Isley, Doris Lee Niemeier
437	Koehl, Rose Olivia Gilliam
98	Laing, Leslie Carol Roach
501	Lewis, Doris Glimp
237	McGuigan, Alma "Fern" Green
76	Moore, Linda Carolyn Ralls
694	Mullens, Amanda
753	Mullens, Christina
502	Mullens, Diane Lewis
33	Niemeier, Rose Block
438	Norton, Patsy Loyce Ann Gilliam
44	Nuinez, Joe Edward, Jr.
43	Nuinez, Tommie Spellman
32	Parr, Reed Brantley
458	Pass, Sharon Fredericka Baker
77	Reinecke, Lillian C. Mueller
95	Roach, Andrew Jackson
186	Saulnier, Amy Ann Brown
71	Schendel, Beth Ann Niemeier
273	Tidwell, M. "Jean" Brantley
96	Waxman, Andrea S. Roach
339	Williams, Dinah Lee Frazier
530	Woods, Ronald Roy
54	Woolsey, Elnora Frazier

Index

Also refer to Bugbee's Old Three Hundred List and Descendants of Austin's Old Three Hundred for additional names; **bold** *numbers denote pictures and land grant maps.*

A

Adcock, Elisha M., 96
Adcock, Rebecca (Mrs. Robert Scobey), 96
Alamo, Battle of the, 9
Allcorn, Elijah, **192**, **202**, **204**
Allen, Benjamin, 3
Allen, Elizabeth Vice, 3
Allen, James Bud, 3
Allen, Katherine, 3
Allen, Martin, 3, **180**, **206**
Allen, Miles N., 3
Allen, Nancy (Mrs. Samuel Isaacks), 57
Allen's Creek, 3
Alley, John, 17, **190**, **198**
Alley, Rawson, **184**, **188**
Alley, Thomas, **182**
Alley, William, **182**
Almanac, 108
Almonte, ——, Colonel, 119
Alsbury, Charles G., 4, 5, **182**
Alsbury, Harvey, 4, 5, **182**
Alsbury, Horace A., 4, 5, **182**
Alsbury, Juana Navarro, 5
Alsbury, Leah Jane Catlett, 6
Alsbury, Thomas, 4, 5, 6, **192**, **202**
Alsbury, Young Perry, 5
Anahuac, Battle of, 7, 35, 101
Anahuac Expedition, 65
Anders, John Demostinie, 46
Anderson, S. A., **190**
Anderson, Thankful (Mrs. Jonathan Whiteside), 125
Andrews, Elizabeth, 7
Andrews, John, 164, **184**, **188**, **190**, **202**
Andrews, Joseph Zabulon, 7
Andrews, Mary Ann, 7
Andrews, Micah, 7
Andrews, Pamelia, 7
Andrews, Richard, 7
Andrews, Susan, 7, 65

Andrews, Susan Clark, 7
Andrews, Walter, 7
Andrews, William, 7, 57, 65, **192**
Andrews, William Alexander, 7
Angier, Eugene Luther, 8
Angier, Mary Ann Kendall, 8
Angier, Mary O'Brien Millard, 8
Angier, Pamelia Picket, 8
Angier, Samuel Tubbs, 8, **182**
Austin, Estevan (*see* Austin, Stephen F.)
Austin, J.E.B. "Santiago," **182**
Austin, John, 63, **182**, **196**
Austin, Moses, 87
Austin, Stephen F., iii, xiii, 6, 7, 9, 10, 20, 21, 22, 25, 26, 34, 36, 41, 43, 52, 65, 67, 68, 72, 74, 76, 77, 81, 87, 90, 99, 101, 105, 111, 123, 127, **182**, **206**
Autrey, Russell, xv

B

Bader, Eddie Wayne, 13
Bailey, Elizabeth, 9
Bailey, James, 9
Bailey, James Britton "Brit," 8, 9, 87
Bailey, Kenneth, 9
Bailey, Mary "Pollie," (Mrs. Joseph Henry Polley), 9, 87
Bailey, Nancy, 9
Bailey, Phelps, 9
Bailey, Smith, 9
Baily, James B., **182**
Balis/Bayliss, Daniel E., **200**
Ball, V., 34
Ballmer, Jonette Henson, 7
Baker, Temperance (Mrs. Jesse Burnam), 19
Baker, Susannah (Mrs. Elisha Flowers), 36
Barnett, Thomas, **192**
Barnhill, Elizabeth (Mrs. Alexander Elliott), 52
Barratt, William, **192**
Barret, Elizabeth (Mrs. Reuben Weir), 11
Barret, Elizabeth Wiant, 11
Barret, Thomas William, 11
Barret, William, 11

Bartlet, J., 122
Bastrop, Baron de, x, 7, 16, 18, 25, 88, 93, 123, 128
Battle, M. M., **200**
Battle, Mills M., **192**
Bayliss/Balis, Daniel E., **200**
Bays, Joseph, 103
Beard, Andrew Jackson, 84
Beard, James, 11
Beard, Mrs. Sidney B., 84
Beard, Sara "Sally" Pentecost, 84
Beard, Sidney, 84
Beale, Martha Jones, 65
Beard, James, **192**
Beason, Abel, 12
Beason, Benjamin, 12, **184**, **188**
Beason, Collins, 12
Beason, Edward, 12
Beason, Elizabeth, 12
Beason, Leander, 12
Beason, Lydia, 12
Beason, Mary Ann, 12
Beason, Nepsey, 12
Belknap, Charles, **192**
Bell, J. H., 63, **182**
Bell, Sally Brumbelow, 84
Bell, Thomas B., **182**
Berry, M., **192**
Berry, Manders, **200**
Best, Ebenezer W. "Eben," 13
Best, Humphrey, 13
Best, Isaac, 13, **202**
Best, John, 13
Best, Margaret "Peggy," 13
Best, Mary Margaret Wilkins, 13
Best, Mary "Polly," 13
Best, Phoebe, 13
Best, Sarah Humphrey, 13
Best, Sarah "Sally," 13
Best, Stephen, 13
Best, Stephen, Jr., 13
Betts, Jacob, **200**
Bexar, Siege of, 5, 16, 30, 47, 75, 97
Biggam, Fras, **182**, **202**, **206**
Billingsley, Jesse, 29, 30
Blakely, Mary L. (Mary Foster), 41
Bloodgood, William, **196**
Boatwright, Amy Rushing, 14, 46

Boatwright, Friend, 14
Boatwright, Pricilla (Mrs. Daniel Gilleland), 14
Boatwright, Richard, 14
Boatwright, Thomas, Sr., 46
Boatwright, Thomas, 14, 68, **180**
Bolstad, Jane Alice Bell, 121
bond marriage, *see* marriage bond
Boone, Daniel, 15
Borden, Thomas, **182**
Bostic, Caleb, 129, **200**
Bowie, James, 5, 53
Bowman, John T., **200**
Bradburn, Juan Davis, 101
Bradbury, Hannah (Mrs. Micajah Byrd and Mrs. James Gray)
Bradley, Edward, 15
Bradley, Edward R., 15, **182**
Bradley, Elizabeth Winn, 15
Bradley, John, **182**
Bradley, Molly Duncan, 15
Bradley, Sarah (Mrs. Archeleus B. Dodson), 15
Bradley, Thomas, 15
Bradley, Thomas W., 8, **182**
Breen, Calton N., 16
Breen, Charles C., 16, **182**
Breen, Christopher, 16
Breen, Hannah Elizabeth (Mrs. John Knox Payne), 16
Breen, Martha, 16
Breen, Mary, 16
Brias/Reels, Patrick, **196**
Bridges, Amanda, 17
Bridges, Carrie, 17
Bridges, Cynthia Ross, 17
Bridges, Eliza Lyons Tribble, 17
Bridges, Elizabeth, 17
Bridges, Harriet, 17
Bridges, John, 17
Bridges, Martha, 17
Bridges, Mary, 17
Bridges, Sophronoa, 17
Bridges, William, 17, **198**
Bridges, William B., Jr., 17
Brigham, Asa, 85
Bright, David, 18, 78, **180**, **192**

Bright, Elizabeth (Mrs. Noel Roberts), 18
Bright, George, 18
Bright, George Adam, 18
Bright, Haney (Mrs. Thomas Jamison), 18
Bright, Judith, 78
Bright, Judith Dinsmore, 18
Bright, Mary (mother of David), 18
Bright, Mary (Mrs. Gabriel Straw Snider, Mrs. Patrick Reels), 18
Bright, Sarah Ann (Mrs. Eli Hunter, Mrs. John McCrosky, Mrs. William D. Lacey), 18, 78
Bringas, Juan, 70
Brinson, Enoch, **196**
Brotherton, Robert, **200**
Brown, George, **192**
Brown, John, **196**, **202**
Brown, William S., **204**
Bruce, Robert, 9
Buckner, Aylett C., 104, **200**
Buena Vista, Battle of, 5
Burks, J. D., 122
Burleson, Edward, 11
Burnam, Adelia Lee, 19
Burnam, Alice, 19
Burnam, Amanda, 19
Burnam, Emily Maria, 19
Burnam, Henry, 19
Burnam, Hickerson, 19
Burnam, James H., 19
Burnam, Jesse, 19, 24, **184**, **188**, **190**
Burnam, Jesse Bennett, 19
Burnam, John, 19
Burnam, Mary, 19
Burnam, Minerva, 19
Burnam, Nancy, 19
Burnam, Nancy Cummins Ross, 19
Burnam, Sadie Ellen, 19
Burnam, Temperance Baker, 19
Burnam, Waddy Linsecum, 19
Burnam, William, 19
Burnet, David G., 12, 70, 75
Burnet, Pumphrey, **200**
Burney, William, 54
Byrd, Hannah Bradbury (Mrs. James Gray), 20

Byrd, Micajah, 20, **204**
Byrd, Nancy, 20

C
Caldwell, Nancy (Mrs. George W. Teel), 117
Calliham, Morris "Moses" A., 118, **196**
Callihan, Susan Haddy, 51
Calloway, Samuel, 73
Calvit, Alexr., **182**, **202**
Campbell III, A. T., xv
Campbell, James P., 85
Campbell, Wincie Chenault, xv, 33, 113, 115
Carey, W. R., 53
Carpenter, David, **196**
Carson, William C., **182**
Carter, Frankie Leland, 14
Carter, Highley (Mrs. Noel Francis Roberts), 93
Carter, Saml., **182**
Cartwright, Jesse H., **192**, **198**
Cartwright, Martha (Mrs. William Stafford), 115
Cartwright, Thomas, **180**, **184**, **188**
Castleman, Benjamin, 21
Castleman, Elizabeth "Betsy" Lucas, 21, 25
Castleman, Jacob, 21
Castleman, Lavena, 21
Castleman, Lavinia Crownover, 25
Castleman, Nancy (Mrs. John Chesney Crownover), 21
Castleman, Sarah Brown, 21, 25
Castleman, Sylvanus, 21, 25, **180**, **190**, **206**
Cavanah, Charles, 36
census, 3, 16, 18, 20, 26, 28, 29, 43, 45, 47, 55, 58, 59, 61, 66, 68, 75, 76, 82, 85, 91, 93, 94, 95, 96, 106, 108, 109, 110, 118, 119, 124, 125, 126, 128
Chance, Samuel, **182**
Charles, Isaac N., **182**
Charlotte (servant to Jackson family), 58
Chojecki, Doug, 125, 126, 127
Chojecki, Traci, 125, 126, 127

Chriesman, Horatio, 18, 20, 67, 71, **180**, **192**

Chrisman, Anna Marie, 111

Clark, ——— (chaincarrier), 105

Clark, John C., 110, **206**

Clark, Susan (Mrs. William Andrews), 7

Clarke, Antony R., **182**

Clayton, Joseph, 68

Coats, Merit M., **202**

Coffey, Elizabeth (Mrs. Robert Whiteside), 126

Coles settlement ("Athens of Texas"), 22

Coles, Jno. P., **182**, **186**, **204**

Coles, John Prince, 22, 127

Coles, Luanne Appel, 23

Coles, Martin, 23

Coles, Mary Eleanor Owen, 22

Comanches, 29, 90

"Come and Take It" flag, 157

Comstock, Amelia "Amy" (Mrs. William White and Mrs. William Swail), 124, 128

Comstock, Rachel (Mrs. Mark Lee), 124

Comstock, William, 124

Cook, James, **184**, **188**

Cook, Jno., **196**

Cook, Gustave, 65

Coonly, Genevieve Hicks, 76

Cooper, William, **180**, **200**, **202**

Cos, ———, General, 7, 101

Cottle, Joseph, 130

Cottle, Minerva (Mrs. Zadock Woods), 130

Cowgill, Winnie Rhea, 41

Craighill, Angeletta (Mrs. George Scott), 97

Crain, Marguerite, 52

Crier, Andrew, 24

Crier, Cynthia, 24

Crier, James, 28

Crier, John, 24, **200**

Crier, Polly Duty, 24

Crier, Rebecca, 28

Crier, Tolitha, 24

Crownover, Arthur (Arter), Jr., 25

Crownover, Chesney, 25

Crownover, Elizabeth Chesney, 25

Crownover, John, 25, 107, **180**, **200**, **206**

Crownover, John Bunyon, 25

Crownover, John Chesney, 25

Crownover, Leona, 25

Crownover, Marian R., 25

Crownover, Mary (Mrs. John Rabb), 25, 89, 114

Crownover, Nancy Castleman, 25, 107

Crownover, Ruffana, 25

Cryer, Barbara Morris, 24

Cryer, Morgan, 24

Cumings, Anthony, 26, 27

Cumings, James, 26, 27

Cumings, John, 26, 27

Cumings, Lucinda Ruggles, 26

Cumings, Rebecca, 26, 27

Cumings, Rebekah Russel, 26, 27

Cumings, Robert, 27

Cumings, Samuel, 26, 27

Cumings, Sarah, 26, 27

Cumings, Thomas, 27

Cumings, Timothy "Tim" Austin, xv, 26, 27

Cumings, William, 26, 27

Cummings, James, **182**

Cummings, John, **182**

Cummings, Rebecca, **182**

Cummings, William, **182**

Cummins, Elinor Mariah Waller, 28

Cummins, Eliza (Mrs. John H. Moore), 28, 81

Cummins, Harriet, 28

Cummins, James, 19, 24, 28, **180**, **184**, **188**

Cummins, Maria, 28

Cummins, Nancy, 28

Cummins, Rebecca, **202**

Cummins, Rebecca Crier, 28

Cummins, Sarah (Mrs. Dennet), 28, 63

Cummins, Willie (Wylie), 28

Cunningham, Helen Shipman, 102, 104

Curtis, Frances Carter, 30

Curtis, Hinton, **200**

Curtis, James, Jr., 29

Curtis, James, Sr., 29, 30, 105, **186**
Curtis, Polly Ann Hide, 29
Curtis, Rebecca, 29
Curtis, Rice III, 30
Curtis, Sarah (Mrs. Bartlett S. Sims), 105
Curtis, Sarah Ann, 29
Curtis, Sarah Hercules, 29, 30
Curtis, Tamer C. Gray, 29

D

Davis, Thomas, **180**
Dawson, ———, Captain, 130
Deckrow, D., **200**
Demos, Charles, **200**
Demos, Peter, **200**
DeMoss, Charles, 31
DeMoss, Elizabeth, 31
DeMoss, John, 31
DeMoss, Lewis, 31
DeMoss, Loraharney, 31
DeMoss, Martha (daughter of Charles), 31
DeMoss, Martha (wife of Charles), 31
DeMoss, Peter, 31, 36
DeMoss, Sally, 31
DeMoss, Susannah Bays, 36
DeMoss, William, 31
Denley, James, 84
Denley, John, 84
Denley, Martha Ellen (Mrs. George S. Pentecost), 84
Denley, Mary (Mrs. Jesse Thompson), 119
Dennet, ———, Mr., 63
Dennet, Sarah Cummins, 28, 63
Dewees, William B., 12, 102, **184**, **188**
DeWitt, Green, 121
DeWitt's Colony, 111, 121
Dick, Elizabeth (Mrs. James Whiteside), 126
Dickinson, John, **196**
Dillard, Nicholas, **182**
Dinsmore, James, 18
Dinsmore, Judith (Mrs. David Bright), 18
Dodson, Archeleus B., 15

Donnell, Martha (Mrs. William Stafford), 113, 115
Dotson, Joy Mellie Gooch, 59
Drake, Clint, xv
Drake, Doris Ballard, 92
Duke, Thomas M., **200**
Duncan, Mrs. Leslie B., 65
Duncan, Molly (Mrs. Edward R. Bradley), 15
Duncan, Peter, 107
Duncan, Sarah "Sally" Lusk Singleton, 107
Duty, George, **190**
Duty, Joseph, **184**, **188**
Duty, Polly (Mrs. John Crier), 24
Dyer, Clement C., 32, 33, **184**, **188**, **202**
Dyer, DeWitt Clinton, 33
Dyer, Florence, 33
Dyer, Harvey, 33
Dyer, James, 33
Dyer, John Eli, 33
Dyer, Josephine, 33
Dyer, Julia, 33
Dyer, Martha, 33
Dyer, Mary, 33
Dyer, Pembrook, 33
Dyer, Sarah Jane, 33
Dyer, Sarah Stafford, 33
Dyer, William, 33

E

Earle, Thomas, **196**
Edwards, G. E., **206**
Edwards, Gustavus, 34, 67
Edwards, Had, xi
Edwards, Hannah Kincheloe, 34
Edwards, Jane (Mrs. William Little), 74
Edwards, John, 34
Edwards, Mary Jane (Mrs. Robert Williamson), 34
Edwards, Susanne Wroe, 34
Elder, Robert, **202**
Elliott, James, 52
Elliott, Mary, 52
Establishing Austin's Colony, 12
Este, Edward, 109
Este, Elizabeth Smith, 109

Everts, George B., 10, 87

F
Falenash, Charles, **186**
Fannin, James W., 80
"Father of Agriculture," 48
Faul, Kathy, 21
Faulk, Priscilla (Mrs. Amos Singleton),
  107
Fenn III, Joseph Johnson, 35
Fenn, Eli, 35
Fenton, David, **200**
Fields, John F., **182**
First Colony of Texas: Austin's Old 300,
  xiii
Fisher, Cynthia (Mrs. Elijah Roark), 92
Fisher, James, **186**
Fitzgerald, David, 35, **192**
Fitzgerald, John, 35
Fitzgerald, Sarah (Mrs. Eli Fenn), 35
Fitzpatrick, Nancy Cecelia (Mrs.
  William Smothers), 111
flags, 15, 75, 81, 87
Flanakin, Isaiah, **180**
Fleming, Mary (Mrs. Joseph Pryor), 88
Flores, Gaspar, x, 16, 123
Flores, Jose Francisco, 106
Flowers, Edward, 36
Flowers, Elisha, 36, **184**, **188**, **200**
Flowers, Elizabeth, 36
Flowers, Martin Van Buren, 36
Flowers, Polly Smalley, 36
Flowers, Rebekkah, 36
Flowers, Romulus Orlando, 36
Flowers, Susannah Baker, 36
Foiles, Ruth T., 73
Fontaine, Paige, 50
Ford, John S., 114
Foster, Augustus Rodney, 39
Foster, Barsheba Hetty, 39
Foster, Carolina Amelia, 41
Foster, Elizabeth, 39
Foster, George Poindexter, 39
Foster, Gideon, 39
Foster, Isaac Guilford, 37, 39, **200**
Foster, Isaac Prestwood, 41
Foster, John, Jr., 39
Foster, John, Sr., 37, 39, 41, **192**

Foster, John Claiborne, 39
Foster, Lucretia Collitanius, 41
Foster, Lucy Matilda, 41
Foster, Lucy Ruffin Hunter, 41
Foster, Mary Elizabeth, 39
Foster, Mary Louise (Mrs. Sid
  Winston), 41
Foster, Mary Smith, 39
Foster, Moses A., 39
Foster, Nancy (Ann) D., 39
Foster, Nancy Adaliza, 41
Foster, Randolph, 39, **40**, 41, **192**, **202**
Foster, Randolph Guilford, 41
Foster, Sarah, 39
Frances, Blanche, 118
Frazier, James, **180**, **192**
Frazier, Joseph, 35
Fredonian Rebellion, 20, 26, 28, 58, 67,
  68, 78, 84, 99, 106
Frontier Life, 101, 102
Fulshear, Benjamin, 43
Fulshear, Betsy Summers, 43, 96
Fulshear, Churchill, Jr., 43
Fulshear, Churchill, Sr., 42, 43, 96, **192**
Fulshear, Graves, 43
Fulshear, Mary L. (Mrs. Robert
  Scobey), 43, 96

G
Galloway, Lucinda (Mrs. George
  Robinson), 95
Garret, Charles, **182**, **202**
Gates, Amos, 44
Gates, Catherine Hardin, 44, 68
Gates, Charles, 44
Gates, Hanna, 44
Gates, Jane, 44
Gates, Ransom, 44
Gates, Samuel, 44, **204**
Gates, Sarah, 44
Gates, Sarah "Sally," (Mrs. Abner
  Kuykendall), 68
Gates, William, 44, 68, **204**
Gates, William, Jr., 44
Gaume, June McCormick, 77
George, David, 45
George, Elenora, 45
George, Freeman, 45, **200**, **202**

George, Freeman, Jr., 45
George, Holman, 45
George, James, 45
George, Jefferson, 45
George, Joseph, 45
George, Nicholas, 45
George, William, 45
Gilbert, Preston, **184**, **188**
Gilbert, Sarah, **192**, **206**
Gilbert, Serena (Mrs. Thomas Rabb), 90
Gilleland family, 14
Gilleland, Daniel, 46, 72, **180**
Gilleland, James, 46
Gilleland, Nancy (Mrs. John D. Anders), 46
Gilleland, Nancy Johnson (Mrs. Thomas Williams), 46, 72, 129
Gilleland, Precilla Boatwright, 46
Gilleland, Sarah Ann (Mrs. Robert H. Kuykendall), 72
Gilleland, William, 46, 72, 129
Gonzales, Battle of, 81, 97
Gonzales, Isabella (Mrs. Montraville Woods), 130
Gorbet, Ann R. Bradley, 47
Gorbet, Chester S., 15, 47, **182**
Gorbet, Dulcenia, 47
Gorbet, Edward B., 47
Gorbet, Elizabeth, 57
Gorbet, John T., 47
Gorbet, Juliana, 47
Gorbet, Lorenzo W., 47
Gorbet, Nancy, 47
Gorbet, Nancy White, 47
Gorbet, Susan B., 47
Gouldrich, Michael, **196**
Grant, —— (chaincarrier), 105
Grass Fight, 47, 97
Gray, Daniel, 29
Gray, Hannah Bradbury Byrd, 20
Gray, James, 20
Gray, Tamer C. (Mrs. James Curtis, Jr.), 29
Gray, Thomas, 81, **182**, **184**, **188**
Greaser, Galen, xii, xvi
Griffin, Carolyn, 95
Grissett, W. H., 54

Groce, Jared E., 13, 48, **182**, **194**, **202**
Groce, Jared Ellison II, 48
Groce, Sarah Ann (Mrs. William H. Wharton), 49
Groce, Sarah Shepherd, 48
Guthrie, Robert, **198**

H
Haddon, Anna, 50
Haddon, Catherine, 50
Haddon, Elizabeth, 50
Haddon, Helen, 50
Haddon, Henry, 50
Haddon, Isabella Elliott, 50
Haddon, Jackson, 50
Haddon, John, 50
Haddon, John B., 50, **184**, **188**
Haddon, William, 50
Haddy, Arnold William, 51
Haddy, Elizabeth Chatham, 51
Haddy, Eunice, 51
Haddy (Hady), Samuel, 51, **202**
Haddy, Sarah (Sarah Kelly), 51
Haddy, Susan (Susan Callihan), 51
Hadley, Bridget, 73
Hadley, Simon, 73
Hady, see Haddy
Haecker, Mary Elizabeth Thompson, 24
Halbert, Esther Smith, 97
Hale, Kathleen Fisk, 81
Hall, George B., 8, 15, **182**
Hall, John W., **182**, **202**
Hall, W. J., **192**
Hallenbake, Matilda (Mrs. William Selkirk), 99
Hamilton, David, **206**
Hancock, Eliza (Mrs. Daniel Shipman), 101
Hancock, Thomas, 101
Hankins, Maria Elizabeth (Mrs. Adam Stafford), 113
Hanna, Letha (Mrs. Henry Whiteside), 125
Harbert, Martha (Mrs. Johnson C. Hunter), 56
Hardin, Catherine (Mrs. William Gates), 44, 68

Harkins, James, xv
Harper, Morning (Mrs. Noel Francis Roberts), 93
Harper's Magazine, 89, 104
Harrell, Milvern, 130
Harrell, Minerva Woods, 130
Harrell, William, 130
Harris, Abner, 11, **192**
Harris, David, **196**
Harris, Dilue Rose, 66
Harris, John R., **196**
Harris, Ruth Hodge, 52
Harris, William, 52, **182, 196**
Harris, William J., **196**
Harrison, George, **182**
Harrison, Mrs. H. G., 3
Harvey, William, **180**
Hatch, Alden, 20
Hays, Nadine Frances Dees, 120
Henderson, Maxine Moses, 110
Hennesey, (Mary) Elizabeth (Mrs. Ezekiel Thomas), 118
Henry, Elizabeth (Mrs. James Selkirk), 99
Hensley, James, **180, 182**
Hercules, Sarah (Mrs. James Curtis, Sr.), 29
Herzer, Anna Beth S., 34, 67
Hicks, Margaret Hall, 76
Hide, Polly Ann (Mrs. James Curtis, Sr.), 29
Higgins, H., 122
Hill, William Warner, 22
historical markers, 3, 13, 22, 46, 99, 117, 130
Hodge, Alexander, 52, **192**
Hodge, Alexander Elliott, 52
Hodge, Archibald, 52
Hodge, Charlotte Reeves, 52
Hodge, Cynthia, 52
Hodge, Elizabeth Barnhill, 52
Hodge, Elsie Smith, 52
Hodge, James, 52
Hodge, John (grandfather of Alexander), 52
Hodge, John (son of Alexander), 52
Hodge, Lucinda (Mrs. Stephen Richardson), 52

Hodge, Margaret Welch, 52
Hodge, Mary (Mrs. James Pevehouse), 52
Hodge, Mary Elliott, 52
Hodge, Nancy, 52
Hodge, Ruth, 52
Hodge, Ruth (Mrs. William Harris), 52
Hodge, William, 52
Hodge, Zulema Kuykendall, 52
Holland, Catherine "Katy," (Mrs. Mill McDowell), 54
Holland, Francis, 53, **194**
Holland, Francis "Frank," Jr., 53, 54
Holland, James, 53, 54
Holland, Margaret Buck, 53
Holland, Mary (Mrs. William Peterson), 54
Holland, Nancy, 53
Holland, Sarah (Mrs. W. H. Grissett), 54
Holland, Susanna, 53
Holland, Susannah Buck, 54
Holland, Tapley, 53
Holland, William, 53, 54, **194**
Houston, Sam, 12, 22, 62, 77, 117, 119, 130
Houston Telegraph, 102
Howard, John Steven, 20
Hubert, Frances (Mrs. Nathaniel Lynch), 75
Hudson, C. S., , **206**
Huff, George, 55, **192, 206**
Huff, Jacob, 55
Huff, John, **206**
Huff, Marian "Mary" Morton, 82
Huff, Mary, 55
Huff, William, 55
Huff, William P., 82
Hunter, Amanda Wilson Calhoun, 56
Hunter, ———, Dr., 122
Hunter, Eli, 18, 78, **206**
Hunter, Harriet Harbert, 56
Hunter, Jacob, 56
Hunter, John Calhoun, 56
Hunter, Johnson, **196**
Hunter, Johnson Calhoun, 56
Hunter, Latisia, 56
Hunter, Lucy Ruffin (mother), 30

Hunter, Lucy Ruffin (daughter), 30
Hunter, Martha, 56
Hunter, Martha Harbert, 56
Hunter, Mary, 56
Hunter, Messina, 56
Hunter, Robert Hancock, 56
Hunter, Sarah Ann Bright, 18
Hunter, Thaddeus Warsaw, 56
Hunter, Thomas Jefferson, 56
Hunter, Walter Crockett, 56
Hunter, William, 41, 56

I

Iiams, John, **196**
Indians, 4, 9, 10, 14, 24, 26, 29, 33, 34,
    35, 36, 46, 50, 53, 58, 66, 68, 69, 72,
    79, 81, 92, 95, 99, 101, 104, 105, 106,
    111, 120, 129, 130
Ingram, Ira, **202**
Ingram, John, 129
Ingram, Seth, **180**, **206**
Inman, Mrs. Gerald Floyd, 43
Irons, John, **202**
Isaacks, Martha "Patsy" Richardson,
    57
Isaacks, Nancy Allen, 57
Isaacks, Samuel, 57, **192**
Isaacks, William, 57

J

Jackson, Alexander, 58, **206**
Jackson, Alexander, Jr., 58
Jackson, Andrew, 130
Jackson, Anna Knox, 58
Jackson, Elizabeth, 59
Jackson, Esther (Mrs. Thomas
    Thatcher), 58
Jackson, F. M., 96
Jackson, Henry, 59
Jackson, Hugh, 58
Jackson, Humphrey, 58, **196**
Jackson, Isaac, Sr., 59, **194**
Jackson, Isaac C., 59
Jackson, James, 59
Jackson, Job, 59
Jackson, John, 59
Jackson, Letitia Thompson, 58
Jackson, Martha, 58

Jackson, Mary Ann, 58
Jackson, Nancy Pollard, 59
Jackson, Sytha Douglas Scobey, 96
Jamison, Haney Bright, 18
Jamison, Thomas, 18, 129, **182**, **200**
Jenkins, J. H., 29
Johnson, Donna McCrosky, 18, 78, 81
Johnson, Francis W., 101
Johnson, Henry, **182**
Johnson, Nancy (Mrs. Daniel
    Gilleland, Sr.), 46, 72, 129
Johnson, Nancy (Mrs. Thomas
    Williams), 129
Johnson, Rebecca (Mrs. George W.
    Teel), 117
Johnson, Sherrill Louise, 16
Jones, Ann Elizabeth, 62
Jones, Anson, 85
Jones, Eliza Jane (Mrs. Joseph
    Kuykendall), 71
Jones, Eliza M., 65
Jones, Elizabeth, 61
Jones, Emily Laura, 61
Jones, Henry, **60**, 61, **192**
Jones, Henry, Jr., 61
Jones, Hetty Stiles, 62
Jones, J. W., **192**, **206**
Jones, James, 61, 65
Jones, James Austin, 65
Jones, James Miller, 65
Jones, James Randall, 62
Jones, James Wales, 62
Jones, James Walter, 62
Jones, John Henry, 61
Jones, John Stiles, 62
Jones, Mark, 80
Jones, Martha (Mrs. Beale), 65
Jones, Mary Moore "Polly," 61
Jones, Mary "Polly" Andrews
    (Andrus), 65
Jones, Nancy Stiles, 61
Jones, Nancy Timelia, 61
Jones, Nettie Ellen, 61
Jones, Oliver, **180**, **182**
Jones, Pamelia Ann, 65
Jones, Polly White, 62
Jones, Randall, 41 **64**, 65, **192**, **206**
Jones, Richard Henry, 62

Jones, Robert Ellis, 62
Jones, Ruth, 61
Jones, Sallie C., 65
Jones, Sam Houston, 65
Jones, Sarah Story Smith, 65
Jones, Stephen Austin, 62
Jones, Sudie E., 65
Jones, Susan "Sudie," 61
Jones, Thomas, 65
Jones, Thomas Walter, 61
Jones, Virginia Claudine, 61
Jones, Vivian Ann, 61
Jones, Wiley Martin, 65
Jones, Wiley Powell, 61
Jones, William, 61
Jones, William Thomas, 62
Justice, Elizabeth J. Scobey, 96
Justice, Stephen Jackson, 96

K
Keels, Flossie Stanley, 75
Keep, Imla, **182**
Kegans, Clarenda Pevehouse, 52
Keith, Keziah (Mrs. Jonathan Woods, Jr.), 130
Keller, John C., **200**
Kelley, John, 101
Kelley, Margaretta (Mrs. Daniel Shipman), 101
Kelley, Sarah, 101
Kelly, Elijah, 66
Kelly, James, 66
Kelly, John, 66
Kelly, Margaretta (Mrs. Daniel Shipman), 66
Kelly, Polly Guthrie, 66
Kelly, Sarah (Fisher?), 66
Kelly, Sarah Haddy, 51
Kelly, William, 51, 66
Kennedy, Samuel, **180, 192**
Kenney, John Wesley, 125
Kennon, Alfred, **186**
Kerr, James, **198**
Kerr, William, **204**
Kian Jane (servant), 98
Kimbrough, William, 117
Kincheloe, Hannah (Mrs. Gustavus Edwards), 67

Kincheloe, Mary (Mrs. Horatio Chriesman), 67
Kincheloe, Mary Betts, 67
Kincheloe, Nancy Taylor, 34, 67
Kincheloe, Thomas Ludwell, 67
Kincheloe, William, 34, 67, **206**
Kingston, William, **200**
Kipp, Abraham H., 96
Kipp, Cheryl B. "Sissie," (Mrs. John Emmette Kipp), 48, 96
Kipp, Elizabeth J. Scobey, 96
Kipp, John Emmette "Dick," 43, 96
Kipp, Mrs. John Emmette, 48
Knight, James, **192**
Kuykendall family, 46
Kuykendall, Abner, 68, 69, 70, **180, 192, 204**
Kuykendall, Adam, 68, 70, 72
Kuykendall, Albert, 72
Kuykendall, Barzillai, 68, 69, **180**
Kuykendall, Eliza Jane Jones, 71
Kuykendall, Elizabeth, 69
Kuykendall, Gibson, 68, 69
Kuykendall, Jane, 72
Kuykendall, Joseph, 68, 69, 70, **192**
Kuykendall, Joseph Felix, 72
Kuykendall, Katherine, 69
Kuykendall, Lucinda, 69
Kuykendall, Margaret Hardin, 68, 70, 72
Kuykendall, Marshall E., 68, 71, 72
Kuykendall, Martha, 69
Kuykendall, Mary "Molly," 72
Kuykendall, Nancy "Nannie," 69
Kuykendall, R. H. "Gill," 72
Kuykendall, Robert H., 68, 70, 72, **206**
Kuykendall, Rosanna, 70
Kuykendall, Sarah (daughter of Barzillai), 69
Kuykendall, Sarah "Sally" Gates, 68
Kuykendall, Sarah Ann Gilleland, 72
Kuykendall, Solomon, 69
Kuykendall, Thomas, 72
Kuykendall, William, 68
Kuykendall, William H., 69
Kuykendall, Zulema (Mrs. James Hodge), 52

L

labor, x, 157
Lacey, Sarah Ann McCrosky, 78
Lacey, William D., 18, 78
Lafever, Mary (Mrs. William Scott), 97
land contract provisions, x
league, x, 157
League, Hosea H., **200**
Leakey, Ann Hadley, 73
Leakey, Anna, 73
Leakey, Elizabeth, 73
Leakey, Joel (Sr.), 73
Leakey, Joel (Jr.), 73
Leakey, Leny, 73
Leakey, Lydia (daughter of Joel), 73
Leakey, Lydia (sister of Joel), 73
Leakey, Mary Asenith, 73
Leakey, Nancy (daughter of Joel), 73
Leakey, Nancy Calloway, 73
Leakey, Ruth, 73
Leakey, Simon, 73
Leakey, Thomas (father of Joel), 73
Leakey, Thomas (son of Joel), 73
Leaming, Thomas F., 38
Lee, Mark, 124
Lee, Rachel White, 124
Lee, Rebecca B., 62
Lindsey, John H., 53
Letters from an Early Settler of Texas, 102
Little, George, 74
Little, Harvey N., 96
Little, James K., 74
Little, Jane Edwards, 74
Little, John, 74, **180**, **192**
Little, Louisa, 74
Little, Martha Jane, 74
Little, Mary Jane Scobey, 96
Little, Rebecca (Mrs. Andrew
    Wilkinson Scobey), 96
Little, Robert, 74
Little, Walter W., 74
Little, William, 74, **192**
Little, William (Jr.), 74
Lively (ship), 4, 35, 74, 82, 85
Long, Ann, 98
Long, James, 98
Long, Jane, 41, 70, 98, **192**, **202**
Lubojacky, Stephen H., 119

Lucas, Betsy (Mrs. Sylvanus
    Castleman), 21, 25
Lusk, Sarah "Sally" (Mrs. George
    Washington Singleton and Mrs.
    Peter Duncan), 106, 107
Lynch, Elizabeth, 75
Lynch, Frances Hubert, 75
Lynch, Franklin, 75
Lynch, James, **204**
Lynch, Nathaniel, 75, **196**
Lynch, William, 75
Lyne, Betty Joyce Upchurch, 111

M

Maddox, Frederick Andrew, 47
Maddox, Lawrence A., Jr., 47
Maps: Boundary of Stephen F.
    Austin's First Contract, 179; Austin
    County, 180; Brazoria County, 183,
    Brazos County, 185; Burleson
    County, 187; Colorado County, 189;
    Fayette County, 191; Fort Bend
    County, 193; Grimes County, 195;
    Harris, Chambers, Galveston coun-
    ties, 197; Jackson and Lavaca coun-
    ties, 199; Matagorda County, 201;
    Waller County, 203; Washington
    County, 205; Wharton County, 207;
Marble, Carolyn, 51
Marion, Francis, 35, 52
marriage bond, 11, 25, 43, 65, 93, 107,
    118
Marriage By Bond in Colonial Texas, 107
Marsh, Elizabeth Foxcroft, 76
Marsh, Lucinda Pitts, 76
Marsh, Shubael, 76, **182**
Marshall, Sarah, 117
Martin, Wiley, 62, **182**
Martin, Wyly, 119
Martinez, ——, Governor, 74
Massengale, Narcissa Frances (Mrs.
    Boland Whiteside), 125
Maxfield, Mary S., 128
Mayes, Francis B., 39
McBee, Charles "Douglas," Jr., 109
McCain, A. W., **184**, **188**
McClelland, Betty, 123
McCormick, Arthur, 77, **196**

McCormick, David, 108, **182**
McCormick, John, 77, **180**, **192**
McCormick, Margaret , 77
McCormick, Michael, 77
McCoy, Thomas, **200**
McCrosky, James, 78
McCrosky, John, 18, 78, **180**, **182**
McCrosky, Sarah Ann Bright, 78
McCrosky, Susan Walker, 78
McCrosky, William Hart, 78
McCullough, Jack, 45
McDowell, Mill, 54
McElhinney, Violet Ranne, 17
McFadden, A., 122
McFarlan, Aechilles, **182**, **202**
McFarlan, John, **202**
McKinney, Thomas F., 122
McKinsey, Hugh, **200**, **206**
McLean, Jane Blagrave (Mrs. William
    Scott), 97
McNair, James, **184**, **188**
McNeel, Daniel, **182**
McNeel, Elizabeth (daughter of John,
    Jr.), 79
McNeel, Elizabeth "Betsy" Mitchell, 79
McNeel, George W., 79, **182**
McNeel, John Greenville, 79, **182**
McNeel, John (Jr.), 79, **182**
McNeel, John, Sr., 79
McNeel, Leander H., 79
McNeel, Nancy (daughter of John, Jr.),
    79
McNeel, Nancy Devine, 79
McNeel, Pleasant D., 79, **182**
McNeel, Sterling, 79, **182**
McNutt, Elizabeth, **198**
McWilliams, William, **186**
Medina, Battle of, 3
Menasco, Judy, 37
Milam, Ben, 47
Milburn, David, **180**
Miller, Catherine (Mrs. James Walker,
    Sr.), 122
Miller, James G., 36
Miller, Samuel, **204**
Miller, Samuel R., **204**
Miller, Simon, **192**
Millican, Andrew, 53

Mims, Benjamin Franklin, 80
Mims, Jane O'Neal, 80
Mims, Joseph, 80, **182**
Mims, Sarah Weakly, 80
Mission Conception, Battle of, 90
Mitchell, Asa, 114, **182**
Mitchell, Elizabeth "Betsy" (Mrs. John
    McNeel), 79
Moczygemba, Betty J., 57
Moore, Eliza (daughter of John H.), 81
Moore, Eliza Cummins, 28, 81
Moore, John H., 28, 81, **182**
Moore, John Henry, Jr., 81
Moore, Luke, **196**
Moore, Mary E., 81
Moore, Robert J., 81
Moore, Sarah (Mrs. Samuel Russel), 27
Moore, Tabitha B., 81
Moore, William Bowen, 81
Morgan, Deurene Oates, 11
Morris, Barbara (Mrs. Morgan Cryer),
    24
Morrison, Moses, 129, **200**
Morton, —— (Mrs. William Little), 82
Morton, Jane, 82
Morton, Marian "Mary" (Mrs. William
    P. Huff), 82
Morton, William, 35, 43, 82, **192**
Moss, Julia Nail, 19, 28
Mouser, David, **202**
Muldoon, Michael, 47, 65, 82

N
Nacogdoches, Battle of, 117
Navarro, Juana, 5
Navasota, Texas, 54
Nelson, James, **184**, **188**
Nettles, Isham, 118
Newman, Ali Joseph, Jr., 83
Newman, Andrew, 83
Newman, Coleman C., 83
Newman, Eliza, 83
Newman, Elizabeth, 83
Newman, Joseph, 83, 89, **180**, **206**
Newman, Mary, 83
Newman, Minerva, 83
Newman, Rachel Rabb, 83, 89
Newman, Sally, 83

Newman, Thomas, 83
Newman, William, 83
Newton, Harry, 96
Newton, Mary Jane Scobey, 96
Nidever, Charles L., 101
Noonan, Katherine Ann, 79
Nuckols, M. B., **182**, **200**

O

Old Plantations and Their Owners of Brazoria County, Texas, 80
O'Neal, Jane (Mrs. Joseph Mims), 80
Only Son (ship), 67
Orrick, James, **180**
Osborn, Nathan, **184**, **188**
Owens, John, 101, 103

P

Pablo, Pedro, 106
Padilla, Juan Antonio, ix
Parker, ——, 63
Parker, Joshua, 126, 127, **206**
Parker, Nancy Whiteside, 126, 127
Parker, William, **182**, **202**
Parr, Mrs. Lewis Asbal, 130
Patrick, Orrell Lee, Jr., 69
Patton, James, 8
Patton, W. H., 11
Payne, John Knox, 16
Payne, Hanna Elizabeth Breen, 16
Pendleton, John Wesley, 130
Pennington, Isaac, **192**
Pentecost, George S., 84, **200**
Pentecost, George Washington, 84
Pentecost, Gracey Elizabeth, 84
Pentecost, James Denley, 84
Pentecost, Jane, 84
Pentecost, Lucy (Mrs. Samuel Pharr), 84
Pentecost, Lucy Ellen, 84
Pentecost, Martha Ellen Denley, 84
Pentecost, Mary Jane, 84
Pentecost, Sara "Sally" (Mrs. Andrew Jackson Beard), 84
Pentecost, Susan Evelyn, 84
Pentecost, William Walter, 84
Perry, Louisiana Morton, 35
Peterson, John, 54

Peterson, Susan Fisher Reid, 54
Peterson, William, 54
Peterson, William, Jr., 54
Pettus, Freeman, 54, **184**, **188**, **190**, **200**
Pettus, William, **192**, **202**, **206**
Petty, John, **190**
Pevehouse, James, 52
Pevehouse, Mary Hodge, 52
Peyton, J. C., **200**
Pharr, Lucy Pentecost, 84
Pharr, Samuel, 84
Phelps, James Aeneas, 85, **182**
Phelps, Orlando, 85
Phelps, Rosetta Adeline Yerby, 85
Philips, I. B., **206**
Philips, Irene T., 91
Philips, Zeno, **182**
Picket, Pamelia, **180**, **200**
Pitts, Lucinda (Mrs. Shubael Marsh), 76
Plageman, Laura, 58
Plageman, William H., Jr., 58
Poffard (Paffard), Rachel (Mrs. Christian Smith), 109
Pollard, Nancy Jackson, 59
Polley, Joseph H., **86**, 87, **192**
Polley, Mary "Pollie" Bailey, 87
Polley, Pollie Bailey, 87
Powell, Peter, **200**
Prater, William, **180**, **182**
Pruitt, Pleasant, **200**
Pryor, Althea Laura, 88
Pryor, Betsy Green Trammell, 88
Pryor, Elizabeth "Betsy" (Mrs. William Roberts), 88, 93
Pryor, Harriet (Mrs. Noel F. Roberts), 88, 93
Pryor, Joseph, 88
Pryor, Mary (daughter of Wm.), 88
Pryor, Mary Fleming, 88
Pryor, Rosannah, 88
Pryor, Trammell, 88
Pryor, William, 88, 93, **202**

R

Rabb, Adelia Ann, 90
Rabb, Andrew, 83, 89, 91, **206**
Rabb, Angeline Thomas, 90

Rabb, Barthenia, 90
Rabb, John, 89, 91, **180**, **192**
Rabb, Lillian Bell, 89
Rabb, Mary Crownover, 89, 114
Rabb, Mary Louisa, 90
Rabb, Mary Polly Smalley, 90, 91
Rabb, Rachel, 91
Rabb, Rachel (Mrs. Joseph Newman), 83, 89, 91
Rabb, Sarah, 90
Rabb, Serena Gilbert, 90
Rabb, Thomas, 89, 90, 91
Rabb, Thomas J., **206**
Rabb, Ulysses, 90, 91
Rabb, William, 83, 89, 90, 91, **190**, **200**
Raleigh, William, **186**
Ramey, L., **200**
Randon, David, **192**
Randon, J., **192**
Rankin, Frederic H., **196**
Rawls, Amos, **200**
Rawls, Benj., **200**
Rawls, Daniel, **200**
Reading, Antoinette Davis, 74
Reed, Mary Elizabeth, 25
Reedy, Mrs. John Wayne, 91
Reels, Mary Bright Snider, 18
Reels, Patrick, 18, **196**
Reid, Charles, 29, 30
Reid, M. Elizabeth Curtis, 30
Reminiscences of Mary Crownover Rabb, 25
Renaud, A. Frederick, 85
Retreat (house), 48
Richardson, Lucinda Hodge, 52
Richardson, Martha "Patsy" (Mrs. Samuel Isaacks), 57
Richardson, Stephen, 52, **182**
Richey, Jean Hicks, 76
rigadore, 22
Roark, Andrew Jackson, 92
Roark, Andy, 92
Roark, Cynthia Fisher, 66, 92
Roark, Elijah, 66, 92, **192**, **202**
Roark, Leo, 92
Roark, Louisa, 92
Roark, Lucinda, 92

Roark, Mary, 92
Roark, Rebecca, 92
Robbins, Earle, **180**
Robbins, William, **180**, **182**
Roberts, Andrew, 94, **192**
Roberts, Elisha, 93
Roberts, Elizabeth (Mrs. Cornelius Smith), 94, 110
Roberts, Elizabeth "Betsy" Pryor, 88, 93
Roberts, Harriet Pryor, 88, 93
Roberts, Highley Carter, 93
Roberts, Hirma, 93
Roberts, James Edgar, 88, 93
Roberts, John, 93
Roberts, John Hardin, 93
Roberts, Josiah, 93
Roberts, Mary, 93
Roberts, Morning Harper, 93
Roberts, Noel, 18
Roberts, Noel Francis, 88, 93, **192**
Roberts, Peggy, 94
Roberts, Thomas, 93
Roberts, William, 88, 94, **182**
Roberts, William Taylor, 93
Robertson, Edward, **192**
Robinette, Sarah, 118
Robinson, A., **182**, **202**, **204**
Robinson, George, 95, **182**
Robinson, John, 101
Robinson, Joyce Gray Clegg, 55
Robinson, Lucinda Galloway, 95
Robinson, Mark Edward, 91
Robinson, Mary (Mrs. Moses Shipman), 101, 103
Robinson, Mrs. W. T., Jr., 82
Rose, Pleasant, 15
Ross, James, 24, **184**, **188**
Ross, James J., 19
Rucker, T. J., 122
Runaway Scrape, 18, 22, 51, 52, 70, 75, 113, 123
Rusk, Betty Jo Ray, 129
Rusk, Thomas J., 70
Russel, Samuel, 27
Russel, Sarah Moore, 27
Russell, Alexander, 85
Rutersville College, 89

S

San Antonio, Battle of, 130
San Jacinto, Battle of, 5, 7, 30, 52, 56, 69, 84, 85, 93, 108, 124, 128
San Pierre, Joseph, **192**
Sanders, Hardy, 31
Santa Anna, Antonio Lopez de, 5, 56, 75, 77, 85, 109, 115, 119
Scarborough, Virginia Davis, xv, 61, 74
Schmidt, Christian, 109
Schoener, Louise, 56
Scobey, Andrew Wilkinson, 96
Scobey, Elizabeth J. (Mrs. Stephen Jackson Justice and Mrs. Abraham H. Kipp), 96
Scobey, Lucy Debow, 96
Scobey, Mary Jane (Mrs. Harvey N. Little and Mrs. Harry Newton), 96
Scobey, Mary L. Fulshear, 43, 96
Scobey, Matthew, 96
Scobey, Rebecca Adcock, 96
Scobey, Rebecca Little, 96
Scobey, Robert, 43, 96, **206**
Scobey, Sytha Douglas (Mrs. F. M. Jackson and Mrs. Albert Brown Sweden), 96
Scott, Angeletta Craighill, 97
Scott, George, 97
Scott, George Russell, 97
Scott, James, 97, **192**
Scott, James William, 97
Scott, Jane Blagrave McLean, 97
Scott, Mary Lafever, 97
Scott, William, 75, 97, **196**
Scott, William Craighill, 97
Selkirk, Charles, 99
Selkirk, Elizabeth Henry, 99
Selkirk, James, 99
Selkirk, James Henry, 99
Selkirk, Matilda Hallenbake, 99
Selkirk, Rachel Elizabeth, 99
Selkirk, William, 99, **200**
Sharper (servant to Jackson family), 58
Shelby, David, **180**
Shelby, James Frazier, **180**
Shipman, Daniel, 66, **100**, 101, 102, 126, **182**

Shipman, Edward Moses, 101
Shipman, Eliza Hancock, 101
Shipman, John Kelley, 101
Shipman, Lucinda, 103
Shipman, Margaretta Kelley, 101
Shipman, Mary Jane, 101
Shipman, Mary Robinson, 101, 103
Shipman, Moses, 4, 101, 103, 104, **180, 192**
Shipman, Moses, Jr., 101
Sim (servant to Jackson family), 58
Sims, Bartlet, **206**
Sims, Bartlett Samuel, 78, 105
Sims, Emily V., 105
Sims, Eugenia Missouria, 105
Sims, James Curtis, 105
Sims, Josephine, 105
Sims, Margaret A., 105
Sims, Mary E., 105
Sims, Sarah, 105
Sims, Sarah Curtis, 105
Sims, Thomas McKinney, 105
Sims, William, 105
Sims, William Anderson, 105
Singleton, Amos, 106
Singleton, G. W., **206**
Singleton, George Washington, 106, 127
Singleton, James W., 108
Singleton, Lavina (Mrs. William Whiteside), 127
Singleton, Marcella (Mrs. Anderson Smith), 106
Singleton, Phillip, 106, 108, 127, **186**
Singleton, Phillip (Jr.), 108
Singleton, Priscilla Faulk, 107
Singleton, Richard, 127
Singleton, Sarah "Sally" Lusk, 106
Singleton, Spyars, 108
Singleton, Susanna Walker, 108
Sinks, Julia, 28
sitio, x, 157
Skillen, Zippora (Mrs. Henry Whiteside), 125
Smalley, Andrew, 36
Smalley, Martha, 36
Smalley, Mary Polly (Mrs. William Rabb), 90, 91

Smeathers, William, **180**
Smith, C. Henry, 110
Smith, Christian, 94, 109, 110, **196**
Smith, Cornelius, 94, 110, **182**
Smith, Cornelius, Jr., 110
Smith, Deaf, 5, 41
Smith, Don Erasmo, 74
Smith, Eleanor, 109
Smith, Elizabeth (daughter of Christian), 109
Smith, Elizabeth (daughter of Cornelius), 110
Smith, Elizabeth (Mrs. Edward Este), 109
Smith, Elizabeth "Betsy" Roberts, 94, 110
Smith, Elsie (Mrs. John Hodge), 52
Smith, Frances Prestwood, 39
Smith, Gaines, 110
Smith, Henry, 87
Smith, James, 110
Smith, John, 106, 109, **200**, **206**
Smith, John B., 110
Smith, Joseph, 109
Smith, Lucriata, 110
Smith, Marcella Singleton, 107
Smith, Margaret Elizabeth, 110
Smith, Mary (Mrs. John Foster), 39
Smith, Mary "Polly," 110
Smith, Molly, 110
Smith, Rachel, 110
Smith, Rachel Poffard (Paffard), 109
Smith, Sarah Story (Mrs. Thomas Jones), 65
Smith, Thomas B., 110
Smith, Wesley Lee, 110
Smith, William Robert, 110
Smith, Zachariah, 39
Smithwick, Noah, 10, 42, 43, 94
Smothers, Anna Marie Chrisman, 111
Smothers, Archibald, 111
Smothers, Betsy, 111
Smothers, Cynthia, 66
Smothers, Elizabeth, 111
Smothers, Jane, 111
Smothers, John, 111
Smothers, Mary, 111
Smothers, Mary Winters, 111

Smothers, Nancy Cecelia Fitzpatrick, 111
Smothers, Smeathers, Smithers, William, 111, **180**
Snider, Gabriel Straw, 18, **184**, **188**
Snider, Mary Bright, 18
Sojourner, Albert S., **200**
Spencer, Nancy, **192**
Spyars, James W., 108
Stafford, Adam, **112**, 113, 115, **202**
Stafford, Harvey, 115
Stafford, John Thomas, 115
Stafford, Margaret "Bettie," 113
Stafford, Maria Elizabeth Hankins, 113
Stafford, Martha, 113, 115
Stafford, Martha Cartwright, 115
Stafford, Martha Donnell, 113, 115
Stafford, Mary, 115
Stafford, Mary Ella, 113
Stafford, Sarah, 113, 115
Stafford, Susan, 115
Stafford, William, 33, 113, 115, 131, **192**, **202**
Stafford, William Hankins, 113
Stafford, William Joseph, Jr., 115
Stedman, Shirley Jean Hanagriff, xv, 107, 108
Stevens, Thomas, **202**
Stevensons (missionaries), 117
Stewart, James, 30
Stewart, John, 30
Stiles, Hetty (Mrs. James W. Jones), 62
Stiles, Nancy (Mrs. Henry Jones), 61
Stout, Owen H., **200**
Strange, James, **196**
Stringer, Aggy (Mrs. Robert Whitlock), 128
Swail, Amelia (Amy) Comstock White, 124
Swail, William, 124
Sweden, Albert Brown, 96
Sweden, Sytha Douglas Scobey, 96

T
Talley, David, 15, **180**, **182**
Tate, Dorothy Shepperd, 53, 54
Taylor, John I., **196**
Teel, Eliza, 117

Teel, George Washington, **116**, 117, **192**
Teel, Lucette, 117
Teel, Nancy Caldwell, 117
Teel, Olive, 117
Teel, Rachel, 117
Teel, Rebecca Johnson, 117
Teel, Wyatt, 117
Telegraph & Texas Register, 122
Texas Rangers, 105, 114, 121
Thacker, Marilyn R., 122
Thatcher, Thomas, 58
Thomas, (Mary) Elizabeth Hennesey, 118
Thomas, Corine Crossland, 105
Thomas, Ezekiel, 118, **196**
Thomas, Frances "Fanny," 118
Thomas, George Warren, 79
Thomas, Jacob, **202**
Thomas, Lindsey, 118
Thomas, Mary, 118
Thomas, Rebecca Jane, 118
Thomas, Samuel E., 118
Thomas, William H., 118
Thompson, Eliza Jane, 119
Thompson, Grace Elizabeth, 119
Thompson, Henry C., 119
Thompson, Hiram M., 119
Thompson, James M., 119
Thompson, Jesse, 119, **182**
Thompson, Jesse M., 119
Thompson, John D., 119
Thompson, Kevin, 46
Thompson, Lavinia, 119
Thompson, Mary, 119
Thompson, Mary Denley, 119
Thompson's Crossing, Battle of, 119
Thompson's Ferry, 62, 119
Thurman, Nancy (Mrs. Boland Whiteside), 125
Tone, Thomas, **200**
Tong, James F., **182**
Toy, Samuel, **180**
Trammell, Betsy Green (Mrs. William Pryor), 88
Travis William B., 39, 53, 88, 126
Tribble, Eliza Lyons (Mrs. William Bridges), 17

Trimmer, Thomas, 122
Triplett, Georgeanna, 99
Tubbs, Katurah Angier, 8
Tubbs, Mary, 8
Tubbs, Samuel, 8
Tumlinson, Diana Mary Wilkerson White, 121
Tumlinson, Elizabeth, 120, 121, **184**, **188**
Tumlinson, George W., 121
Tumlinson, J. J., 30
Tumlinson, James, **184**, **188**, **206**
Tumlinson, James, Jr., 121
Tumlinson, John Jackson, Sr., 120

V
Vandorn, Isaac, **200**
Varner, Martin, 71, 94, **182**, **202**
Velasco, Battle of, 7, 10
Veramendi family, 56
Veramendi, Juan, 5
Vice, Elizabeth (Mrs. Martin Allen), 3
Viesca, Jose Maria, 10
Vince, Allen, **196**
Vince, Robert, **196**
Vince, William, **196**
Visit to Texas, 79
Von-Maszewski, Matthew E., xv
Von-Maszewski, Wolfram M., xv, 178

W
Waites, Jackie Thompson, 15
Walker, Andrew, 122
Walker, Catherine, 122
Walker, Catherine Miller, 122
Walker, Charles, 122
Walker, Elizabeth, 122
Walker, Gideon, 122
Walker, James, Sr., 106, 122, **204**
Walker, James, Jr., 122
Walker, John, 122
Walker, Lucinda, 122
Walker, Lucretia, 122
Walker, Sally, 122
Walker, Sanders, 122
Walker, Susan (Mrs. James McCrosky), 78
Walker, Susanna (Mrs. Phillip Singleton), 108, 122

Walker, Thomas, 122, **182**
Walker, William, 122
Wallace, Caleb, 123, **194**
Wallace, Elizabeth Wingfield, 123
Wallace, Elvira Wingfield, 123
Waller, Elinor Mariah (Mrs. James Cummins), 28
Wauer, Betty Newman, 91
Weakly, Sarah (Mrs. Joseph Mims), 80
Wegenhoft, Victor C., 90
Weir, Elizabeth Barret, 11
Weir, Reuben, 11
Welch, Margaret (Mrs. William Hodge), 52
Wells, Francis F., **182**, **198**
Wells, Jane Boyd (Mrs. Norman Woods and Mrs. Henry Gonsalvo Woods), 130
Westall, Thomas, **180**, **192**, **206**
Wharton, John A., 85
Wharton, William H., 49
Whitaker, Delbert W., 4, 5, 6
White, —— (silversmith), 49
White, Amelia (Amy) Comstock, 124, 128, **196**
White, Diana Mary Wilkerson (Mrs. James Tumlinson, Jr.), 121
White, Elizabeth L., 44
White, Gifford, 124
White, Jesse, 124
White, John, 124
White, Joseph, **182**
White, Mary (Mrs. William Whitlock), 124, 128
White, Rachel (Mrs. Mark Lee), 124
White, Reuben, 124, **196**
White, Sarah Gambill, 124
White, Walter C., **192**
White, William, 124, 128, **180**
White, William, Jr., 124
White Settlement, 124
Whiteside, Ann Eliza, 127
Whiteside, Betty, 4
Whiteside, Boland, 125, 127
Whiteside, Davis, 127
Whiteside, Elisha, 127
Whiteside, Elizabeth Coffey, 126
Whiteside, Elizabeth Dick, 126

Whiteside, George Washington, 127
Whiteside, Henry, 125, 127
Whiteside, James, 106, 125, 126, 127, **194**
Whiteside, James Anderson, 125
Whiteside, John J., 127
Whiteside, Jonathan, 125
Whiteside, Lavina Singleton, 127
Whiteside, Letha Hanna, 125
Whiteside, Mary, 127
Whiteside, ——, Mrs., 20
Whiteside, Nancy (Mrs. Joshua Parker), 126, 127
Whiteside, Nancy Thurman, 125
Whiteside, Narcissa Frances Massengale, 125
Whiteside, Phillip, 127
Whiteside, Robert, 126, 127
Whiteside, Thankful Anderson, 125
Whiteside, William, 125, 127
Whiteside, William, Jr., 127
Whiteside, Zippora Skillen, 125
Whitesides, James, **202**
Whitesides, William, **202**
Whiting, Nathaniel, **184**, **188**
Whitlock, Aggy Stringer, 128
Whitlock, Amanda, 128
Whitlock, Bernard, 128
Whitlock, Elizabeth, 128
Whitlock, Henry, 128
Whitlock, Martha, 128
Whitlock, Mary White, 124, 128
Whitlock, Rachel, 128
Whitlock, Robert, 128
Whitlock, William, 124, 128, **196**
Wiant, Elizabeth (Mrs. William Barret), 11
Wightman, Elias, 99, **200**
Wilbeck, Dorothy W., xvi
Wilkins, Jane, **192**
Wilkins, John, 13
Wilkins, Mary Margaret (Mrs. Isaac Best), 13
Williams, Benjamin, 129
Williams, George I., **200**
Williams, Henry, **200**
Williams, John, 78, **192**, **200**, **202**
Williams, Mary Diane, 129

Williams, Nancy Johnson Gilleland, 129

Williams, Robert H., **200**

Williams, Samuel M., 108, **180**, **182**, **202**

Williams, Solomon, **200**, **202**

Williams, Thomas, 46, 129, **200**

Williams, Thomas Johnson, 129

Williamson, Hoxie Collinsworth, 34

Williamson, James Bennett, 34

Williamson, Robert McAlpin "Three-Legged Willie," 34

Williamson, Susan Bruce, 34

Williamson, Willie Annexus, 34

Wilson, Joe Darrell, 66

Wilson, Nancy White (Mrs. Chester S. Gorbet), 47

Wingfield, Elizabeth (Mrs. Caleb Wallace), 123

Wingfield, Elvira (Mrs. Caleb Wallace), 123

Winn, Elizabeth (Mrs. Edward R. Bradley), 15

Winn, George, 15

Winston, Sid, 41

Winston, Mary Louise Foster, 41

Winters, Mary (Mrs. William Smothers), 111

Woll, ——, General, 130

Woods, Ardelia, 130

Woods, Henry Gonsalvo, 130

Woods, Isabella Gonzales, 130

Woods, Jane Boyd Wells, 130

Woods, Jonathan, Jr., 130

Woods, Keziah Keith, 130

Woods, Leander, 130

Woods, Minerva (Mrs. William Harrell), 130

Woods, Minerva Cottle, 130, 131

Woods, Montraville, 130

Woods, Norman, 130

Woods, Zadock, 130, **200**

Woods Fort, 130

Wooten, Nancy Jane Perry, 12

Wright, LaNell Lee Moses, 94

Y-Z

Yerby, Rosetta Adeline (Mrs. James Aeneas Phelps), 85

York, Captain, 5

Zavala, Lorenzo de, 108

Zvolanek, Nadine Foster, 39